A General Selection from
the Works of Sigmund Freud

Sigmund Freud, the founder of psychoanalysis, was born in Moravia in 1856 and lived most of his life in Vienna where he took his medical degree in 1881. He published his first work, *On the Psychical Mechanism of Hysterical Phenomena*, in collaboration with Josef Breuer, after he had completed his medical training in Paris under J. M. Charcot (1885–86). His researches into hidden emotional energies that become transformed in man's conscious life led to his publication of *The Interpretation of Dreams* (1900), *The Psychopathology of Everyday Life* (1901) and *Three Contributions to the Theory of Sexuality* (1905). In 1906 he was joined by Eugen Bleuler, C. G. Jung, Alfred Adler, and others who helped to establish The International Psychoanalytical Association (1910) with Jung as president. Jung and Adler soon left the Association after rejecting Freud's theory that psychological phenomena were sexual in origin. Freud persisted in his theories in the face of much opposition, founding and editing several psychiatric journals, and expanding his analysis of the individual psyche to society and culture in his later works, *Totem and Taboo* (1912–13), *The Future of an Illusion* (1927), *Civilization and Its Discontents* (1930), and *Moses and Monotheism* (1939). He died in England in 1939 after migrating from the Nazi occupation. Other writings by Freud include: *Wit and Its Relation to the Unconscious* (1905), *A General Introduction to Psychoanalysis* (1916–17), *Beyond the Pleasure Principle* (1920), *The Problem of Anxiety* (1926), *New Introductory Lectures on Psychoanalysis* (1933), and *An Outline of Psychoanalysis* (1940).

The following works are available in Anchor Book editions: *The Future of an Illusion* by Sigmund Freud, *The Question of Lay Analysis* (with Freud's 1927 Postscript) by Sigmund Freud, *Freud: The Mind of the Moralist* by Philip Rieff, and *The Life and Work of Sigmund Freud* by Ernest Jones, which has been edited and abridged in one volume by Lionel Trilling and Steven Marcus.

A General Selection from the Works of SIGMUND FREUD

Edited by
JOHN RICKMAN, M.D.

With an Appendix by
CHARLES BRENNER, M.D.

Doubleday Anchor Books
Doubleday & Company, Inc.
Garden City, New York

Cover by Leonard Baskin
Typography by Edward Gorey

A *General Selection from the Works of Sigmund Freud* was originally published by the Hogarth Press, Ltd., in 1937.

The Anchor Books edition is published by arrangement with The Hogarth Press, Ltd., London. In this edition, Dr. Brenner's Appendix replaces the selection from *Inhibitions, Symptoms and Anxiety*. The selections from *Beyond the Pleasure Principle*, *Group Psychology and the Analysis of the Ego* and *New Introductory Lectures on Psychoanalysis* are reprinted here with the permission of the Liveright Publishing Corporation and W. W. Norton & Company, Inc.

Library of Congress Catalog Card Number 57–11436

CONTENTS

PREFACE TO FIRST IMPRESSION

THE reader of a volume of Selections should know the principle on which the selections have been made.

In order that this book should merit the title of an Epitome it has been confined as far as possible to the General Theory of Psychoanalysis. It is therefore an exposition of psychoanalytical theories regarding the interplay of the forces of instinct in the human mind, the mechanisms employed in this interplay and the principles governing the reduction of "tension" or strain in the mind. It deals also with the topography of the mental apparatus, particularly in respect to those parts of the mind that are concerned with instinct-impulses, with consciousness, with conscience and with the regulating or executive mental functions. The Special Theories of the Neuroses, Psychoses, and Character-Difficulties are included only as far as is needed to throw light on the General Theory.

No attempt has been made to include the evidence on which the theories have been built up, i.e. there are no Case Histories; nor are highly technical discussions included, since these cannot be adequately grasped, still less udged, apart from the details of the case material.

The Technique of Therapy has been omitted for a different reason. There are many who do not scruple to call themselves psychoanalysts and their therapy psychoanalytic without having first submitted themselves to the discipline of a psychoanalytical training in the technique of this therapy, and without even having made a careful study of the literature on the subject. Therefore it is not in the public interest to publish accounts of the therapeutic procedures without giving details of the precautions necessary to avoid mistakes; this cannot be done in epitome. Those who wish to *read* the case histories and to *read about* the therapeutic method are referred to the periodical literature and to the *Library Series* of books, those who

wish to *learn* the therapeutic method may apply to the
branch of the International Psychoanalytical Association
in the country where they reside (in England, to the Institute of Psychoanalysis, London).

Psychoanalysis is a term having two meanings. Freud
describes it as a "particular method of treating nervous and
mental disorders and as the science of unconscious mental
processes, which has been appropriately called *depth
psychology*." The method of treatment gives access to the
unconscious part of the mind, which is shut off from consciousness on account of *mental suffering*.

One can roughly distinguish psychoanalysis from the
other branches of psychology by the fact that it takes
cognizance of the causes and the effects of mental suffering. This does not mean that psychoanalysis takes no account of pleasure, on the contrary it shows in what way
and how much the individual is deprived of pleasure by
anxiety and guilt, and how the capacity for pleasure may
be restored when the mental conflicts which give rise to
the anxiety and guilt have been overcome. Indeed one can
go further and say that psychology has come most closely
into touch with human affairs when it has faced the problem of suffering. True to medical tradition psychoanalysis
has been most effective in bringing a remedy when it has
discovered the causes of the trouble—it does not offer
advice, encouragement, or vague hopes for the future, but
like the other branches of medicine it gives diagnosis and
therapy based on causation.

The book is an attempt to show the *development of
psychoanalytical theories*. Just as each page is dated so
the reader is urged to remember that each concept is dated
too. I think that the evolution of Freud's thought is shown
more clearly in this book than in any other.

An endeavor has been made to include the concepts
which are most useful in *the psychoanalytical method of
dealing with problems of the mind*. Freud's "Group Psychology" is an excellent instance of this method. There is
no attempt "to solve the whole problem," but to seek for
a few elements, which have been well studied and see

how they are related to this new field of research. It is once more a matter of putting the right questions. Freud's success in many aspects of medical and applied psychology is due to the simplicity of the questions he puts.

This volume is the main stem upon which will be attached several branches, which could not flourish by themselves because it is not possible in a small compass to show both the analysis of a problem and at the same time to give at all an adequate account of the theoretical instrument employed. These branches, which to many may be the most interesting part of psychoanalysis, relate to Aesthetics, Character, the Love Life, Religion, the Supernatural, War and Death, and other topics.

In the forthcoming *Epitomes*, as in this one, the method of approach to the problem is stressed rather than the conclusions, for in the long run the method of science is its most valuable contribution to mankind. Freud has developed a new theoretical instrument and has opened up a new field of knowledge—nothing less than the inner life of man. Though these discoveries were made in the course of relieving suffering they throw light on our everyday activities, because our mental life is so largely shaped by pain. Those who choose to deny the importance of the role of mental suffering in the lives of men can neither receive much from nor give much to psychology—or to their fellow men.

* * * * *

Four points of editing require explanation: (*a*) All words added by myself or a translator are in square brackets; (*b*) Every omission of importance is marked by three dots . . . ; (*c*) In order not to make the pages look too scrappy I have in a few instances disregarded the paragraphing of the original version and have put footnotes into the text; (*d*) If a page heading is in small capitals it is the title of a book or paper, if in italics it refers to a chapter or section only.

For the roughness caused by the omission of sentences and paragraphs in a smooth-flowing exposition, I ask pardon of the author and indulgence of the reader, and I would like to remind the student that this little book contains only about one-twentieth of Freud's work.

J. R.

11 Kent Terrace,
Regent's Park,
London, N.W.1.
October 1937

EDITOR'S NOTE

THE German words *Besetzung, Libidinös, Angst* sometimes present difficulties, and in these selections from Freud's works the translation is not uniform. *Besetzung,* as in *Energiebesetzung* or *Besetzungsenergie,* was in the early twenties rendered by the words "investment" or "charge"; as this was not always clear enough the word "cathexis" was invented.

The German word *Libidinös* is an adjectival derivative from the technical term "Libido," it is rendered "libidinal" in order to avoid the highly colored connotation of the English "libidinous."

The "anxiety" group of words needs a little explanation. *Angst* (a condition as of expectation of danger and preparation for it, even though it be an unknown one) is translated as a rule by the word "anxiety," *Furcht* (the fear that has a definite object) by "fear," and *Schreck* by "fright." Sometimes translators sacrifice appearance in order to avoid complexity and have inserted the word *Angst* into the English text.

All other words are explained in the text or Glossary if they are used in a special sense.

A General Selection from
the Works of Sigmund Freud

IT has been my guiding purpose to make no sacrifice in favor of apparent simplicity, completeness, and finality, not to hide any problems, and not to deny the existence of gaps and uncertainties.

In no other field of scientific work would it be necessary to insist upon the modesty of one's claims. In every other subject this is taken for granted; the public expect nothing else. No reader of a work on astronomy would feel disappointed and contemptuous of that science, if he were shown the point at which our knowledge of the universe melts into obscurity. Only in psychology is it otherwise; here the constitutional incapacity of men for scientific research comes into full view. It looks as though people did not expect from psychology progress in knowledge, but some other kind of satisfaction; every unsolved problem, every acknowledged uncertainty is turned into a ground of complaint against it.

Anyone who loves the science of the mind must accept these hardships. . . .

From the Preface to
"New Introductory Lectures on Psychoanalysis"

1932

THE ORIGIN AND DEVELOPMENT OF PSYCHOANALYSIS [1]

Five Lectures delivered at the Celebration of the Twentieth Anniversary of Clark University, Worcester, Mass., in September 1909

First Lecture. Ladies and Gentlemen,—It is a new and somewhat embarrassing experience for me to appear as lecturer before students of the New World. I assume that I owe this honor to the association of my name with the theme of psychoanalysis, and consequently it is of psychoanalysis that I shall aim to speak. I shall attempt to give you in very brief form an historical survey of the origin and further development of this new method of research and cure. . . .

I was a student, busy with the passing of my last examinations, when another physician of Vienna, Dr. Joseph

[1] This first appeared in the *American Journal of Psychology*, 1910, XXI, ii, 181-218, later in *G.S. iv*, 349-406. It was published in German under the title "Ueber Psychoanalyse", by Verlag F. Deuticke, Leipzig u. Wein, and grateful acknowledgments are made to this firm, to the Internationaler Psychoanalytischer Verlag and to the Editor of the *Am. J. Psych.* for permission to print these extracts. Trans. by Harry W. Chase, revised by author.

Breuer [was experimenting with methods of treating hysterical patients (1880-2)].... Dr. Breuer's patient was a girl of twenty-one, of a high degree of intelligence. She had developed in the course of her two years' illness a series of physical and mental disturbances which well deserved to be taken seriously. She had a severe paralysis of both right extremities with anesthesia, and at times the same affection of the members of the left side of the body; disturbance of eye-movements, and much impairment of vision; difficulty in maintaining the position of the head, an intense *Tussis nervosa,* nausea when she attempted to take nourishment, and at one time for several weeks a loss of the power to drink, in spite of tormenting thirst. Her power of speech was also diminished, and this progressed so far that she could neither speak nor understand her mother tongue; and, finally, she was subject to states of "absence," of confusion, delirium, alteration of her whole personality. These states will later claim our attention.... The illness first appeared while the patient was caring for her father, whom she tenderly loved, during the severe illness which led to his death, a task which she was compelled to abandon because she herself fell ill....

You must not think that the outlook of a patient with regard to medical aid is essentially bettered when the diagnosis points to hysteria rather than to organic disease of the brain. Against the serious brain diseases medical skill is in most cases powerless, but also in the case of hysterical affections the doctor can do nothing. He must leave it to benign nature, when and how his hopeful prognosis will be realized.[2] Accordingly with the recognition of the disease as hysteria, little is changed in the situation of the patient, but there is a great change in the attitude of the doctor. We can observe that he acts quite differently toward hystericals than toward patients suffering from organic diseases. He will not bring the same interest to

[2] I know that this view no longer holds today, but in the lecture I take myself and my hearers back to the time before 1880. If things have become different since that time it has been largely due to the work the history of which I am sketching.

the former as to the latter, since their suffering is much less serious and yet seems to set up the claim to be valued just as seriously. . . .

Now Dr. Breuer did not deserve this reproach in this case; he gave his patient sympathy and interest, although at first he did not understand how to help her. . . . His sympathetic observation soon found the means which made the first help possible. It had been noticed that the patient, in her states of "absence," of psychic alteration, usually mumbled over several words to herself. These seemed to spring from associations with which her thoughts were busy. The doctor, who was able to get these words, put her in a sort of hypnosis and repeated them to her over and over, in order to bring up any associations that they might have. The patient yielded to his suggestion and reproduced for him those psychic creations which controlled her thoughts during her "absences," and which betrayed themselves in these single spoken words. These were fancies, deeply said, often poetically beautiful, day dreams we might call them, which commonly took as their starting point the situation of a girl beside the sickbed of her father. Whenever she had related a number of such fancies, she was, as it were, freed and restored to her normal mental life. This state of health would last for several hours, and then give place on the next day to a new "absence," which was removed in the same way by relating the newly created fancies. It was impossible not to get the impression that the psychic alteration which was expressed in the "absence" was a consequence of the excitations originating from these intensely emotional fancy-images. The patient herself, who at this time of her illness strangely enough understood and spoke only English, gave this new kind of treatment the name "talking cure," or jokingly designated it as "chimney sweeping."

The doctor soon hit upon the fact that through such cleansing of the soul more could be accomplished than a temporary removal of the constantly recurring mental "clouds." Symptoms of the disease would disappear when in hypnosis the patient could be made to remember the situation and the associative connections under which they first appeared, provided free vent was given to the emotions which they aroused. "There was in the summer a time of intense heat, and the patient had suffered very much from thirst; for, without any apparent reason, she had suddenly become unable to drink. She would take a glass of water in her hand, but as soon as it touched her lips she would push it away as though suffering from hydrophobia. Obviously for these few seconds she was in her absent state. She ate only fruit, melons, and the like in order to relieve this tormenting thirst. When this had been going on about six weeks, she was talking one day in hypnosis about her English governess, whom she disliked, and finally told, with every sign of disgust, how she had come into the room of the governess, and how that lady's little dog, that she abhorred, had drunk out of a glass. Out of respect for the conventions the patient had remained silent. Now, after she had given energetic expression to her restrained anger, she asked for a drink, drank a large quantity of water without trouble, and woke from hypnosis with the glass at her lips. The symptom thereupon vanished permanently."

Permit me to dwell for a moment on this experience. No one had ever cured an hysterical symptom by such means before, or had come so near understanding its cause. This would be a pregnant discovery if the expectation could be confirmed that still other, perhaps the majority of symptoms, originated in this way and could be removed by the same method. Breuer spared no pains to convince himself of this and investigated the pathogenesis of the other more serious symptoms in a more orderly way. Such was indeed the case; almost all the symptoms originated in exactly this way, as remnants, as precipitates, if you like, of affectively toned experiences, which for that reason we later called "psychic traumata." The nature of the symptoms became clear through their relation to the scene which caused them. They were, to use the technical term, "determined" by the scene whose memory traces they embodied, and so could no longer be described as arbitrary or enigmatical functions of the neurosis.

Only one variation from what might be expected must be mentioned. It was not always a single experience which occasioned the symptom, but usually several, perhaps many similar, repeated traumata co-operated in this effect. It was necessary to repeat the whole series of pathogenic memories in chronological sequence, and of course in reverse order, the last first and the first last. It was quite impossible to reach the first and often most essential trauma directly, without first clearing away those coming later....

When, a number of years later, I began to use Breuer's researches and treatment on my own patients, my experiences completely coincided with his. ... If you will permit me to generalize, as is indispensable in so brief a presentation, we may express our results up to this point in the formula: *Our hysterical patients suffer from reminiscences.* Their symptoms are the remnants and the memory symbols of certain (traumatic) experiences ... they cannot escape from the past and neglect present reality in its favor. This fixation of the mental life on the pathogenic traumata is an essential, and practically a most significant characteristic of the neurosis. I will willingly concede the objection which you are probably formulating as you think over the history of Breuer's patient. All her traumata originated at the time when she was caring for her sick father, and her symptoms could only be regarded as memory symbols of his sickness and death. They corresponded to mourning, and a fixation on thoughts of the dead so short a time after death is certainly not pathological, but rather corresponds to normal emotional behavior. I concede this: there is nothing abnormal in the fixation of feeling on the trauma shown by Breuer's patient....

We have so far only explained the relation of the hysterical symptoms to the life history of the patient; now by considering two further factors which Breuer observed, we may get a hint as to the processes of the beginning of the illness and those of the cure. With regard to the first, it is especially to be noted that Breuer's patient in almost all pathogenic situations had to suppress a strong excitement, instead of giving vent to it by appropriate words and deeds. In the little experience with her governess' dog, she suppressed, through regard for the conventions, all manifestations of her very intense disgust. While she was seated by her father's sickbed, she was careful to betray nothing of her anxiety and her painful depression to the patient. When, later, she reproduced the same scene before the physician, the emotion which she had suppressed on the occurrence of the scene burst out with especial strength, as though it had been pent up all along. The symptom which had been caused by that scene reached its greatest intensity while the doctor was striving to revive the memory of the scene, and vanished after it had been fully laid bare. On the other hand, experience shows that if the patient is reproducing the traumatic scene to the physician, the process has no curative effect if, by some peculiar chance, there is no development of emotion. It is apparently these emotional processes upon which the illness of the patient and the restoration to health are dependent. We feel justified in regarding "emotion" as a quantity which may become increased, derived, and displaced. So we are forced to the conclusion that the patient fell ill because the emotion developed in the pathogenic situation was prevented from escaping normally, and that the essence of the sickness lies in the fact that these "imprisoned" emotions undergo a series of abnormal changes. In part they are preserved as a lasting charge and as a source of constant disturbance in psychical life; in part they undergo a change into unusual bodily innervations and inhibitions, which present themselves as the physical symptoms of the case. We have coined the name "hysterical conversion" for the latter process. Part of our mental energy is, under normal conditions, conducted off by way of physical innervation and gives what we call "the expression of emotions." Hysterical conversion exaggerates this part of the course of a mental process which is emotionally colored; it corresponds to a far more intense emotional expression, which finds outlet by new paths. If a stream flows in two channels, an overflow of one will take place as soon as the current in the other meets with an obstacle.

You see that we are in a fair way to arrive at a purely psychological theory of hysteria, in which we assign the first rank to the affective processes. A second observation of Breuer compels us to ascribe to the altered condition of consciousness a great part in determining the characteristics of the disease. His patient showed many sorts of mental states, conditions of "absence," confusion and alteration of character, besides her normal state. In her normal state she was entirely ignorant of the pathogenic scenes and of their connection with her symptoms. She had forgotten those scenes, or at any rate had dissociated them from their pathogenic connection. When the patient was hypnotized, it was possible, after considerable difficulty, to recall those scenes to her memory, and by this means of recall the symptoms were removed. It would have been extremely perplexing to know how to interpret this fact, if hypnotic practice and experiments had not pointed out the way. Through the study of hypnotic phenomena, the conception, strange though it was at first, has become familiar, that in one and the same individual several mental groupings are possible, which may remain relatively independent of each other, "know nothing" of each other, and which may cause a splitting of consciousness along lines which they lay down. . . . In the same way it is quite possible to explain the facts in hysterical cases. Breuer came to the conclusion that the hysterical symptoms originated in peculiar mental states, which he called "hypnoidal states." . . . Later I shall at least suggest what other influences and processes have been disclosed besides that of the hypnoidal states, to which Breuer limited the causal factor.

You have probably also felt, and rightly, that Breuer's investigations gave you only a very incomplete theory and insufficient explanation of the phenomena which we have observed. But complete theories do not fall from heaven,

and you would have had still greater reason to be dis-
trustful had anyone offered you at the beginning of his
observations a well-rounded theory, without any gaps;
such a theory could only be the child of his speculations
and not the fruit of an unprejudiced investigation of the
facts.

Second Lecture. ... The great French observer [Char-
cot], whose student I was during the years 1885-86, had
no natural bent for creating psychological theories. His
student, P. Janet, was the first to attempt to penetrate
more deeply into the psychic processes of hysteria, and
we followed his example when we made the mental splitting and the dissociation of personality the central points
of our theory. Janet propounds a theory of hysteria which
draws upon the principal theories of heredity and de-
generation which are current in France. According to his
view hysteria is a form of degenerative alteration of the
nervous system, manifesting itself in a congenital "weakness" of the function of psychic synthesis. ...

When I undertook to continue on my own account the
investigations begun by Breuer I soon came to another
view of the origin of hysterical dissociation (or splitting
of consciousness). ... The cathartic treatment, as Breuer
had made use of it, presupposed that the patient should
be put in deep hypnosis, for only in hypnosis was available
the knowledge of his pathogenic associations, which were
unknown to him in his normal state. Now hypnosis, as a
fanciful, and so to speak, mystical, aid, I soon came to
dislike; and when I discovered that, in spite of all my
efforts, I could not hypnotize by any means all of my
patients, I resolved to give up hypnotism and to make the
cathartic method independent of it.

Since I could not alter the psychic state of most of my
patients at my wish, I directed my efforts to working with
them in their normal state. This seems at first sight to be
a particularly senseless and aimless undertaking. The problem was this: to find out something from the patient that
the doctor did not know and the patient himself did not

know. How could one hope to make such a method succeed? The memory of a very noteworthy and instructive proceeding came to my aid, which I had seen in Bernheim's clinic at Nancy. Bernheim showed us that persons put in a condition of hypnotic somnambulism, and subjected to all sorts of experiences, had only apparently lost the memory of those somnambulic experiences, and that their memory of them could be awakened even in the normal state. If he asked them about their experiences during somnambulism, they said at first that they did not remember, but if he persisted, urged, assured them that they did know, then every time the forgotten memory came back.

Accordingly I did this with my patients. When I had reached in my procedure with them a point at which they declared that they knew nothing more, I would assure them that they did know, that they must just tell it out, and I would venture the assertion that the memory which would emerge at the moment that I laid my hand on the patient's forehead would be the right one. In this way I succeeded, without hypnosis, in learning from the patient all that was necessary for a construction of the connection between the forgotten pathogenic scenes and the symptoms which they had left behind. This was a troublesome and in its length an exhausting proceeding, and did not lend itself to a finished technique. But I did not give it up without drawing definite conclusions from the data which I had gained. I had substantiated the fact that the forgotten memories were not lost. They were in the possession of the patient, ready to emerge and form associations with his other mental content, but hindered from becoming conscious, and forced to remain in the unconscious by some sort of a force. The existence of this force could be assumed with certainty, for in attempting to drag up the unconscious memories into the consciousness of the patient, in opposition to this force, one got the sensation of his own personal effort striving to overcome it. One could get an idea of this force, which maintained the pathological situation, from the resistance of the patient.

It is on this idea of *resistance* that I based my theory of the psychic processes of hystericals. It had been found that in order to cure the patient it was necessary that this force should be overcome. Now with the mechanism of the cure as a starting point, quite a definite theory could be constructed. These same forces, which in the present situation as resistances opposed the emergence of the forgotten ideas into consciousness, must themselves have caused the forgetting, and repressed from consciousness the pathogenic experiences. I called this hypothetical process "repression," and considered that it was proved by the undeniable existence of resistance.

But now the question arose: What were those forces, and what were the conditions of this repression, in which we were now able to recognize the pathogenic mechanism of hysteria? A comparative study of the pathogenic situations, which the cathartic treatment has made possible, allows us to answer this question. In all those experiences, it had happened that a wish had been aroused, which was in sharp opposition to the other desires of the individual, and was not capable of being reconciled with the ethical, aesthetic and personal pretensions of the patient's personality. There had been a short conflict, and the end of this inner struggle was the repression of the idea which presented itself to consciousness as the bearer of this irreconcilable wish. This was, then, repressed from consciousness and forgotten. The incompatibility of the idea in question with the "ego" of the patient was the motive of the repression, the ethical and other pretensions of the individual were the repressing forces. The presence of the incompatible wish, or the duration of the conflict, had given rise to a high degree of mental pain; this pain was avoided by the repression. This latter process is evidently in such a case a device for the protection of the personality.

I will not multiply examples, but will give you the history of a single one of my cases, in which the conditions and the utility of the repression process stand out clearly enough. Of course for my purpose I must abridge the history of the case and omit many valuable theoretical considerations. It is that of a young girl who was deeply attached to her father, who had died a short time before, and in whose care she had shared—a situation analogous to that of Breuer's patient. When her older sister married, the girl grew to feel a peculiar sympathy for her new brother-in-law, which easily passed with her for family tenderness. This sister soon fell ill and died, while the patient and her mother were away. The absent ones were hastily recalled, without being told fully of the painful situation. As the girl stood by the beside of her dead sister, for one short moment there surged up in her mind an idea, which might be framed in these words: "Now he is free and can marry me." We may be sure that this idea, which betrayed to her consciousness her intense love for her brother-in-law, of which she had not been conscious, was the next moment consigned to repression by her revolted feelings. The girl fell ill with severe hysterical symptoms, and, when I came to treat the case, it appeared that she had entirely forgotten that scene at her sister's bedside and the unnatural, egoistic desire which had arisen in her. She remembered it during the treatment, reproduced the pathogenic moment with every sign of intense emotional excitement, and was cured by this treatment. . . .[3]

The difference between our theory and that of Janet [is that we] do not derive the psychic fission from a congenital lack of capacity on the part of the mental apparatus to synthesize its experiences, but we explain it dynamically by the conflict of opposing mental forces, we recognize in it the result of an active striving of each mental complex against the other.

New questions at once arise in great number from our theory. The situation of psychic conflict is a very frequent one; an attempt of the ego to defend itself from painful memories can be observed everywhere, and yet the result is not a mental fission. We cannot avoid the assumption that still other conditions are necessary, if the

[3] This case has been translated by Dr. Brill in *Selected Papers on Hysteria.*

conflict is to result in dissociation. I willingly concede that with the assumption of "repression" we stand, not at the end, but at the very beginning of a psychological theory. But we can advance only one step at a time, and the completion of our knowledge must await further and more thorough work. . . .

We come to the conclusion, from working with hysterical patients and other neurotics, that they have not fully succeeded in repressing the idea to which the incompatible wish is attached. They have, indeed, driven it out of consciousness and out of memory, and apparently saved themselves a great amount of psychic pain, *but in the unconscious the suppressed wish still exists,* only waiting for its chance to become active, and finally succeeds in sending into consciousness, instead of the repressed idea, a disguised and unrecognizable surrogate-creation, to which the same painful sensations associate themselves that the patient thought he was rid of through his repression. This surrogate of the suppressed idea—the symptom—is secure against further attacks from the defenses of the ego, and instead of a short conflict there originates now a permanent suffering. We can observe in the symptom, besides the tokens of its disguise, a remnant of traceable similarity with the originally repressed idea; the way in which the surrogate is built up can be discovered during the psychoanalytic treatment of the patient, and for his cure the symptom must be traced back over the same route to the repressed idea. If this repressed material is once more made part of the conscious mental functions—a process which supposes the overcoming of considerable resistance —the psychic conflict which then arises, the same which the patient wished to avoid, is made capable of a happier termination, under the guidance of the physician, than is offered by repression. There are several possible suitable decisions which can bring conflict and neurosis to a happy end; in particular cases the attempt may be made to combine several of these. Either the personality of the patient may be convinced that he has been wrong in rejecting the pathogenic wish, and he may be made to accept it either wholly or in part; or this wish may itself be directed to a higher goal which is free from objection, by what is called sublimation; or the rejection may be recognized as rightly motivated, and the automatic and therefore insufficient mechanism of repression be reinforced by the higher, more characteristically human mental faculties; one succeeds in mastering his wishes by conscious thought.

Forgive me if I have not been able to present more clearly these main points of the treatment which is today known as "psychoanalysis." The difficulties do not lie merely in the newness of the subject.

Regarding the nature of the unacceptable wishes, which succeed in making their influence felt out of the unconscious, in spite of repression; and regarding the question of what subjective and constitutional factors must be present for such a failure of repression and such a surrogate or symptom creation to take place, we will speak in later remarks.

Third Lecture. . . . .In the patients whom I treated there were two opposing forces: on the one hand the conscious striving to drag up into consciousness the forgotten experience which was present in the unconscious; and on the other hand the resistance which we have seen, which set itself against the emergence of the suppressed idea or its associates into consciousness. In cases where this resistance was non-existent or very slight, the forgotten material could become conscious without disguise. It was then a natural supposition that the disguise would be the more complete, the greater the resistance to the emergence of the idea. Thoughts which broke into the patient's consciousness instead of the ideas sought for, were accordingly made up just like symptoms; they were new, artificial, ephemeral surrogates for the repressed ideas, and differed from these just in proportion as they had been more completely disguised under the influence of the resistances. These surrogates must, however, show a certain similarity with the ideas which are the object of our search, by virtue of their nature as symptoms; and when the resistance is not too intensive it is possible from the nature of these irruptions to discover the hidden object of our search. This must be related to the repressed thought as a sort of allusion, as a statement of the same things in *indirect* terms.

We know cases in normal psychology in which analogous situations to the one which we have assumed give rise to similar experiences. Such a case is that of wit. By my study of psychoanalytic technique I was necessarily led to a consideration of the problem of the nature of wit. I will give one example of this sort, which, too, is a story that originally appeared in English.

The anecdote runs: "Two unscrupulous business men had succeeded by fortunate speculations in accumulating a large fortune, and then directed their efforts to breaking into good society. Among other means they thought it would be of advantage to be painted by the most famous and expensive artist of the city, a man whose paintings were considered as events. The costly paintings were first shown at a great soiree and both hosts led the most influential connoisseur and art critic to the wall of the salon on which the portraits were hung, to elicit his admiring judgment. The artist looked for a long time, looked about as though in search of something, and then merely asked, pointing out the vacant space between the two pictures: 'And where is the Saviour?' " ...

We understand that the critic means to say: "You are a couple of malefactors, like those between whom the Saviour was crucified." But he does not say this, he expresses himself instead in a way that at first seems not to the purpose and not related to the matter in hand, but which at the next moment we recognize as an *allusion* to the insult at which he aims, and as a perfect surrogate for it. We cannot expect to find in the case of wit all those relations that our theory supposes for the origin of the irruptive ideas of our patients, but it is my desire to lay stress on the similar motivation of wit and irruptive idea. Why does not the critic say directly what he has to say to the two rogues? Because in addition to his desire to say it straight out, he is actuated by strong opposite motives. It is a proceeding which is liable to be dangerous to offend people who are one's hosts, and who can call to their aid the strong arms of numerous servants. . . . On this ground the critic does not express the particular insult directly, but in a disguised form, as an allusion with omission. The same constellation comes into play, according to our hypothesis, when our patient produces the irruptive idea as a surrogate for the forgotten idea which is the object of the quest. . . .

It is very useful to designate a group of ideas which belong together and have a common emotive tone, according to the custom of the Zurich school (Bleuler, Jung, and others), as a "complex." So we can say that if we set out from the last memories of the patient to look for a repressed complex, that we have every prospect of discovering it, if only the patient will communicate to us a sufficient number of the ideas which come into his head. So we let the patient speak along any line that he desires, and cling to the hypothesis that nothing can occur to him except what has some indirect bearing on the complex that we are seeking. If this method of discovering the repressed complexes seems too circumstantial, I can at least assure you that it is the only available one.

In practicing this technique, one is further bothered by the fact that the patient often stops, is at a standstill, and considers that he has nothing to say; nothing occurs to him. If this were really the case and the patient were right, our procedure would again be proven inapplicable. Closer observation shows that such an absence of ideas never really occurs, and that it only appears to when the patient holds back or rejects the ideas which he perceives, under the influence of the resistance, which disguises itself as critical judgment of the value of the idea. The patient can be protected from this if he is warned in advance of this circumstance, and told to take no account of the critical attitude. He must say anything that comes into his mind, fully laying aside such critical choice, even though he may think it unessential, irrelevant, nonsensical, especially when the idea is one which is unpleasant to dwell on. By following this prescription we secure the material which sets us on the track of the repressed complex. . . .

This method of work with whatever comes into the patient's head when he submits to psychoanalytic treatment, is not the only technical means at our disposal for the widening of consciousness. Two other methods of procedure serve the same purpose, the interpretation of his dreams and the evaluation of acts which he bungles or does without intending to. . . .

You must remember that our nightly dream productions show the greatest outer similarity and inner relationship to the creations of the insane, but on the other hand are compatible with full health during waking life. It does not sound at all absurd to say that whoever regards these normal sense illusions, these delusions and alterations of character as matter for amazement instead of understanding, has not the least prospect of understanding the abnormal creations of diseased mental states in any other than the lay sense. . . .

In our waking state we usually treat dreams with as little consideration as the patient treats their irruptive ideas which the psychoanalyst demands from him. It is evident that we reject them, for we forget them quickly and completely. The slight valuation which we place on them is based, with those dreams that are not confused and nonsensical, on the feeling that they are foreign to our personality. . . . [But] not all dreams are so foreign to the character of the dreamer, are incomprehensible and confused. If you will undertake to consider the dreams of young children from the age of a year and a half on, you will find them quite simple and easy to interpret. The young child always dreams of the fulfillment of wishes which were aroused in him the day before and were not satisfied. You need no art of interpretation to discover this simple solution, you only need to inquire into the experiences of the child on the day before (the "dream day"). Now it would certainly be a most satisfactory solution of the dream-riddle, if the dreams of adults, too, were the same as those of children, fulfillments of wishes which had been aroused in them during the dream day. This is actually the fact; the difficulties which stand in the way of this solution can be removed step by step by a thorough analysis of the dream.

There is, first of all, the most weighty objection, that the dreams of adults generally have an incomprehensible content, which shows wish-fulfillment least of anything. The answer is this: these dreams have undergone a process of disguise, the psychic content which underlies them was originally meant for quite different verbal expression. You must differentiate between the *manifest dream-content*, which we remember in the morning only confusedly, and with difficulty clothe in words which seem arbitrary, and the *latent dream-thoughts*, whose presence in the unconscious we must assume. This distortion of the dream is the same process which has been revealed to you in the investigations of the creations (symptoms) of hysterical subjects; it points to the fact that the same opposition of psychic forces has its share in the creation of dreams as in the creation of symptoms.

The manifest dream-content is the disguised surrogate for the unconscious dream thoughts, and this disguising is the work of the defensive forces of the ego, of the resistances. These prevent the repressed wishes from entering consciousness during the waking life, and even in the relaxation of sleep they are still strong enough to force them to hide themselves by a sort of masquerading. The dreamer, then, knows just as little the sense of his dream as the hysterical knows the relation and significance of his symptoms. That there are latent dream-thoughts and that between them and the manifest dream-content there exists the relation just described—of this you may convince yourselves by the analysis of dreams, a procedure the technique of which is exactly that of psychoanalysis. You must abstract entirely from the apparent connection of the elements in the manifest dream and seek for the irruptive ideas which arise through free association, according to the psychoanalytic laws, from each separate dream-element. From this material the latent dream-thoughts may be discovered, exactly as one divines the concealed complexes of the patient from the fancies connected with his symptoms and memories. From the latent dream-thoughts which you will find in this way, you will see at once how thoroughly justified one is in interpreting the dreams of adults by the same rubrics as those of children. What is now substituted for the manifest dream-content is the real sense of the dream, is always clearly comprehensible, associated with the impressions of the day before, and appears as the fulfilling of an unsatisfied wish. The manifest dream, which we remember after waking, may then be described as a *disguised* fulfillment of *repressed* wishes.

It is also possible by a sort of synthesis to get some insight into the process which has brought about the disguise of the unconscious dream-thoughts as the manifest dream-content. We call this process "dream-work." This deserves our fullest theoretical interest, since here as nowhere else we can study the unsuspected psychic processes which are existent in the unconscious, or, to express it more exactly, *between* two such separate systems as the conscious and the unconscious. Among these newly discovered psychic processes, two, condensation and displacement, or transvaluation, change of psychic accent, stand out most prominently. Dream-work is a special case of the reaction of different mental groupings on each other, and as such is the consequence of psychic fission. In all essential points it seems identical with the work of disguise, which changes the repressed complex in the case of failing repression into symptoms.

You will furthermore discover by the analysis of dreams, most convincingly your own, the unsuspected importance of the role which impressions and experiences from early childhood exert on the development of men. In the dream life the child, as it were, continues his existence in the man, with a retention of all his traits and wishes, including those which he was obliged to allow to fall into disuse in his later years. With irresistible might it will be impressed on you by what processes of development, of

symbols in dreams

repression, sublimation, and reaction there arises out of the child, with its peculiar gifts and tendencies, the so-called normal man, the bearer and partly the victim of our painfully acquired civilization. I will also direct your attention to the fact that we have discovered from the analysis of dreams that the unconscious makes use of a sort of symbolism, especially in the presentation of sexual complexes. This symbolism in part varies with the individual, but in part is of a typical nature, and seems to be identical with the symbolism which we suppose to lie behind our myths and legends. It is not impossible that these latter creations of the people may find their explanation from the study of dreams.

Finally I must remind you that you must not be led astray by the objection that the occurrence of anxiety-dreams, contradicts our idea of the dream as a wish-fulfillment. Apart from the consideration that anxiety-dreams also require interpretation before judgment can be passed on them, one can say quite generally that the anxiety does not depend in such a simple way on the dream content as one might suppose without more knowledge of the facts, and more attention to the conditions of neurotic anxiety. Anxiety is one of the ways in which the ego relieves itself of repressed wishes which have become too strong, and so is easy to explain in the dream, if the wish has gone too far towards the fulfilling of the objectionable wish. . . .

I may now pass to that group of everyday mental phenomena whose study has become a technical help for psychoanalysis. These are the bungling of acts [parapraxes] among normal men as well as among neurotics, to which no significance is ordinarily attached; the forgetting of things which one is supposed to know and at other times really does know (for example the temporary forgetting of proper names); mistakes in speaking, which occur so frequently; analogous mistakes in writing and in reading; the automatic execution of purposive acts in wrong situations and the loss or breaking of objects, etc. These are trifles for which no one has ever sought a psychological determination, which have passed unchallenged as chance experiences, as consequences of absent-mindedness, inattention, and similar conditions. Here, too, are included the acts and gestures executed without being noticed by the subject, to say nothing of the fact that he attaches no psychic importance to them; as playing and trifling with objects, humming melodies, handling one's person and clothing and the like.[4]

These little things, the bungling of acts, like the symptomatic and chance acts are not so entirely without meaning as is generally supposed by a sort of tacit agreement. They have a meaning, generally easy and sure to interpret from the situation in which they occur, and it can be demonstrated that they either express impulses and purposes which are repressed, hidden if possible from the consciousness of the individual, or that they spring from exactly the same sort of repressed wishes and complexes which we have learned to know already as the creators of symptoms and dreams.

It follows that they deserve the rank of symptoms, and their observation, like that of dreams, can lead to the discovery of the hidden complexes of the psychic life. With their help one will usually betray the most intimate of his secrets. If these occur so easily and commonly among people in health, with whom repression has on the whole succeeded fairly well, this is due to their insignificance and their inconspicuous nature. But they can lay claim to high theoretic value, for they prove the existence of repression and surrogate creations even under the conditions of health. You have already noticed that the psychoanalyst is distinguished by an especially strong belief in the determination of the psychic life. For him there is in the expressions of the psyche nothing trifling, nothing arbitrary and lawless. ...

Fourth Lecture. ... Psychoanalytic investigations trace back the symptoms of disease with really surprising regularity to impressions from the sexual life, show us that the

[4] See *The Psychopathology of Everyday Life.*

pathogenic wishes are of the nature of erotic impulse-components, and necessitate the assumption that to disturbances of the erotic sphere must be ascribed the greatest significance among the etiological factors of the disease. This holds of both sexes. I know that this assertion will not willingly be credited. Even those investigators who gladly follow my psychological labors, are inclined to think that I overestimate the etiological share of the sexual factors. They ask me why other mental excitations should not lead to the phenomena of repression and surrogate-creation which I have described. I can give them this answer; that I do not know why they should not do this, I have no objection to their doing it, but experience shows that they do not possess such a significance, and that they merely support the effect of the sexual factors, without being able to supplant them. . . .

The conduct of the patients does not make it any easier to convince one's self of the correctness of the view which I have expressed. Instead of willingly giving us information concerning their sexual life, they try to conceal it by every means in their power. Men generally are not candid in sexual matters. They do not show their sexuality freely, but they wear a thick overcoat—a fabric of lies—to conceal it, as though it were bad weather in the world of sex. And they are not wrong; sun and wind are not favorable in our civilized society to any demonstration of sex life. In truth no one can freely disclose his erotic life to his neighbor. But when your patients see that in your treatment they may disregard the conventional restraints, they lay aside this veil of lies, and then only are you in a position to formulate a judgment on the question in dispute. Unfortunately physicians are not favored above the rest of the children of men in their personal relationship to the questions of the sex life. Many of them are under the ban of that mixture of prudery and lasciviousness which determines the behavior of most *Kulturmenschen* in affairs of sex. . . .

The work of analysis which is necessary for the thorough explanation and complete cure of a case of sickness does not stop in any case with the experience of the time of onset of the disease, but in every case it goes back to the adolescence and the early childhood of the patient. Here only do we hit upon the impressions and circumstances which determine the later sickness. Only the childhood experiences can give the explanation for the sensitivity to later traumata and only when these memory traces, which almost always are forgotten, are discovered and made conscious, is the power developed to banish the symptoms. We arrive here at the same conclusion as in the investigation of dreams—that it is the incompatible, repressed wishes of childhood which lend their power to the creation of symptoms. Without these the reactions upon later traumata discharge normally. But we must consider these mighty wishes of childhood very generally as sexual in nature. . . .

Is there an infantile sexuality? you will ask. Is childhood not rather that period of life which is distinguished by the lack of the sexual impulse? No . . . it is not at all true that the sexual impulse enters into the child at puberty, as the devils in the gospel entered into the swine. The child has his sexual impulses and activities from the beginning, he brings them with him into the world, and from these the so-called normal sexuality of adults emerges by a significant development through manifold stages. It is not very difficult to observe the expressions of this childish sexual activity; it needs rather a certain art to overlook them or to fail to interpret them.[5] . . .

Lay aside your doubts and let us evaluate the infantile sexuality of the earliest years. The sexual impulse of the child manifests itself as a very complex one, it permits of an analysis into many components, which spring from different sources. It is entirely disconnected from the function of reproduction which it is later to serve. It permits the child to gain different sorts of pleasure sensations, which we include, by the analogues and connections which they show, under the term sexual pleasures. The

[5] See *Three Contributions to the Theory of Sexuality.*

great source of infantile sexual pleasure is the ___
tion of certain particularly sensitive parts of
besides the genitals, are included the rectur
opening of the urinary canal, and also the skin __ other
sensory surfaces. Since in this first phase of child sexual
life the satisfaction is found on the child's own body
and has nothing to do with any other object, we call this
phase after a word coined by Havelock Ellis, that of
"auto-erotism." The parts of the body significant in giving
sexual pleasure we call "erotogenic zones." The thumb-
sucking or passionate sucking of very young children is a
good example of such an auto-erotic satisfaction of an
erotogenic zone. The first scientific observer of this phenomenon, a specialist in children's diseases in Budapest
by the name of Lindner, interpreted these rightly as
sexual satisfaction and described exhaustively their transformation into other and higher forms of sexual gratification.[6] Another sexual satisfaction of this time of life is
the excitation of the genitals by masturbation, which has
such a great significance for later life and, in the case
of many individuals, is never fully overcome. Besides this
and other auto-erotic manifestations we see very clearly
in the child the impulse-components of *sexual pleasure*,
or, as we may say, of the *libido*, which presupposes a second person as its object. These impulses appear in opposed pairs, as active and passive. The most important
representatives of this group are the pleasure in inflicting
pain (sadism) with its passive opposite (masochism) and
active and passive exhibition-pleasure. From the first of
these later pairs splits off the curiosity for knowledge, as
from the latter the impulse toward artistic and theatrical
representation. Other sexual manifestations of the child can
already be regarded from the viewpoint of object-choice,
in which the second person plays the prominent part. The
significance of this was primarily based upon motives of
the impulse of self-preservation. The difference between
the sexes plays, however, in the child no very great role.

[6] *Jb. Kinderheilkunde,* 1879.

One may attribute to every child, without wronging him, a bit of the homosexual disposition.

The sexual life of the child, rich, but dissociated, in which each single impulse goes about the business of arousing pleasure independently of every other, is later correlated and organized in two general directions, so that by the close of puberty the definite sexual character of the individual is practically finally determined. The single impulses subordinate themselves to the overlordship of the genital zone, so that the whole sexual life is taken over into the service of procreation, and their gratification is now significant only so far as they help to prepare and promote the true sexual act. On the other hand, object-choice prevails over auto-erotism, so that now in the sexual life all components of the sexual impulse are satisfied in the loved person. But not all the original impulse-components are given a share in the final shaping of the sexual life. Even before the advent of puberty certain impulses have undergone the most energetic repression under the impulse of education, and mental forces like shame, disgust, and morality are developed, which, like sentinels, keep the repressed wishes in subjection. When there comes, in puberty, the high tide of sexual desire, it finds dams in this creation of reactions and resistances. These guide the outflow into the so-called normal channels, and make it impossible to revivify the impulses which have undergone repression. . . .

A sentence of general pathology says that every process of development brings with it the germ of pathological dispositions, in so far as it may be inhibited, delayed, or incompletely carried out. This holds for the development of the sexual function, with its many complications. It is not smoothly completed in all individuals, and may leave behind either abnormalities or disposition to later diseases by the way of later falling back or regression. It may happen that not all the partial impulses subordinate themselves to the rule of the genital zone Such an impulse which has remained disconnected brings about what we call a perversion, which may replace the normal sexual goal by one of its own. It may happen, as has been said before, that the auto-erotism is not fully overcome, as many sorts of disturbances testify. The originally equal value of both sexes as sexual objects may be maintained and an inclination to homosexual activities in adult life result from this, which, under suitable conditions, rises to the level of exclusive homosexuality. This series of disturbances corresponds to the direct inhibition of development of the sexual function, it includes the perversions and the general *infantilism* of the sex life that are not seldom met with.

The disposition to neuroses is to be derived in another way from an injury to the development of the sex life. The neuroses are related to the perversions as the negative to the positive; in them we find the same impulse-components as in perversions, as bearers of the complexes and as creators of the symptoms; but here they work from out the unconscious. They have undergone a repression, but in spite of this they maintain themselves in the unconscious. Psychoanalysis teaches us that overstrong expression of the impulse in very early life leads to a sort of fixation, which then offers a weak point in the articulation of the sexual function. If the exercise of the normal sexual function meets with hindrances in later life, this repression, dating from the time of development, is broken through at just that point at which the infantile fixation took place.

You will now perhaps make the objection: "But all that is not sexuality." I have used the word in a very much wider sense than you are accustomed to understand it. This I willingly concede. But it is a question whether you do not rather use the word in much too narrow a sense when you restrict it to the realm of procreation. You sacrifice by that the understanding of perversions; of the connection between perversion, neurosis, and normal sexual life; and have no means of recognizing, in its true significance, the easily observable beginning of the somatic and mental sexual life of the child. But however you decide about the use of the word, remember that the psychoanalyst understands sexuality in that full sense to which he is led by the evaluation of infantile sexuality.

Now we turn again to the sexual development of the child. We still have much to say here, since we have given more attention to the somatic than to the mental expressions of the sexual life. The primitive object-choice of the child, which is derived from his need of help, demands our further interest. It first attaches to all persons to whom he is accustomed, but soon these give way in favor of his parents. The relation of the child to his parents is, as both direct observation of the child and later analytic investigation of adults agree, not at all free from elements of sexual accessory-excitation. The child takes both parents, and especially one, as an object of his erotic wishes. Usually he follows in this the stimulus given by his parents, whose tenderness has very clearly the character of a sex manifestation, though inhibited so far as its goal is concerned. As a rule, the father prefers the daughter, the mother the son; the child reacts to this situation, since, as son, he wishes himself in the place of his father, as daughter, in the place of the mother. The feelings awakened in these relations between parents and children, and, as a resultant of them, those among the children in relation to each other, are not only positively of a tender, but negatively of an inimical sort. The complex built up in this way is destined to quick repression, but it still exerts a great and lasting effect from the unconscious. We must express the opinion that this with its ramifications presents the *nuclear complex* of every neurosis, and so we are prepared to meet with it in a not less effectual way in the other fields of mental life. The myth of King Oedipus, who kills his father and wins his mother as a wife, is only the slightly altered presentation of the infantile wish, rejected later by the opposing barriers of incest. Shakespeare's tale of Hamlet rests on the same basis of an incest complex, though better concealed. At the time when the child is still ruled by the still unrepressed nuclear complex, there begins a very significant part of his mental activity which serves sexual interest. He begins to investigate the question of where children come from and guesses more than adults imagine of the true relations by deduction from the signs which he sees. Usually his interest in this investigation is awakened by the threat to his welfare through the birth of another child in the family, in whom at first he sees only a rival. Under the influence of the partial impulses which are active in him he arrives at a number of "infantile sexual theories," as that the same male genitals belong to both sexes, that children are conceived by eating and born through the opening of the intestine and that sexual intercourse is to be regarded as an inimical act, a sort of overpowering.

But just the unfinished nature of his sexual constitution and the gaps in his knowledge brought about by the hidden condition of the feminine sexual canal, cause the infant investigator to discontinue his work as a failure. The facts of this childish investigation itself as well as the infant sex theories created by it are of determinative significance in the building of the child's character, and in the content of his later neuroses.

It is unavoidable and quite normal that the child should make his parents the objects of his first object-choice. But his *libido* must not remain fixed on these first chosen objects, but must take them merely as a prototype and transfer from these to other persons in the time of definite object-choice. The breaking loose of the child from his parents is thus a problem impossible to escape if the social virtue of the young individual is not to be impaired. During the time that the repressive activity is making its choice among the partial sexual impulses and later, when the influence of the parents, which in the most essential way has furnished the material for these repressions, is lessened, great problems fall to the work of education, which at present certainly does not always solve them in the most intelligent and economic way....

Do not think that with these explanations of the sexual life and the sexual development of the child we have too far departed from psychoanalysis and the cure of neurotic disturbances. If you like, you may regard the psychoanalytic treatment only as a continued education for the overcoming of childhood-remnants.

Fifth Lecture. ... With the discovery of infantile sexuality and the tracing back of the neurotic symptoms to erotic impulse-components we have arrived at several unexpected formulae for expressing the nature and tendencies of neurotic disease. We see that the individual falls ill when in consequence of outer hindrances or inner lack of adaptability the satisfaction of the erotic needs in the sphere of reality is denied. We see that he then flees to sickness, in order to find with its help a surrogate satisfaction for that denied him. We recognize that the symptoms of illness contain fractions of the sexual activity of the individual, or his whole sexual life, and we find in the turning away from reality the chief tendency and also the chief injury of the sickness. We may guess that the resistance of our patients against the cure is not a simple one, but is composed of many motives. Not only does the ego of the patient strive against the giving up of the repressions by which it has changed itself from its original constitution into its present form, but also the sexual impulses may not renounce their surrogate satisfaction so long as it is not certain that they can be offered anything better in the sphere of reality.

The flight from the unsatisfying reality into what we call, on account of its biologically injurious nature, disease, but which is never without an individual gain in pleasure for the patient, takes place over the path of regression, the return to earlier phases of the sexual life, when satisfaction was not lacking. This regression is seemingly a twofold one, a *temporal,* in so far as the *libido* or erotic need falls back to a temporally earlier stage of development, and a *formal,* since the original and primitive psychic means of expression are applied to the expression of this need. Both sorts of regression focus in childhood and have their common point in the production of an infantile condition of sexual life.

The deeper you penetrate into the pathogenesis of

neurotic diseases, the more the connection of neuroses with other products of human mentality, even the most valuable, will be revealed to you. You will be reminded that we men, with the high claims of our civilization and under the pressure of our repressions, find reality generally quite unsatisfactory and so keep up a life of fancy in which we love to compensate for what is lacking in the sphere of reality by the production of wish-fulfillments. In these fantasies is often contained very much of the particular constitutional essence of personality and of its tendencies, repressed in real life. The energetic and successful man is he who succeeds by dint of labor in transforming his wish-fancies into reality. Where this is not successful in consequence of the resistance of the outer world and the weakness of the individual, there begins the turning away from reality. The individual takes refuge in his satisfying world of fancy. Under certain favorable conditions it still remains possible for him to find another connecting link between these fancies and reality, instead of permanently becoming a stranger to it through the regression into the infantile. If the individual who is displeased with reality is in possession of that *artistic talent* which is still a psychological riddle, he can transform his fancies into artistic creations. So he escapes the fate of a neurosis and wins back his connection with reality by this roundabout way. Where this opposition to the real world exists, but this valuable talent fails or proves insufficient, it is unavoidable that the *libido*, following the origin of the fancies, succeeds by means of regression in revivifying the infantile wishes and so producing a neurosis. The neurosis takes, in our time, the place of the cloister, in which were accustomed to take refuge all those whom life had undeceived or who felt themselves too weak for life. Let me give at this point the main result at which we have arrived by the psycho-analytic investigation of neurotics, namely, that neuroses have no peculiar psychic content of their own, which is not also to be found in healthy states; or, as C. G. Jung has expressed it, neurotics fall ill of the same complexes with which we sound people struggle. It depends on quantitative relationships, on the relations of the forces wrestling with each other, whether the struggle leads to health, to a neurosis, or to compensatory over-functioning. . . .

I have still withheld from you the most remarkable experience which corroborates our assumptions of the sexual impulse-forces of neurotics. Every time that we treat a neurotic psychoanalytically, there occurs in him the so-called phenomenon of *transference,* that is, he applies to the person of the physician a great amount of tender emotion, often mixed with enmity, which has no foundation in any real relation, and must be derived in every respect from the old wish-fancies of the patient which have become unconscious. Every fragment of his emotive life, which can no longer be called back into memory, is accordingly lived over by the patient in his relations to the physician, and only by such a living of them over in the "transference" is he convinced of the existence and the power of these unconscious sexual excitations. The symptoms, which to use a simile from chemistry, are the precipitates of earlier love experiences (in the widest sense), can only be dissolved in the higher temperature of the experience of transference and transformed into other psychic products. The physician plays in this reaction, to use an excellent expression of S. Ferenczi, the role of a *catalytic ferment,* which temporarily attracts to itself the affect which has become free in the course of the process. The study of transference can also give you the key to the understanding of hypnotic suggestion, which we at first used with our patients as a technical means of investigation of the unconscious. Hypnosis showed itself at that time to be a therapeutic help, but a hindrance to the scientific knowledge of the real nature of the case, since it cleared away the psychic resistances from a certain field, only to pile them up in an unscalable wall at the boundaries of this field. You must not think that the phenomenon of transference, about which I can unfortunately say only too little here, is created by the influence of the psychoanalytic treatment. The transference arises spontaneously in all

human relations and in the relations of the patient to the
physician; it is everywhere the especial bearer of therapeutic influences, and it works the stronger the less one
knows of its presence. Accordingly psychoanalysis does
not create it, it merely discloses it to consciousness, and
avails itself of it, in order to direct the psychic processes
to the wished-for goal. But I cannot leave the theme of
transference without stressing the fact that this phenomenon is of decisive importance to convince not only the
patient, but also the physician. I know that all my ad-
herents were first convinced of the correctness of my views
through their experience with transference, and I can
very well conceive that one may not win such a surety
of judgment so long as he makes no psychoanalysis, and
so has not himself observed the effects of transference. . . .

I am of the opinion that there are, on the intellectual
side, two hindrances to acknowledging the value of the
psychoanalytic viewpoint: first, the fact that we are not
accustomed to reckon with a strict determination of mental
life, which holds without exception, and second, the lack
of knowledge of the peculiarities through which unconscious mental processes differ from those conscious ones
with which we are familiar. One of the most widespread
resistances against the work of psychoanalysis with patients as with persons in health reduces to the latter of
the two factors. One is afraid of doing harm by psychoanalysis, one is anxious about calling up into consciousness
the repressed sexual impulses of the patient, as though
there were danger that they could overpower the higher
ethical strivings and rob him of his cultural acquisitions.
One can see that the patient has sore places in his mental
life, but one is afraid to touch them, lest his sufferings be
increased. We may use this analogy. It is, of course, better
not to touch diseased places when one can only cause
pain. But we know that the surgeon does not refrain from
the investigation and reinvestigation of the seat of illness,
if his invasion has as its aim the restoration of lasting
health. Nobody thinks of blaming him for the unavoidable
difficulties of the investigation or the phenomena of re-

action from the operation, if these only accomplish their purpose, and gain for the patient a final cure by temporarily making his condition worse. The case is similar in psychoanalysis; it can lay claim to the same things as surgery; the increase of pain which takes place in the patient during the treatment is very much less than that which the surgeon imposes upon him, and especially negligible in comparison with the pains of serious illness. But the consequence which is feared, that of a disturbance of the cultural character by the impulse which has been freed from repression, is wholly impossible. In relation to this anxiety we must consider what our experiences have taught us with certainty, that the somatic and mental power of a wish, if once its repression has not succeeded, is incomparably stronger when it is unconscious than when it is conscious, so that by being made conscious it can only be weakened. The unconscious wish cannot be influenced, is free from all strivings in the contrary direction, while the conscious is inhibited by those wishes which are also conscious and which strive against it. The work of psychoanalysis accordingly presents a better substitute, in the service of the highest and most valuable cultural strivings, for the repression which has failed.

Now what is the fate of the wishes which have become free by psychoanalysis, by what means shall they be made harmless for the life of the individual? There are several ways. The general consequence is that the wish is consumed during the work by the correct mental activity of those better tendencies which are opposed to it. The repression is supplanted by a condemnation carried through with the best means at one's disposal. This is possible, since for the most part we have to abolish only the effects of earlier developmental stages of the ego. The individual for his part only repressed the useless impulse, because at that time he was himself still incompletely organized and weak; in his present maturity and strength he can, perhaps, conquer without injury to himself that which is inimical to him. A second issue of the work of psychoanalysis may be that the revealed unconscious impulses can now arrive at those useful applications which, in the case of undisturbed development, they would have found earlier. The extirpation of the infantile wishes is not at all the ideal aim of development. The neurotic has lost, by his repressions, many sources of mental energy whose contributions would have been very valuable for his character building and his life activities. We know a far more purposive process of development, the so-called *sublimation,* by which the energy of infantile wish-excitations is not secluded, but remains capable of application, while for the particular excitations, instead of becoming useless, a higher, eventually no longer sexaul, goal is set up. The components of the sexual instinct are especially distinguished by such a capacity for the sublimation and exchange of their sexual goal for one more remote and socially more valuable. We probably owe the highest achievements of our culture to energy which has been liberated in this way. A repression taking place at an early period precludes the sublimation of the repressed impulse; after the removal of the repression the way to sublimation is again free.

We must not neglect, also, to glance at the third of the possible issues. A certain part of the suppressed libidinous excitation has a right to direct satisfaction and ought to find it in life. The claims of our civilizaton make life too hard for the greater part of humanity, and so further the aversion to reality and the origin of neuroses, without producing an excess of cultural gain by this excess of sexual repression. We ought not to go so far as fully neglect the original animal part of our nature, we ought not to forget that the happiness of individuals cannot be dispensed with as one of the aims of our culture. The plasticity of the sexual-components, manifest in their capacity for sublimation, may induce the temptation to accomplish ever greater achievements of culture by a more and more far-reaching sublimation. But just as with our machines we expect to change only a certain fraction of the applied heat into useful mechanical work, so we ought not to try to separate the sexual impulse in its whole extent of energy from its peculiar goal. It cannot be done, and if the narrowing of sexuality is pushed too far it will have all the evil effects of a robbery.

I do not know whether you will regard the exhortation with which I close as a presumptuous one. I only venture the indirect presentation of my conviction, if I relate an old tale, whose application you may make yourselves. German literature knows a town called Schilda, to whose inhabitants were attributed all sorts of clever pranks. The wiseacres, so the story goes, had a horse, with whose powers of work they were well satisfied, and against whom they had only one grudge, that he consumed so much expensive oats. They concluded that by good management they would break him of this bad habit, by cutting down his rations by several stalks each day, until he had learned to do without them altogether. Things went finely for a while, the horse was weaned to one stalk a day, and on the next day he would at last work without fodder. On the morning of this day the malicious horse was found dead; the citizens of Schilda could not understand why he had died. We should be inclined to believe that the horse had starved, and that without a certain ration of oats no work could be expected from an animal.

By a process of development against which it would have been useless to struggle, the word "psychoanalysis" has itself become ambiguous. While it was originally the name of a particular therapeutic method, it has now become the name of a science—the science of unconscious mental processes. By itself this science is seldom able to deal with a problem completely, but it seems destined to give valuable contributory help in a large number of regions of knowledge. The sphere of application of psychoanalysis extends as far as that of psychology, to which it forms a complement of the greatest moment.

From "An Autobiographical Study."

1924

FORMULATIONS REGARDING THE TWO PRINCIPLES IN MENTAL FUNCTIONING [1]

(1911)

WE have long observed that every neurosis has the result, and therefore probably the purpose, of forcing the patient out of real life, of alienating him from actuality. Nor could a fact such as this escape the observation of Pierre Janet; he spoke of a loss of *"la fonction du réel* as being a special characteristic of the neurotic, but without discovering the connection of this disturbance with the fundamental conditions of neurosis. By introducing the concept of repression into the genesis of the neuroses we have been able to gain some insight into this connection. The neurotic turns away from reality because he finds it unbearable—either the whole or parts of it. The most extreme type of this alienation from reality is shown in certain cases of hallucinatory psychosis which aim at denying the existence of the particular event that occasioned the outbreak of insanity. But actually every neurotic does the same with some fragment of reality. And

[1] *Jb. f. Ps.-An. iii,* 1-8; *G.S. v,* 409-17; *S.k.S.N. iii,* 271-79; *C.P. iv,* 13-21. Trans. by M. N. Searl, revised by Joan Riviere.

now we are confronted with the task of investigating the development of the relation of the neurotic and of mankind in general to reality, and of so bringing the psychological significance of the real outer world into the structure of our theory.

In the psychology which is founded on psychoanalysis we have accustomed ourselves to take as our starting point the unconscious mental processes, with the peculiarities of which we have become acquainted through analysis. These we consider to be the older, primary processes, the residues of a phase of development in which they were the only kind of mental processes. The sovereign tendency obeyed by these primary processes is easy of recognition; it is called the pleasure-pain (*Lust-Unlust*) principle, or more shortly the pleasure-principle. These processes strive towards gaining pleasure; from any operation which might arouse unpleasantness ("pain") mental activity draws back (repression). Our nocturnal dreams, our waking tendency to shut out painful impressions, are remnants of the supremacy of this principle and proofs of its power.

In presupposing that the state of mental equilibrium was originally disturbed by the peremptory demands of inner needs, I am returning to lines of thought which I have developed in another place.[2] In the situation I am considering, whatever was thought of (desired) was simply imagined in an hallucinatory form, as still happens today with our dream-thoughts every night.[3] This attempt at satisfaction by means of hallucination was abandoned only in consequence of the absence of the expected gratification, because of the disappointment experienced. Instead, the mental apparatus had to decide to form a conception of the real circumstances in the outer world and to exert itself to alter them. A new principle of mental functioning was thus introduced; what was conceived of was no longer that which was pleasant, but that which was

[2] The General Section of *The Interpretation of Dreams*.

[3] The state of sleep can recover the likeness of mental life as it was before the recognition of reality, because a prerequisite of sleep is a deliberate rejection of reality (the wish to sleep).

real, even if it should be unpleasant.[4] This institution of the *reality-principle* proved a momentous step.

1. In the first place the new demand made a succession of adaptations necessary in the mental apparatus, which, on account of insufficient or uncertain knowledge, we can only detail very cursorily.

The increased significance of external reality heightened the significance also of the sense-organs directed towards that outer world, and of the *consciousness* attached to them; the latter now learned to comprehend the qualities of sense in addition to the qualities of pleasure and "pain" which hitherto had alone been of interest to it. A special function was instituted which had periodically to search the outer world in order that its data might be already familiar if an urgent inner need should arise; this function was *attention*. Its activity meets the sense-impressions halfway, instead of awaiting their appearance. At the same time there was probably introduced a system of *notation*, whose task was to deposit the results of this periodical activity of consciousness—a part of that which we call *memory*.

In place of repression, which excluded from cathexis as productive of "pain" some of the emerging ideas, there

---

[4] I will attempt to amplify the above schematic presentation with some further details. It will rightly be objected that an organization which is a slave to the pleasure-principle and neglects the reality of the outer world could not maintain itself alive for the shortest time, so that it could not have come into being at all. The use of a fiction of this kind is, however, vindicated by the consideration that the infant, if one only includes the maternal care, does almost realize such a state of mental life. Probably it hallucinates the fulfillment of its inner needs; it betrays its "pain" due to increase of stimulation and delay of satisfaction by the motor discharge of crying and struggling and then experiences the hallucinated satisfaction. Later, as a child, it learns to employ intentionally these modes of discharge as means of expression. Since the care of the infant is the prototype of the later care of the child, the supremacy of the pleasure-principle can end in actuality only with complete mental detachment from the parents.

cathexis: the investment of emotional significance in a thought, object or idea

developed an impartial *passing of judgment,* which had to decide whether a particular idea was true or false, that is, was in agreement with reality or not; decision was determined by comparsion with the memory-traces of reality.

A new function was now entrusted to motor discharge, which under the supremacy of the pleasure-principle had served to unburden the mental appartus of accretions of stimuli, and in carrying out this task had sent innervations into the interior of the body (mien, expressions of affect); it was now employed in the appropriate alteration of reality. It was converted into *action.*

Restraint of motor discharge (of action) had now become necessary, and was provided by means of the process of *thought,* which was developed from ideation. Thought was endowed with qualities which made it possible for the mental apparatus to support increased tension during a delay in the process of discharge. It is essentially an experimental way of acting, accompanied by displacement of smaller quantities of cathexis together with less expenditure (discharge) of them. For this purpose conversion of free cathexis into "bound" cathexes was imperative, and this was brought about by means of raising the level of the whole cathectic process. It is probable that thinking was originally unconscious, in so far as it rose above mere ideation and turned to the relations between the object-impressions, and that it became endowed with further qualities which were perceptible to consciousness only through its connection with the memory-traces of words.

2. There is a general tendency of our mental apparatus which we can trace back to the economic principle of saving in expenditure; it seems to find expression in the tenacity with which we hold on to the sources of pleasure at our disposal, and in the difficulty with which we renounce them. With the introduction of the reality-principle one mode of thought-activity was split off; it was kept free from reality-testing and remained subordinated to the

pleasure-principle alone.[5] This is the act of *fantasy-making*, which begins already in the games of children, and later, continued as *day-dreaming*, abandons its dependence on real objects.

3. The supersession of the pleasure-principle by the reality-principle with all the mental consequences of this, which is here schematically condensed in a single sentence, is not in reality accomplished all at once; nor does it take place simultaneously along the whole line. For while this development is going on in the ego-instincts, the sexual instincts become detached from them in very significant ways. The sexual instincts at first behave auto-erotically; they find their satisfaction in the child's own body and therefore do not come into the situation of frustration which enforces the installation of the reality-principle. Then when later on they begin to find an object, this development undergoes a long interruption in the latency period, which postpones sexual development until puberty. These two factors—auto-erotism and latency period—bring about the result that the mental development of the sexual instincts is delayed and remains far longer under the supremacy of the pleasure-principle, from which in many people it is never able to withdraw itself at all.

In consequence of these conditions there arises a closer connection, on the one hand, between the sexual instincts and fantasy and, on the other hand, between the ego-instincts and the activities of consciousness. Both in healthy and in neurotic people this connection strikes us as very intimate, although the considerations of genetic psychology put forward above lead us to recognize it as *secondary*. The perpetuated activity of auto-erotism makes possible a long retention of the easier momentary and fantastic satisfaction in regard to the sexual object, in place of real satisfaction in regard to its, the latter requiring effort and delay. In the realm of fantasy, repression remains all-

---

[5] Just as a nation whose wealth rests on the exploitation of its land yet reserves certain territory to be preserved in its original state and protected from cultural alterations, *e.g.* Yellowstone Park.

powerful; it brings about the inhibition of ideas *in statu nascendi* before they can be consciously noticed, should cathexis of them be likely to occasion the release of "pain." This is the weak place of our mental organization, which can be utilized to bring back under the supremacy of the pleasure-principle thought-processes which had already become rational. An essential part of the mental predisposition to neurosis thus lies in the delayed training of the sexual instincts in the observance of reality and, further, in the conditions which make this delay possible.

4. Just as the pleasure-ego can do nothing but *wish*, work towards gaining pleasure and avoiding "pain," so the reality-ego need do nothing but strive for what is *useful* and guard itself against damage.[6] Actually, the substitution of the reality-principle for the pleasure-principle denotes no dethronement of the pleasure-principle, but only a safeguarding of it. A momentary pleasure, uncertain in its results, is given up, but only in order to gain in the new way an assured pleasure coming later. But the endopsychic impression made by this substitution has been so powerful that it is mirrored in a special religious myth. The doctrine of reward in a future life for the—voluntary or enforced—renunciation of earthly lusts is nothing but a mythical projection of this revolution in the mind. In logical pursuit of this prototype, *religions* have been able to effect absolute renunciation of pleasure in this life by means of the promise of compensation in a future life; they have not, however, achieved a conquest of the pleasure-principle in this way. It is *science* which comes nearest to succeeding in this conquest; science, however, also offers intellectual pleasure during its work and promises practical gain at the end.

5. *Education* can without further hesitation be described as an incitement to the conquest of the pleasure-

---

[6] The superiority of the reality-ego over the pleasure-ego is aptly expressed by Bernard Shaw in these words: "To be able to choose the line of greatest advantage instead of yielding in the direction of least resistance." (*Man and Superman: A Comedy and a Philosophy.*)

principle, and to its replacement by the reality-principle;
it offers its aid, that is, to that process of development
which concerns the ego; to this end it makes use of
rewards of love from those in charge, and thus it fails
if the spoiled child thinks it will possess this love whatever
happens and can in no circumstances lose it.

6. *Art* brings about a reconciliation of the two principles in a peculiar way. The artist is originally a man who
turns from reality because he cannot come to terms with
the demand for the renunciation of instinctual satisfaction
as it is first made, and who then in fantasy-life allows full
play to his erotic and ambitious wishes. But he finds a
way of return from this world of fantasy back to reality;
with his special gifts he molds his fantasies into a new
kind of reality, and men concede them a justification as
valuable reflections of actual life. Thus by a certain path
he actually becomes the hero, king, creator, favorite he
desired to be, without pursuing the circuitous path of
creating real alterations in the outer world. But this he can
only attain because other men feel the same dissatisfaction
as he with the renunciation demanded by reality, and because this dissatisfaction, resulting from the displacement
of the pleasure-principle by the reality-principle, is itself
a part of reality.[7]

7. While the ego goes through its transformation from
a *pleasure-ego* into a *reality-ego*, the sexual instincts undergo the changes that lead them from their original auto-
erotism through various intermediate phases to object-love
in the service of procreation. If it is correct that every step
of these two processes of development may become the
seat of a predisposition to later neurotic illness, it seems to
follow that the decision as regards the form of the subsequent illness (election of neurosis) will depend on the
particular phase of ego-development and libido-develop-
ment in which the inhibition of development has occurred.
The chronological characteristics of the two developments,

[7] Cf. the similar position taken by Otto Rank in *Der Künstler*,
1907.

as yet unstudied, their possible variations in speed with respect to each other, thus receive unexected significance.

8. There is a most surprising characteristic of unconscious (repressed) process to which every investigator accustoms himself only by exercising great self-control; it results from their entire disregard of the reality-test; thought-reality is placed on an equality with external actuality, wishes with fulfilment and occurrence, just as happens without more ado under the supremacy of the old pleasure-principle. Hence also the difficulty of distinguishing unconscious fantasies from memories which have become unconscious. One must, however, never allow oneself to be misled into applying to the repressed creations of the mind the standards of reality; this might result in undervaluing the importance of fantasies in symptom-formation on the ground that they are not actualities; or in derving a neurotic sense of guilt from another source because there is no proof of actual committal of any crime. One is bound to employ the currency that prevails in the country one is exploring; in our case it is the neurotic currency. . . .

The deficiencies of this short paper, which is rather introductory than expository, are perhaps only to a slight extent excused if I acknowledge them to be unavoidable. In the meager sentences on the mental consequences of adaptation to the reality-principle I was obliged to intimate opinions which I should have preferred to withhold, the vindication of which will certainly require no small exertion. But I hope that benevolent readers will not fail to observe how even in this work the sway of the reality-principle is beginning.

A NOTE ON THE UNCONSCIOUS IN PSYCHOANALYSIS [1]

(1912)

I WISH to expound in a few words and as plainly as possible what the term "unconscious" has come to mean in psychoanalysis and in psychoanalysis alone.

A conception—or any other mental element—which is now *present* to my consciousness may become *absent* the next moment, and may become *present again*, after an interval, unchanged, and, as we say, from memory, not as a result of a fresh perception by our senses. It is this fact which we are accustomed to account for by the supposition that during the interval the conception has been present in our mind, although *latent* in consciousness. In what shape it may have existed while present in the mind and latent in consciousness we have no means of guessing.

At this very point we may be prepared to meet with the philosophical objection that the latent conception did not exist as an object of psychology, but as a physical disposi-

[1] Written (in English) at the request of the Society for Psychical Research and first published in a Special Medical Supplement of their *Proceedings*, Part lxvi, Vol. xxvi, 1912. Z. *i*, 117-23; *G.S. v*, 433-42; *S.k.S.N. iv*, 157-67; *C.P. iv*, 22-29.

tion for the recurrence of the same physical phenomenon, i.e. of the said conception. But we may reply that this is a theory far overstepping the domain of psychology proper; that it simply begs the question by asserting "conscious" to be an identical term with "mental," and that it is clearly at fault in denying psychology the right to account for its most common facts, such as memory, by its own means.

Now let us call "conscious" the conception which is present to our consciousness and of which we are aware, and let this be the only meaning of the term "conscious." As for latent conceptions, if we have any reason to suppose that they exist in the mind—as we had in the case of memory—let them be denoted by the term "unconscious."

Thus an unconscious conception is one of which we are not aware, but the existence of which we are nevertheless ready to admit on account of other proofs or signs.

This might be considered an uninteresting piece of descriptive or classificatory work if no experience appealed to our judgment other than the facts of memory, or the cases of association by unconscious links. The well-known experiment, however, of "post-hypnotic suggestion" teaches us to insist upon the importance of the distinction between *conscious* and *unconscious* and seems to increase its value.

In this experiment, as performed by Bernheim, a person is put into a hypnotic state and is subsequently aroused. While he was in the hypnotic state, under the influence of the physician, he was ordered to execute a certain action at a certain fixed moment after his awakening, say half an hour later. He awakes, and seems fully conscious and in his ordinary condition; he has no recollection of his hypnotic state, and yet at the pre-arranged moment there rushes into his mind the impulse to do such and such a thing, and he does it consciously though not knowing why. It seems impossible to give any other description of the phenomenon than to say that the order had been present in the mind of the person in a condition of latency, or had been present unconsciously, until the given moment came, and then had become conscious. But not the whole of it emerged into consciousness: only the conception of the act to be executed. All the other ideas associated with this conception—the order, the influence of the physician, the recollection of the hypnotic state—remained unconscious even then.

But we have more to learn from such an experiment. We are led from the purely descriptive to a *dynamic* view of the phenomenon. The idea of the action ordered in hypnosis not only became an object of consciousness at a certain moment, but the more striking aspect of the fact is that this idea grew *active*: it was translated into action as soon as consciousness became aware of its presence. The real stimulus to the action being the order of the physician, it is hard not to concede that the idea of the physician's order became active too. Yet this last idea did not reveal itself to consciousness, as did its outcome, the idea of the action; it remained unconscious, and so it was *active and unconscious* at the same time.

A post-hypnotic suggestion is a laboratory production, an artificial fact. But if we adopt the theory of hysterical phenomena first put forward by Pierre Janet and elaborated by Breuer and myself, we shall not be at a loss for plenty of natural facts showing the psychological character of the post-hypnotic suggestion even more clearly and distinctly.

The mind of the hysterical patient is full of active yet unconscious ideas; all her symptoms proceed from such ideas. It is in fact the most striking character of the hysterical mind to be ruled by them. If the hysterical woman vomits, she may do so from the idea of being pregnant. She has, however, no knowledge of this idea, although it can easily be detected in her mind, and made conscious to her, by one of the technical procedures of psychoanalysis. If she is executing the jerks and movements constituting her "fit," she does not even consciously represent to herself the intended actions, and she may perceive those actions with the detached feelings of an onlooker. Nevertheless analysis will show that she was acting her part in the dramatic reproduction of some incident in her life, the memory of which was unconsciously active during the attack. The same preponderance of active unconscious ideas is revealed by analysis as the essential fact in the psychology of all other forms of neurosis.

We learn therefore by the analysis of neurotic phenomena that a latent or unconscious idea is not necessarily a weak one, and that the presence of such an idea in the mind admits of indirect proofs of the most cogent kind, which are equivalent to the direct proof furnished by consciousness. We feel justified in making our classification agree with this addition to our knowledge by introducing a fundamental distinction between different kinds of latent or unconscious ideas. We were accustomed to think that every latent idea was so because it was weak and that it grew conscious as soon as it became strong. We have now gained the conviction that there are some latent ideas which do not penetrate into consciousness, however strong they may have become. Therefore we may call the latent ideas of the first type *preconscious*, while we reserve the term *unconscious* (proper) for the latter type which we came to study in the neuroses. The term *unconscious*, which was used in the purely descriptive sense before, now comes to imply something more. It designates not only latent ideas in general, but especially ideas with a certain dynamic character, ideas keeping apart from consciousness in spite of their intensity and activity.

Before continuing any exposition I will refer to two objections which are likely to be raised at this point. The first of these may be stated thus: intead of subscribing to the hypothesis of unconscious ideas of which we know nothing, we had better assume that consciousness can be split up, so that certain ideas or other psychical acts may constitute a consciousness apart, which has become detached and estranged from the bulk of conscious psychical activity. Well-known pathological cases like that of Dr. Azam seem to go far to show that the splitting up of consciousness is no fanciful imagination.

I venture to urge against this theory that it is a gratuitous assumption, based on the abuse of the word "conscious." We have no right to extend the meaning of this word so far as to make it include a consciousness of which its owner is not aware. If philosophers find difficulty in accepting the existence of unconscious ideas, the existence of an unconscious consciousness seems to me even more objectionable. The cases described as splitting of consciousness, like Dr. Azam's, might better be denoted as shifting of consciousness—that function—or whatever it be—oscillating between two different psychical complexes which become conscious and unconscious in alternation.

The other objection that may probably be raised would be that we apply to normal psychology conclusions which are drawn chiefly from the study of pathological conditions. We are enabled to answer it by another fact, the knowledge of which we owe to psychoanalysis. Certain deficiencies of function of most frequent occurrence among healthy people, e.g. *lapsus linguae*, errors in memory and speech, forgetting of names, etc., may easily be shown to depend on the action of strong unconscious ideas in the same way as neurotic symptoms. We shall meet with another still more convincing argument at a later stage of this discussion.

By the differentiation of preconscious and unconscious ideas, we are led on to leave the field of classification and to form an opinion about functional and dynamical relations in the action of the mind. We have found a *preconscious activity* passing into consciousness with no difficulty, and an *unconscious activity* which remains so and seems to be cut off from consciousness.

Now we do not know whether these two modes of psychical activity are identical or essentially divergent from their beginning, but we may ask why they should become different in the course of mental action. To this last question psychoanalysis gives a clear and unhesitating answer. It is by no means impossible for the product of unconscious activity to pierce into consciousness, but a certain amount of exertion is needed for this task. When we try to do it in ourselves, we become aware of a distinct feeling of *repulsion* which must be overcome, and when we produce it in a patient we get the most unquestionable signs of what we call his *resistance* to it. So we learn that the unconscious idea is excluded from consciousness by living forces which oppose themselves to its reception, while they do not object to other ideas, the preconscious ones. Psychoanalysis leaves no room for doubt that the repulsion from unconscious ideas is only provoked by the tendencies embodied in their contents. The next and most probable theory which can be formulated at this stage of our knowledge is the following. Unconsciousness is a regular and inevitable phase in the processes constituting our mental activity; every mental act begins as an unconscious one, and it may either remain so or go on developing into consciousness, according as it meets with resistance or not. The distinction between preconscious and unconscious activity is not a primary one, but comes to be established after repulsion has sprung up. Only then the difference between preconscious ideas, which can appear in consciousness and reappear at any moment, and unconscious ideas which cannot do so gains a theoretical as well as a practical value. A rough but not inadequate analogy to this supposed relation of conscious to unconscious activity might be drawn from the field of ordinary photography. The first stage of the photograph is the "negative"; every photographic picture has to pass through the "negative process," and some of these negatives which have held good in examination are admitted to the "positive process" ending in the picture.

But the distinction between preconscious and unconscious activity, and the recognition of the barrier which keeps them asunder, is not the last or the most important result of the psychoanalytic investigation of mental life. There is one mental product to be met with in the most normal persons, which yet presents a very striking analogy to the wildest productions of insanity, and was no more intelligible to philosophers than insanity itself. I refer to dreams. Psychoanalysis is founded upon the analysis of dreams; the interpretation of dreams is the most complete piece of work the young science has done up to the present. One of the most common types of dream-formation may be described as follows: a train of thoughts has been aroused by the working of the mind in the daytime, and retained some of its activity, escaping from the general inhibition of interests which introduces sleep and constitutes the mental preparation for sleeping. During the night this train of thoughts succeeds in finding connections with one of the unconscious tendencies present ever since his childhood in the mind of the dreamer, but ordinarily *repressed* and excluded from his conscious life. By the borrowed force of this unconscious help, the thoughts, the residue of the day's mental work, now become active again, and emerge into consciousness in the shape of the dream. Now three things have happened:

(1) The thoughts have undergone a change, a disguise, and a distortion, which represents the part of the unconscious helpmate.
(2) The thoughts have occupied consciousness at a time when they ought not.
(3) Some part of the unconscious, which could not otherwise have done so, has emerged into consciousness.

We have learned the art of finding out the "residual thoughts," the *latent thoughts of the dream*, and, by comparing them with the *manifest dream*, we are able to form a judgment on the changes they underwent and the manner in which these were brought about.

The latent thoughts of the dream differ in no respect from the products of our regular conscious activity; they deserve the name of preconscious thoughts, and may indeed have been conscious at some moment of waking life. But by entering into connection with the unconscious tendencies during the night they have become assimilated to the latter, degraded, as it were to the condition of unconscious thoughts, and subjected to the laws by which unconscious activity is governed. And here is the opportunity to learn what we could not have guessed from speculation, or from another source of empirical information—that the laws of unconscious activity differ widely from those of the conscious. We gather in detail what the peculiarities of the *Unconscious* are, and we may hope to learn still more about them by a profounder investigation of the processes of dream-formation.

This inquiry is not yet half finished, and an exposition of the results obtained hitherto is scarcely possible without entering into the most intricate problems of dream-analysis. But I would not break off this discussion without indicating the change and progress in our comprehension of the Unconscious which are due to our psychoanalytic study of dreams.

Unconsciousness seemed to us at first only an enigmatical characteristic of a definite mental act. Now it means more for us. It is a sign that this act partakes of the nature of a certain mental category known to us by other and more important features, and that it belongs to a system of mental activity which is deserving of our fullest attention. The index-value of the unconscious has far outgrown its importance as a property. The system revealed by the sign that the single acts forming parts of it are unconscious we designate by the name "The Unconscious," for want of a better and less ambiguous term. . . .

NEGATION [1]

(1925)

THE manner in which our patients bring forward their associations during the work of analysis gives us an opportunity for making some interesting observations. "Now you'll think I mean to say something insulting, but really I've no such intention." We see at once that this a repudiation, by means of projection, of an association that has just emerged. . . .

There is a most convenient method by which one can sometimes obtain a necessary light upon a piece of unconscious and repressed material. "What," one asks, "would you consider was about the most unlikely thing in the world in that situation?" If the patient falls into the trap and names what he thinks most incredible, he almost invariably in so doing makes the correct admission. A nice counterpart of this experiment is often met with in obsessional neurotics who have been initiated into the meaning of their symptoms. "A new obsessive idea came over me; and it immediately occurred to me that it might mean so and so. But of course that can't be true, or it couldn't have oc-

[1] *I. xi*, 217-221; *J. vi*, 367-71. Trans. by Joan Riviere.

curred to me." ... The subject-matter of a repressed image or thought can make its way into consciousness on condition that it is *denied*. Negation is a way of taking account of what is repressed; indeed, it is actually a removal of the repression, though not, of course, an acceptance of what is repressed. It is to be seen how the intellectual function is here distinct from the affective process. Negation only assists in undoing *one* of the consequences of repression— namely, the fact that the subject-matter of the image in question is unable to enter consciousness. The result is a kind of intellectual acceptance of what is repressed, though in all essentials the repression persists. (The same process is at the root of the familiar superstition that boasting is dangerous. "How lovely that I've not had one of my headaches for such a long time!" But this is in fact the first announcement of a new attack, of whose approach the patient is already aware, though he is as yet unwilling to believe it.) ...

Since it is the business of the function of intellectual judgment to affirm or deny the subject-matter of thoughts, we have been led by the foregoing remarks to the psychological origin of that function. To deny something in one's judgment is at bottom the same thing as to say: "That is something that I would rather repress." A negative judgment is the intellectual substitute for repression; the "No" in which it is expressed is the hallmark of repression, a certificate of origin, as it were, like "Made in Germany." By the help of the symbol of negation, the thinking-process frees itself from the limitations of repression and enriches itself with the subject-matter without which it could not work efficiently.

The function of judgment is concerned ultimately with two sorts of decision. It may assert or deny that a thing has a particular property; or it may affirm or dispute that a particular image or presentation (*Vorstellung*) exists in reality. Originally the property to be decided about might be either good or bad, useful or harmful. Expressed in the language of the oldest, that is, of the oral, instinctual impulses, the alternative runs thus: "I should like to eat that, or I should like to spit it out"; or, carried a stage further: "I should like to take this into me and keep that out of me." That is to say: it is to be either *inside me* or *outside me*. As I have shown elsewhere, the original pleasure-ego tries to introject into itself everything that is good and to reject from itself everything that is bad. From its point of view what is bad, what is alien to the other ego, and what is external are, to begin with, identical.

The other sort of decision made by the function of judgment, namely, as to the real existence of something imagined, is a concern of the final reality-ego, which develops out of the previous pleasure-ego (a concern, that is, of the faculty that tests the reality of things). It is now no longer a question of whether something perceived (a thing) shall be taken into the ego or not, but of whether something which is present in the ego as an image can also be rediscovered in perception (that is, in reality). Once more, it will be seen, the question is one of *external* and *internal*. What is not real, what is merely imagined or subjective, is only *internal*; while on the other hand what is real is also present *externally*. When this stage is reached the pleasure-principle is no longer taken into account. Experience has taught that it is important not only whether a thing (an object from which satisfaction is sought) possesses the "good" property, that is, whether it deserves to be taken into the ego, but also whether it is there in the external world, ready to be seized when it is wanted. In order to understand this step forward, we must recollect that all images originate from perceptions and are repetitions of them. So that originally the mere existence of the image serves as a guarantee of the reality of what is imagined. The contrast between what is subjective and what is objective does not exist from the first. It only arises from the faculty which thought possesses for reviving a thing that has once been perceived, by reproducing it as an image, without its being necessary for the external object still to be present. Thus the first and immediate aim of the process of testing reality is not to discover an object in real perception corresponding to what is imagined, but to *re-*

discover such an object, to convince oneself that it is still there. The differentiation between what is subjective and what is objective is further assisted by another faculty of the power of thought. The reproduction of a perception as an image is not always a faithful one; it can be modified by omissions or by the fusion of a number of elements. The process for testing the thing's reality must then investigate the extent of these distortions. But it is evident that an essential pre-condition for the institution of the function for testing reality is that objects shall have been lost which have formerly afforded real satisfaction.

Judging is the intellectual action which decides the choice of motor-action, which puts an end to the procrastination of thinking, and which leads over from thinking to acting. This procrastinating character of thought, too, has been discussed by me elsewhere.[2] Thought is to be regarded as an experimental action, a kind of groping forward, involving only a small expenditure of energy in the way of discharge. Let us consider where the ego can have made a previous use of this kind of groping forward, where it can have learned the technique which it now employs in thought-processes. It was at the sensory end of the mental apparatus, in connection with sensory perceptions. For upon our hypothesis perception is not a merely passive process; we believe rather that the ego periodically sends out small amounts of cathetic energy into the perceptual system and by their means samples the external stimuli, and after every such groping advance draws back again.

The study of judgment affords us, perhaps for the first time, an insight into the derivation of an intellectual function from the interplay of the primary instinctual impulses. Judging has been systematically developed out of what was in the first instance introduction into the ego or expulsion from the ego carried out according to the pleasure-principle. Its polarity appears to correspond to the opposition between the two groups of instincts which we have

[2] Cf. "Formulations regarding the Two Principles in Mental Functioning" (1911).

assumed to exist. Affirmation, as being a substitute for union, belongs to Eros; while negation, the derivative of expulsion, belongs to the instinct of destruction. The passion for universal negation, the "negativism," displayed by many psychotics, is probably to be regarded as a sign of "defusion" of instincts due to the withdrawal of the libidinal components. The achievements of the function of judgment only become feasible, however, after the creation of the symbol of negation has endowed thought with a first degree of indepedence from the results of repression and at the same time from the sway of the pleasure-principle.

This view of negation harmonizes very well with the fact that in analysis we never discover a "No" in the unconscious, and that a recognition of the unconscious on the part of the ego is expressed in a negative formula. . . .

[A General Etiological Formula] [1]

I THINK we can effect a presentation of the probably very complicated etiological conditions which exists in the pathology of the neuroses, if we establish the following etiological concepts:

(a) *Predisposition,* (b) *Specific Cause,* (c) *Contributory Cause* and, as a term not equivalent to the former, (d) *Exciting* or *Releasing Cause.*

In order to satisfy all possibilities let us assume that we are dealing with etiological factors capable of quantitative alterations, and consequently of increase or decrease.

If we may use the conception of a compound etiological formula which must be fulfilled if the effect is to take place, then we may designate as exciting or releasing cause that which last makes its appearance in the formula, so that it immediately precedes the manifestation of the effect. It is this temporal element alone which constitutes the essence of an incitement; each of the other factors can in individual cases play the part of an incite-

[1] [This extract is taken from a paper entitled "A Reply to Criticisms of the Anxiety-Neurosis" ("Zur Kritik der 'Angstneurose.'") *Wiener Klinischen Rundschau.* 1895. *G.S. i.* 343-62. The page heading in this instance is not the title of a book or paper. Trans. by John Rickman, revised by Joan Riviere.—ED.]

ment, and this part can even alternate within this same etiological conglomeration.

The factors which are to be described as *predisposition* are those in whose absence the effect would never come about; but which, however, are incapable of alone bringing about the effect, no matter to what degree they may be present. For the specific cause is lacking.

The *specific cause* is one which is never absent when the effect actually takes place, and which also suffices, in the required quantity or intensity, to bring about the effect, provided that the predisposition is present as well.

As *contributory causes* we may comprehend such factors as are not necessarily present every time nor able in any degree to produce the effect alone, but which co-operate with the predisposition and the specific etiological cause to make up the etiological formula.

The peculiar position of the contributory or auxiliary causes seems clear; but how are we to distinguish between predisposition and specific causes, since both are indispensable and no one of them alone is sufficient as a cause?

In these circumstances the following considerations would seem to make a decision possible. Among the "indispensable causes" we find several which are also present in the etiological formulae of many other conditions beside anxiety-neurosis, thus showing that they have no particular relation to individual disorders; *one* of these causes, however, stands out with special prominence, in that it is found in no other or in very few etiological formulae, and this has a claim to be called the *specific* cause of the disease in question. Further predisposing factors and specific causes are particularly clearly distinguished in cases where the former have the quality of long duration and little alteration in their condition, whereas the specific cause corresponds to a factor which has recently come into action.

I will attempt to give an example of this complete etiological scheme:

Effect: Pulmonary tuberculosis.

Predisposition: For the most part hereditary disposition of the organs concerned.

Specific Cause: Koch's bacillus.

Contributory Causes: Everything that lowers resistance: emotion as well as infections or colds.

TYPES OF NEUROTIC NOSOGENESIS [1]

(1912)

In the ensuing remarks, which are based on impressions obtained empirically, it is proposed to describe those changes of conditions which operate to bring about the onset of neurotic illness in a person predisposed to it. We are concerned, that is, with the exciting cause of illness; scarcely at all with the form of it. The following view is distinguishable from other formulations concerning the exciting causes of illness in that it connects the changes to be described entirely with the libido of the person concerned. Psychoanalysis has shown us that the course taken by the libido is decisive for nervous health or ill-health. The concept of pre-disposition needs no discussion in this connection; for psychoanalytic research has made it possible for us to trace back the pre-disposition to neurosis to its source in the developmental history of the libido, and to reveal the factors operative in this pre-disposition as inborn varieties of the sexual constitution and the effects of external experiences in early childhood.

(a) The most immediate, most easily discerned, and

---

[1] *Zbt. ii*, 297-302; *S.k.S.N. iii*, 306-13; *C.P. ii*, 105-12. Trans. by E. Colburn Mayne, revised by Joan Riviere.

most comprehensible exciting cause of the onset of neurotic illness lies in that external factor which may generally be described as *frustration*. The person was healthy as long as his erotic need was satisfied by an actual object in the outer world; he becomes neurotic as soon as he is deprived of this object and no substitute is forthcoming. Happiness here coincides with health, unhappiness with neurosis. By providing a substitute for the lost source of gratification, fate can effect a cure more easily than the physician.

For this type, which may be said to include the majority of mankind, the possibility of an outbreak of illness begins only with abstinence—which may give us some indication of the significance for the causation of neuroses of cultural restrictions in facilities for satisfaction. Frustration operates pathogenically in that it dams up the libido, and thus puts to the test both the person's power of tolerating the increase of mental tension, and his manner of taking steps to release himself from it. There are only two possible methods of retaining health in a continuous state of actual frustration of satisfaction: first, that of transposing the mental tension into active energy which remains directed towards the outer world and finally wrests from that world an actual satisfaction for the libido; and secondly, that of renouncing the libidinal satisfaction, sublimating the stored-up libido, and making use of it to ends which are no longer erotic and thus elude the frustration. Both possibilities can be realized in the destinies of mankind, which shows that unhappiness does not necessarily coincide with neurosis, and frustration is not alone decisive for the health or ill-health of the person concerned. The effect of frustration lies principally in its bringing into action dispositional factors which have hitherto remained inoperative.

When these are present in sufficient strength there arises the danger of the libido becoming *introverted*.[2] It turns away from reality, which on account of the unrelenting frustration experienced has lost all its value for the person concerned, and takes refuge in the life of fantasy where it

[2] A term introduced by C. G. Jung.

creates new wish-formations and reanimates the vestiges of earlier, forgotten ones. In consequence of the intimate connection between fantasy-activity and the infantile, repressed, and now unconscious material existing in every individual, and thanks to that attribute to the life of fantasy which exempts it from the "testing of reality,"[3] the libido may now begin to flow backward, may seek out infantile paths in the course of its regression, and may strive after corresponding aims. When such strivings, which are incompatible with the person's state of mind in real life, have become sufficiently intensified, there must enuse a conflict between them and the other part of the personality which has remained in relation with reality. This conflict issues in symptom-formations and ends in manifest illness. That the whole process originates in the actual frustration may be clearly perceived from the circumstance that the symptoms by means of which the sphere of reality is regained represent substitutive gratifications.

(b) The second type of occasion for the outbreak of illness is by no means so obvious as the first, and could not indeed be discerned before the searching analytic studies stimulated by the complex-theory of the Zürich School.[4] In these cases the person falls ill not as a result of some alteration in the outer world which has replaced gratification by frustration, but as a result of an inner effort to seize a gratification which reality offers to him. He falls ill of the attempt to adapt himself to reality and to fulfill the *requisitions of reality*, for in doing so he is confronted with insurmountable inward obstacles.

It will be convenient to set these two types of falling ill in sharp antithesis to one another—sharper, indeed, than observation for the most part warrants. In the first type an alteration in the external world is prominent; in the second, the accent falls upon an internal change. In the first type, the person falls ill from an event; in the second,

[3] Cf. Freud, "Formulations regarding the two Principles in Mental Functioning."

[4] Cf. Jung, *Die Bedeutung des Vaters für das Schicksal des Einzelnen*, 1909.

from a developmental process. In the first case the task is one of renouncing a gratification, and the person falls ill because of his lack of resistance; in the second case the task is that of exchanging one kind of gratification for another, and the person is wrecked by his rigidity. In the second case the conflict between the endeavor to keep as he is and the other endeavor to alter himself in accordance with new aims and new demands in reality already exists in him; in the first case, the conflict does not begin until the damned-up libido has chosen other and incompatible possibilities of gratification. The part played by the conflict and the previous fixation of the libido is in the second type incomparably more striking than in the first, for in the first it may well be that undesirable fixations of this kind only re-establish themselves in consequence of the external frustration. . . .

Despite the very evident distinctions between the two types of falling ill here described, they have essential points in common, and it is not hard to find a formula which will apply to both. Falling ill of a deprivation (frustration) likewise comes under the head of incapacity for adaptation to reality, only that the incapacity is confined to occasions when reality denies gratification to the libido. Falling ill under the conditions belonging to the second type points merely to a necessary peculiarity in the frustration. What is denied is not every form of gratification in reality, but merely just the one which the person declares to be the one and only form for him; further, the frustration does not derive directly from the outer world but primarily from certain trends within the ego. Yet the factor of frustration remains common to both, and the most significant one for both. As a result of the conflict which forthwith ensues in the second type, both kinds of gratification, the customary as well as the desired, become equally inhibited; damming-up of the libido and its attendant results follow as they did in the first case. The mental processes involved in the course of symptom-formation are in the second type more easily discoverable than in the first, since the pathogenic fixations of the libido had not first to be re-established but had been potentially active during the healthy period. A certain degree of introversion of the libido was mostly already existent; some degree of the regression to the infantile is spared because the development had never traversed its entire course.

(c) The next type seems an exaggeration of the second type, that of succumbing before the requisitions of reality; I shall describe it as an outbreak of illness through *inhibition of development*. There would be no theoretical reason for distinguishing this from the rest, but there is a practical need to do so; since here we have to deal with those persons who fall ill as soon as they pass beyond the irresponsible age of childhood, and thus never attain a phase of health—that of unrestricted capacity in general for production and enjoyment. The essential part played by the dispositional processes is in these cases quite apparent. The libido has never forsaken its infantile fixations; the demands of reality do not suddenly confront an individuality which is wholly or partially matured, but arise out of the bare fact of its having grown older, and are of course continually changing with the age of the person concerned. The conflict is subordinate in importance to the incapacity; but if we take into account the other results of our researches, we must postulate a striving to overcome the infantile fixations, for otherwise the outcome of the process would never be neurosis but only stationary infantilism.

(d) Just as the third type shows us the dispositional condition in an almost isolated form, so the now following fourth one directs our attention to another factor, the operation of which has to be reckoned with in all cases, and for that very reason might easily be overlooked in a theoretical discussion. That is to say, we see people fall ill who have hitherto been healthy, to whom no new experience has presented itself, whose relation to the outer world has undergone no change, so that their falling ill makes an inevitable impression of spontaneity. Closer scrutiny of such cases shows us, nevertheless, that a change *has* taken place in them which we cannot but regard as highly significant in the causation of the illness. As a result of reaching a certain period of life, and in accordance with regular biological processes, the *quantity* of libido in their mental economy has increased to an extent which by itself suffices to upset the balance of health and establish the conditions for neurosis. As is well known, such rather sudden intensifications in libido are regularly connected with puberty and the menopause, with the reaching of a certain age in women; in many people they may in addition manifest themselves in periodicities as yet unrecognized. The damming-up of the libido is here the primary factor; it becomes pathogenic as a result of the *relative* frustration coming from the outer world, which would have afforded sufficient gratification to a lesser need in the libido. The dissatisfied and dammed-up libido may now open up the path to regression and excite the same conflicts as those found in cases of absolute external frustration. This warns us never to leave the quantitative factor out of consideration when we are dealing with the outbreak of illness. All the other factors—frustration, fixation, inhibition in development—remain inoperative as long as they do not involve a certain amount of libido and produce a definite degree of damming-up. We cannot, it is true, measure the amount of libido essential to produce pathological effects; we can only postulate it after the effects of the illness have evinced themselves. In only one direction can we define it more closely; we may assume that it is not a question of an absolute quantity, but of the relation of this effective amount of libido to that quantity of libido which the particular ego in question can control, that is, can hold in suspension, sublimate, or make direct use of. Therefore a relative increase in the quantity of libido may have the same effects as one that is absolute. An enfeeblement of the ego through organic illness or an unusual demand upon its energy will be capable of producing neuroses which would otherwise have remained latent in spite of all dispositional tendencies.

The significance which we must attribute to the quantity of libido in the causation of illness is in satisfactory accord with two axioms of the new theory of neurosis which have emerged from psycho-analysis: first, with the axiom that the neuroses have their source in a conflict between the ego and the libido; secondly, with the view that no qualitative distinction exists between the conditions of health and those of neurosis, but rather that the healthy have to contend with the same difficulties in controlling the libido—only they succeed better in doing so.

There still remain a few words to be said about the relation of these "types" to clinical experience. When I review the number of patients with whose analysis I am at this moment occupied, I must admit that none of them represents any of the four types in its pure form. Instead, I find in each an element of frustration operating along with a certain degree of incapacity for adaptation to reality; the standpoint of inhibition in development, which of course coincides with a tenacity of fixations, is to be reckoned with in all of them; and the significance of the quantity of libido we can never, as was set forth above, afford to overlook. Indeed, it is my experience that in several of these patients the illness has been manifested in accesses, between which there were intervals of health, and that every one of these accesses was to be traced to a different type of exciting cause. The formulation of these four types has therefore no great theoretical value; they are merely different paths by which a definite pathogenic constellation in the mental economy may be achieved—I refer to a damming-up of the libido which the ego is not able to master with the means at its disposal without some damage. The situation itself, however, becomes pathogenic only as a result of a quantitative factor; it is in no way a novelty in the mental economy, nor is it created by the advent of a so-called "cause of illness."

A certain practical importance may readily be granted to these types of falling ill. . . . The first type reveals to us the extraordinarily powerful influence of the outer world; the second that, no less significant, of the peculiarities of the individual who opposes himself to that influence. Pathology could never master the problem of the outbreak of illness in the neurotic so long as it was occupied merely with deciding whether these affections were of an endogenous or an exogenous nature. To all the experience which points to the significance of abstinence (in the broadest sense) as an exciting cause, pathology then necessarily objected that other persons suffered a similar fate without falling ill. But if it elected to lay emphasis upon individual peculiarities as essential in sickness or health, it was obliged to bow to the objection that persons with such peculiarities could permanently retain their health provided only that they could preserve their peculiarity. Psychoanalysis warns us to abandon the unfruitful antithesis of external and internal factors, of fate and constitution, and has taught us regularly to discover the cause of an outbreak of neurosis in a definite mental situation, which can be brought into being in different ways.

INSTINCTS AND THEIR VICISSITUDES [1]

(1915)

THE view is often defended that sciences should be built up on clear and sharply defined basal concepts. In actual fact no science, not even the most exact, begins with such definitions. The true beginning of scientific activity consists rather in describing phenomena and then in proceeding to group, classify and correlate them. Even at the stage of description it is not possible to avoid applying certain abstract ideas to the material in hand, ideas derived from various sources and certainly not the fruit of the new experience only. Still more indispensable are such ideas—which will later become the basal concepts of the science—as the material is further elaborated. They must at first necessarily possess some measure of uncertainty; there can be no question of any clear delimitation of their content. So long as they remain in this condition, we come to an understanding about their meaning by repeated references to the material of observation, from which we seem to have deduced our abstract ideas, but which is in point of fact subject to them. Thus, strictly

[1] Z. *iii*, 84-100; S.k.S.N. *iv*, 252-78; G.S. *v*, 443-62; *C.P. iv*, 60-83. Trans. by Cecil M. Baines, revised by Joan Riviere.

speaking, they are in the nature of conventions; although everything depends on their being chosen in no arbitrary manner, but determined by the important relations they have to the empirical material—relations that we seem to divine before we can clearly recognize and demonstrate them. It is only after more searching investigation of the field in question that we are able to formulate with increased clarity the scientific concepts underlying it, and progressively so to modify these concepts that they become widely applicable, and at the same time consistent logically. Then, indeed, it may be time to immure them in definitions. The progress of science, however, demands a certain elasticity even in these definitions. The science of physics furnishes an excellent illustration of the way in which even those "basal concepts" that are firmly established in the form of definitions are constantly being altered in their content.

A conventional but still rather obscure basal concept of this kind, which is nevertheless indispensable to us in psychology, is that of an *instinct*. Let us try to ascertain what is comprised in this conception by approaching it from different angles.

First, from the side of physiology. This has given us the concept of *stimuli* and the scheme of the reflex arc, according to which a stimulus applied *from the outer world* to living tissue (nervous substance) is discharged by action *towards the outer world*. The action answers the purpose of withdrawing the substance affected from the operation of the stimulus, removing it out of range of the stimulus.

Now what is the relation between "instinct" and "stimulus"? There is nothing to prevent our including the concept of "instinct" under that of "stimulus" and saying that an instinct is a stimulus to the mind. But we are immediately set on our guard against treating instinct and mental stimulus as one and the same thing. Obviously, besides those of instinctual origin, there are other stimuli to the mind which behave far more like physiological stimuli. For example, a strong light striking upon the eye is not a stimulus of instinctual origin; it is one, however, when the mucous membrane of the esophagus becomes parched or when a gnawing makes itself felt in the stomach.[2]

We have now obtained material necessary for discriminating between stimuli of instinctual origin and the other (physiological) stimuli which operate on our minds. First, a stimulus of instinctual origin does not arise in the outside world but from within the organism itself. For this reason it has a different mental effect and different actions are necessary in order to remove it. Further, all that is essential in an external stimulus is contained in the assumption that it acts as a single impact, so that it can be discharged by a single appropriate action.... An instinct, on the other hand, never acts as a momentary impact but always as a constant force. As it makes its attack not from without but from within the organism, it follows that no flight can avail against it. A better term for a stimulus of instinctual origin is a "need"; that which does away with this need is "satisfaction." This can be attained only by a suitable (adequate) alteration of the inner source of stimulation....

Now ... we cannot fail to be struck by a fact which compels us to a further admission. We do not merely accept as basal concepts certain conventions which we apply to the material we have acquired empirically, but we also make use of various complicated postulates to guide us in dealing with psychological phenomena. We have already cited the most important of these postulates; it remains for us expressly to lay stress upon it. It is of a biological nature, and makes use of the concept of "purpose" (one might say, of adaptation of the means to the end) and runs as follows: the nervous system is an apparatus having the function of abolishing stimuli which reach it, or of reducing excitation to the lowest possible level: an apparatus which would even, if this were feasible, maintain itself in an altogether unstimulated condition.

[2] Assuming, of course, that these internal processes constitute the organic basis of the needs described as thirst and hunger.

Let us for the present not take exception to the indefiniteness of this idea and let us grant that the task of the nervous system is—broadly speaking—*to master stimuli.* We see then how greatly the simple physiological reflex scheme is complicated by the introduction of instincts. External stimuli impose upon the organism the single task of withdrawing itself from their action: this is accomplished by muscular movements, one of which reaches the goal aimed at and, being the most appropriate to the end in view, is thenceforward transmitted as an hereditary disposition. Those instinctual stimuli which emanate from within the organism cannot be dealt with by this mechanism. Consequently, they make far higher demands upon the nervous system and compel it to complicated and interdependent activities, which effect such changes in the outer world as enable it to offer satisfaction to the internal source of stimulation; above all, instinctual stimuli oblige the nervous system to renounce its ideal intention of warding off stimuli, for they maintain an incessant and unavoidable afflux of stimulation. So we may probably conclude that instincts and not external stimuli are the true motive forces in the progress that has raised the nervous system, with all its incomparable efficiency, to its present high level of development. Of course there is nothing to prevent our assuming that the instincts themselves are, at least in part, the precipitates of different forms of external stimulation, which in the course of phylogenesis have effected modifications in the organism. . . .

We are now in a position to discuss certain terms used in reference to the concept of an instinct, for example, its impetus, its aim, its object, and its source.

By the *impetus* of an instinct we understand its motor element, the amount of force or the measure of the demand upon energy which it represents. The characteristic of impulsion is common to all instincts, is in fact the very essence of them. Every instinct is a form of activity; if we speak loosely of passive instincts, we can only mean those whose aim is passive.

The *aim* of an instinct is in every instance satisfaction, which can only be obtained by abolishing the condition of stimulation in the source of the instinct. But although this remains invariably the final goal of every instinct, there may yet be different ways leading to the same goal, so that an instinct may be found to have various nearer or intermediate aims, capable of combination or interchange. Experience permits us also to speak of instincts which are *inhibited in respect of their aim,* in cases where a certain advance has been permitted in the direction of satisfaction and then an inhibition or deflection has occurred. We may suppose that even in such cases a partial satisfaction is achieved.

The *object* of an instinct is that in or through which it can achieve its aim. It is the most variable thing about an instinct and is not originally connected with it, but becomes attached to it only in consequence of being peculiarly fitted to provide satisfaction. The object is not necessarily an extraneous one: it may be part of the subject's own body. It may be changed any number of times in the course of the vicissitudes the instinct undergoes during life; a highly important part is played by this capacity for displacement in the instinct. It may happen that the same object may serve for the satisfaction of several instincts simultaneously, a phenomenon which Adler calls a "confluence" of instincts. A particularly close attachment of the instinct to its object is distinguished by the term *fixation*: this frequently occurs in very early stages of the instinct's development and so puts an end to its mobility, through the vigorous resistance it sets up against detachment.

By the *source* of an instinct is meant that somatic process in an organ or part of the body from which there results a stimulus represented in mental life by an instinct. We do not know whether this process is regularly of a chemical nature or whether it may also correspond with the release of other, e.g. mechanical, forces. The study of the sources of instinct is outside the scope of psychology; although its source in the body is what gives the instinct its distinct and essential character, yet in mental life we know it merely by its aims. A more exact knowledge of the sources of instincts is not strictly necessary for purposes of psychological investigation; often the source may be with certainty inferred from the aims. . . .

Now what instincts and how many should be postulated? There is obviously a great opportunity here for arbitrary choice. No objection can be made to anyone's employing the concept of an instinct of play or of destruction, or that of a social instinct, when the subject demands it and the limitations of psychological analysis allow of it. Nevertheless, we should not neglect to ask whether such instinctual motives, which are in one direction so highly specialized, do not admit of further analysis in respect of their sources, so that only those primal instincts which are not to be resolved further could really lay claim to the name.

I have proposed that two groups of such primal instincts should be distinguished: the *self-preservative* or *ego*-instincts and the *sexual* instincts. But this proposition has not the weight of a necessary postulate, such as, for instance, our assumption about the biological "purpose" in the mental apparatus (v. *supra*); it is merely an auxiliary construction, to be retained only so long as it proves useful, and it will make little difference to the results of our work of description and classification if we replace it by another. . . .

I am altogether doubtful whether work upon psychological material will afford any decisive indication for the distinction and classification of instincts. Rather it would seem necessary to apply to this material certain definite assumptions in order to work upon it, and we could wish that these assumptions might be taken from some other branch of knowledge and transferred to psychology. . . .

Since a study of the instincts from the side of consciousness presents almost insuperable difficulties, psychoanalytic investigation of mental disturbances remains the principal source of our knowledge. The development of this line of investigation, however, has necessarily produced hitherto information of a more or less definite nature only in regard to the sexual instincts, for it is this group in particular which can be observed in isolation, as it were, in the psychoneuroses. With the extension of psychoanalysis to other neurotic affections we may be sure that we shall find a basis for our knowledge of the ego-instincts also, though it would be optimistic to expect equally favorable conditions for observation in this field of research.

An attempt to formulate the general characteristics of the sexual instincts would run as follows: they are numerous, emanate from manifold organic sources, act in the first instance independently of one another and only at a late stage achieve a more or less complete synthesis. The aim which each strives to attain is "organ-pleasure"; only when the synthesis is complete do they enter the service of the function of reproduction, becoming thereby generally recognizable as sexual instincts. At their first appearance they support themselves upon the instincts of self-preservation, from which they only gradually detach themselves; in their choice of object also they follow paths indicated by the ego-instincts. Some of them remain throughout life associated with these latter and furnish them with libidinal components, which with normal functioning easily escape notice and are clearly recognizable only when disease is present. They have this distinctive characteristic—that they have in a high degree the capacity to act vicariously for one another and that they can readily change their objects. In consequence of the last-mentioned properties they are capable of activities widely removed from their original modes of attaining their aims (sublimation).

Our inquiry into the various vicissitudes which instincts undergo in the process of development and in the course of life must be confined to the sexual instincts, for these are the more familiar to us. Observation shows us that an instinct may undergo the following vicissitudes:

Reversal into its opposite
Turning round upon the subject
Repression
Sublimation

Since I do not intend to treat of sublimation here and since repression requires a special chapter to itself, it only remains for us to describe and discuss the two first points. Bearing in mind that there are tendencies which are opposed to the instincts pursuing a straightforward course, we may regard these vicissitudes as modes of defense against the instincts.

The *reversal* of an instinct *into its opposite* may on closer scrutiny be resolved into two different processes: a change from active to passive, and a reversal of the content. The two processes, being essentially distinct, must be treated separately.

Examples of the first process are met with in the two pairs of opposites: sadism-masochism and scoptophilia-exhibitionism. The reversal here concerns only the aims of the instincts. The passive aim (to be tortured, or looked at) has been substituted for the active aim (to torture, to look at). Reversal of content is found in the single instance of the change of love into hate.

The *turning round* of an instinct *upon the subject* is suggested to us by the reflection that masochism is actually sadism turned round upon the subject's own ego, and that exhibitionism includes the love of gazing at the subject's own body. Further, analytic observation leaves us in no doubt that the masochist also enjoys the *act* of torturing when this is being applied to himself, and the exhibitionist the exposing of someone in being exposed himself. So the essence of the process is the change of the object, while the aim remains unchanged.

We cannot fail to note, however, that in these examples turning round upon the subject's self and transformation from active to passive coincide or occur in one process. To elucidate the relation between the two processes, a more thorough investigation must be undertaken.

With the pair of opposites sadism-masochism, the process may be represented as follows:

(*a*) Sadism consists in the exercise of violence or power upon some other person as its object.

(*b*) This object is abandoned and replaced by the subject's self. Together with the turning round upon the self the change from an active to a passive aim in the instinct is also brought about.

(*c*) Again another person is sought as object; this person, in consequence of the alteration which has taken place in the aim of the instinct, has to take over the original role of the subject.

Case (*c*) is the condition commonly termed masochism. Satisfaction follows in this case also by way of the original sadism, the passive ego placing itself in fantasy back in its former situation, which, however, has now been given up to another subject outside the self.... That it is not superfluous to make the assumption of stage (*b*) is quite clear when we observe the behavior of the sadistic impulse in cases of obsessional neurosis. In these we have the turning upon the subject's self, without the attitude of passivity towards another: the reversal has only reached the second stage. Self-torment and self-punishment have arisen from the desire to torture, but not masochism. The active voice is changed, not into the passive, but into the reflexive middle voice.

The conception of sadism is made more complicated by the circumstance that this instinct, side by side with its general aim (or perhaps rather, within it), seems to press towards a quite special aim:—the infliction of pain, in addition to subjection and mastery of the object. Now psycho-analysis would seem to show that the infliction of pain plays no part in the original aims sought by the instinct ... but when once the transformation into masochism has taken place, the experience of pain is very well adapted to serve as a passive masochistic aim, for we have every reason to believe that sensations of pain, like other unpleasant sensations, extend into sexual excitation and produce a condition which is pleasurable, for the sake of which the subject will even willingly experience the unpleasantness of pain. Where once the suffering of pain has been experienced as a masochistic aim, it can be carried back into the sadistic situation and result in a sadistic aim of *inflicting pain*, which will then be masochistically enjoyed by the subject while inflicting pain upon others, through his identification of himself with the suffering object. Of course, in either case it is not the pain itself which is enjoyed, but the accompanying sexual excitement, and this is especially easy for the sadist. . . . In order to complete my exposition I would add that pity cannot be described as a result of the reversal of the sadistic instinct, but necessitates the conception of a *reaction-formation* against that instinct (for the difference, *v. infra*).

Rather different and simpler results are afforded by the investigation of another pair of opposites, namely, those instincts whose aim is sexual gazing (scoptophilia) and self-display (the "voyeur" and exhibitionist tendencies as they are called in the language of the perversions). Here again we may postulate the same stages as in the previous instance: (*a*) scoptophilia as an activity directed towards an extraneous object; (*b*) abandonment of the object and a turning of the scoptophilic instinct towards a part of the subject's own person; therewith a transformation to passivity and the setting up of a new aim—that of being looked at; (*c*) the institution of a new subject to whom one displays oneself in order to be looked at. Here too, it is hardly possible to doubt that the active aim appears before the passive, that scoptophilia precedes exhibitionism. . . . [With regard to both of the instincts examined above, it must be said that transformation of them by a reversal from active to passive and by a turning round upon the subject never in fact concerns the whole amount of impelling force pertaining to the instinct. To some extent its earlier active direction always persists side by side with the later passive direction, even when the transformation is very extensive. . . . The fact that, at that later period of development, the instinct in its primary form may be observed side by side with its (passive) opposite deserves to be distinguished by the highly appropriate name introduced by Bleuler: *ambivalence*. . . .

The transformation of the "content" of an instinct into its opposite is observed in a single instance only—the changing of *love into hate*. It is particularly common to find both these directed simultaneously towards the same object, and this phenomenon of their co-existence furnishes the most important example of ambivalence of feeling.

The case of love and hate acquires a special interest from the circumstance that it resists classification in our scheme of the instincts. It is impossible to doubt the existence of a most intimate relation between these two contrary feelings and sexual life, but one is naturally unwilling to conceive of love as being a kind of special component-instinct of sexuality in the same way as are the others just discussed. One would prefer to regard loving rather as the expression of the whole sexual current of feeling, but this idea does not clear up our difficulties and we are at a loss how to conceive of an essential opposite to this striving.

Loving admits of not merely one, but of three antitheses. First there is the antithesis of loving—hating; secondly, there is loving—being loved; and, in addition to these, loving and hating together are the opposite of the condition of neutrality or indifference. The second of these two antitheses, loving—being loved, corresponds exactly to the transformation from active to passive and may be traced to a primal situation in the same way as the scoptophilic instinct. This situation is that of *loving oneself*, which for us is the characteristic of narcissism. Then, according to whether the self as object or subject is exchanged for an extraneous one, there results the active aim of loving or the passive one of being loved, the latter remaining nearly related to narcissism.

Perhaps we shall come to a better understanding of the manifold opposites of loving if we reflect that our mental life as a whole is governed by *three polarities*, namely, the following antitheses:

Subject (ego)—Object (external world)
Pleasure—Pain
Active—Passive

The antithesis of *ego—non-ego* (outer), i.e. *subject—object*, is thrust upon the individual being at an early stage, by the experience that it can abolish external stimuli by means of muscular action but is defenseless against those stimuli that originate in instinct. This antithesis remains sovereign above all in our intellectual activity and provides research with a fundamental situation which no amount of effort can alter. The polarity of *pleasure—pain* depends upon a feeling-series, the significance of which in determining our actions (will) is paramount and has already been emphasized. The antithesis of active and passive must not be confounded with that of *ego-subject—external object*. The relation of the ego to the outer world is passive in so far as it receives stimuli from it, active when it reacts to these. Its instincts compel it to a quite special degree of activity towards the outside world, so that, if we wished to emphasize the essence of the matter, we might say that the ego-subject is passive in respect of external stimuli, active in virtue of its own instincts. The antithesis of *active—passive* coalesces later with that of *masculine—feminine*, which, until this has taken place, has no psychological significance. The fusion of activity with masculinity and passivity with femininity confronts us, indeed, as a biological fact, but it is by no means so invariably complete and exclusive as we are inclined to assume.

The three polarities within the mind are connected with one another in various highly significant ways. There is a certain primal psychic situation in which two of them coincide. Originally, at the very beginning of mental life, the ego's instincts are directed to itself and it is to some extent capable of deriving satisfaction for them on itself. This condition is known as narcissism and this potentiality for satisfaction is termed auto-erotic. The outside world is at this time, generally speaking, not cathected with any interest and is indifferent for purposes of satisfaction. At this period, therefore, the ego-subject coincides with what is pleasurable and the outside world with what is indifferent (or even painful as being a source of stimulation). Let us for the moment define loving as the relation of the ego to its sources of pleasure: then the situation in which the ego loves itself only and is indifferent to the outside world illustrates the first of the polarities in which "loving" appeared.

In so far as it is auto-erotic, the ego has no need of the outside world, but, in consequence of experiences undergone by the instincts of self-preservation, it tends to find objects there and doubtless it cannot but for a time perceive inner instinctual stimuli as painful. Under the sway of the pleasure-principle there now takes place a further development. The objects presenting themselves, in so far as they are sources of pleasure, are absorbed by the ego into itself, "introjected" (according to an expression coined by Ferenczi); while, on the other hand, the ego thrusts forth upon the external world whatever within itself gives rise to pain (v. infra: the mechanism of projection).

Thus the original *reality-ego*, which distinguished outer and inner by means of a sound objective criterion, changes into a purified *pleasure-ego*, which prizes above all else the quality of pleasure. For this pleasure-ego the outside world is divided into a part that is pleasurable, which it has incorporated into itself, and a remainder that is alien to it. A part of itself it has separated off, and this it projects into the external world and regards as hostile. According to this new arrangement the congruence of the two polarities,

ego-subject with pleasure,

outside world with pain (or earlier with neutrality), is once more established. . . .

As we have heard, the ego's objects are presented to it from the outside world in the first instance by the instincts of self-preservation, and it is undeniable also that hate originally betokens the relation of the ego to the alien external world with its afflux of stimuli. Neutrality may be classified as a special case of hate or rejection, after having made its appearance first as the forerunner of hate. Thus at the very beginning, the external world, objects and that which was hated were one and the same thing. When later on an object manifests itself as a source of pleasure, it becomes loved, but also incorporated into the ego, so that for the purified pleasure-ego the object once again coincides with what is extraneous and hated.

Now, however, we note that just as the antithesis *love–indifference* reflects the polarity *ego–external world*, so the second antithesis, *love–hate*, reproduces the polarity *pleasure–pain*, which is bound up with the former. When the purely narcissistic stage gives place to the object-stage, pleasure and pain denote the relations of the ego to the object. When the object becomes a source of pleasurable feelings, a motor tendency is set up which strives to bring the object near to and incorporate it into the ego; we then speak of the "attraction" exercised by the pleasure-giving object, and say that we "love" that object. Conversely, when the object is the source of painful feelings, there is a tendency which endeavours to increase the distance between object and ego and to repeat in relation to the former the primordial attempt at flight from the external world with its flow of stimuli. We feel a "repulsion" from the object, and hate it; this hate can then be intensified to the point of an aggressive tendency towards the object, with the intention of destroying it.

We might at a pinch say of an instinct that it "loves" the objects after which it strives for purposes of satisfaction, but to say that it "hates" an object strikes us as odd; so we become aware that the attitudes of love and hate cannot be said to characterize the relations of instincts to their objects, but are reserved for the relations of the ego as a whole to objects. But, if we consider a colloquial usage which is certainly full of meaning, we see that there is yet another limitation to the significance of love and hate. We do not say of those objects which serve the interests of self-preservation that we love them;

rather we emphasize the fact that we need them, and perhaps add an element of a different kind in our relation to them by words which denote a much lesser degree of love—for example, to be fond of, to like, to find agreeable.

So the word "to love" becomes shifted ever further into the sphere of the pure pleasure-relation existing between the ego and its object and finally attaches itself to sexual objects in the narrower sense and to those which satisfy the needs of sublimated sexual instincts. The discrimination of the ego-instincts from the sexual, a discrimination which we have imposed upon our psychology, is seen, therefore, to be in conformity with the spirit of our speech. Since we do not customarily say that the single sexual component-instinct loves its object, but see the most appropriate case in which to apply the word "love" in the relation of the ego to its sexual object, we learn from this fact that the applicability of the word in this relation begins only with the synthesis of all the component-instincts under the primacy of the genitals and in the service of the function of reproduction.

It is noteworthy that in the use of the word "hate" no such intimate relation to sexual pleasure and the sexual function appears: on the contrary, the painful character of the relation seems to be the sole decisive feature. The ego hates, abhors, and pursues with intent to destroy all objects which are for it a source of painful feelings, without taking into account whether they mean to it frustration of sexual satisfaction or of gratification of the needs of self-preservation. Indeed, it may be asserted that the true prototypes of the hate-relation are derived not from sexual life, but from the struggle of the ego for self-preservation and self-maintenance.

So we see that love and hate, which present themselves to us as essentially antithetical, stand in no simple relation to each other. They did not originate in a cleavage of any common primal element, but sprang from different sources and underwent each its own development before the influence of the pleasure-pain relation constituted them antitheses to each other. At this point we are confronted with the task of putting together what we know of the genesis of love and hate.

Love originates in the capacity of the ego to satisfy some of its instincts auto-erotically through the obtaining of "organ-pleasure." It is primarily narcissistic, is then transferred to those objects which have been incorporated in the ego, now much extended, and expresses the motor striving of the ego after these objects as sources of pleasure. It is intimately connected with the activity of the later sexual instincts and, when these have been completely synthetized, coincides with the sexual trend as a whole. The preliminary stages of love reveal themselves as temporary sexual aims, while the sexual instincts are passing through their complicated development. First among these we recognize the phase of incorporating or devouring, a type of love which is compatible with abolition of any separate existence on the part of the object, and which may therefore be designated ambivalent. At the higher stage of the pregenital sadistic-anal organization, the striving after the object appears in the form of an impulsion to mastery, in which injury or annihilation of the object is a matter of indifference. This form and preliminary stage of love is hardly to be distinguished from hate in its behavior towards the object. Only when the genital organization is established does love become the antithesis of hate.

The relation of hate to objects is older than that of love. It is derived from the primal repudiation by the narcissistic ego of the external world whence flows the stream of stimuli. As an expression of the pain-reaction induced by objects, it remains in constant intimate relation with the instincts of self-preservation, so that sexual and ego-instincts readily develop an antithesis which repeats that of love and hate. When the sexual function is governed by the ego-instincts, as at the stage of the sadistic-anal organization, they impart the qualities of hate to the instinct's aim as well.

The history of the origin and relations of love makes

us understand how it is that love so constantly manifests itself as "ambivalent," i.e. accompanied by feelings of hate against the same object. This admixture of hate in love is to be traced in part to those preliminary stages of love which have not been wholly outgrown, and in part is based upon reactions of aversion and repudiation on the part of the ego-instincts which, in the frequent conflicts between the interests of the ego and those of love, can claim to be supported by real and actual motives. In both cases, therefore, the admixture of hate may be traced to the source of the self-preservative instincts. When a love-relationship with a given object is broken off, it is not infrequently succeeded by hate, so that we receive the impression of a transformation of love into hate. This descriptive characterization is amplified by the view that, when this happens, the hate which is motivated by considerations of reality is reinforced by a regression of the love to the sadistic preliminary stage, so that the hate acquires an erotic character and the continuity of a love-relation is ensured.

The third antithesis of love, the transformation of loving into being loved, represents the operation of the polarity of active and passive, and is to be judged in the same way as in scoptophilia and sadism. We may sum up by saying that the essential feature in the vicissitudes undergone by instincts is *their subjection to the influences of the three great polarities that govern mental life.* Of these three polarities we might describe that of activity—passivity as the *biological,* that of ego—external world as the *real,* and finally that of pleasure—pain as the *economic* respectively. . . .

REPRESSION [1]

(1915)

ONE of the vicissitudes an instinctual impulse may undergo
is to meet with resistances the aim of which is to make
the impulse inoperative. Under certain conditions, which
we shall presently investigate more closely, the impulse
then passes into the state of *repression*. If it were a question of the operation of an external stimulus, obviously
flight would be the appropriate remedy; with an instinct,
flight is of no avail, for the ego cannot escape from itself.
Later on, rejection based on judgment (*condemnation*)
will be found to be a good weapon against the impulse.
Repression is a preliminary phase of condemnation, something between flight and condemnation; it is a concept
which could not have been formulated before the time
of psychoanalytic research.

It is not easy in theory to deduce the possibility of
such a thing as repression. Why should an instinctual
impulse suffer such a fate? For this to happen, obviously
a necessary condition must be that attainment of its aim

[1] Z. *iii*, 129-138; S.k.S.N. *iv*, 279-94; G.S. *v*, 463-80; C.P. *iv*,
84-97. Trans. by Cecil M. Baines, revised by Joan Riviere.

by the instinct should produce "pain" instead of pleasure. But we cannot well imagine such a contingency. There are no such instincts; satisfaction of an instinct is always pleasurable. We should have to assume certain peculiar circumstances, some sort of process which changes the pleasure of satisfaction into "pain."

In order the better to define repression we may discuss some other situations in which instincts are concerned. It may happen that an external stimulus becomes internal, for example, by eating into and destroying a bodily organ, so that a new source of constant excitation and increase of tension is formed. The stimulus thereby acquires a far-reaching similarity to an instinct. We know that a case of this sort is experienced by us as *physical pain*. . . .

The case of physical pain is too obscure to help us much in our purpose. Let us suppose that an instinctual stimulus such as hunger remains unsatisfied. It then becomes imperative and can be allayed by nothing but the appropriate action for satisfying it; it keeps up a constant tension of need. Anything like a repression seems in this case to be utterly out of the question.

So repression is certainly not an essential result of the tension produced by lack of satisfaction of an impulse being raised to an unbearable degree. The weapons of defense of which the organism avails itself to guard against that situation must be discussed in another connection.

Let us instead confine ourselves to the clinical experience we meet with in the practice of psychoanalysis. We then see that the satisfaction of an instinct under repression is quite possible; further, that in every instance such a satisfaction is pleasurable in itself, but is irreconcilable with other claims and purposes; it therefore causes pleasure in one part of the mind and "pain" in another. We see then that it is a condition of repression that the element of avoiding "pain" shall have acquired more strength than the pleasure of gratification. Psycho-analytic experience of the transference neuroses, moreover, forces us to the conclusion that repression is not a defense-mechanism present from the very beginning, and that it cannot occur until a sharp distinction has been established between what is conscious and what unconscious: that the *essence of repression lies simply in the function of rejecting and keeping something out of consciousness.* This conception of repression would be supplemented by assuming that, before the mental organization reaches this phase, the other vicissitudes which may befall instincts, e.g. reversal into the opposite or turning round upon the subject, deal with the task of mastering the instinctual impulses.

It seems to us now that in view of the very great extent to which repression and the unconscious are correlated, we must defer probing more deeply into the nature of repression until we have learned more about the structure of the various institutions in the mind—and about what differentiates consciousness from the unconscious. Till we have done this, all we can do is to put together in purely descriptive fashion some characteristics of repression noted in clinical practice, even though we run the risk of having to repeat unchanged much that has been said elsewhere.

Now we have reason for assuming *a primal repression,* a first phase of repression, which consists in a denial of entry into consciousness to the mental (ideational) presentation of the instinct. This is accompanied by a *fixation*; the ideational presentation in question persists unaltered from then onwards and the instinct remains attached to it. This is due to certain properties of unconscious processes of which we shall speak later.

The second phase of repression, *repression proper,* concerns mental derivatives of the repressed instinct-presentation, or such trains of thought as, originating elsewhere, have come into associative connection with it. On account of this association, these ideas experience the same fate as that which underwent primal repression. Repression proper, therefore, is actually an after-expulsion. Moreover, it is a mistake to emphasize only the rejection which operates from the side of consciousness upon what is to be repressed. We have to consider just as much the attraction exercised by what was originally repressed upon everything with which it can establish a connection. Probably the tendency to repression would fail of its purpose if these forces did not co-operate, if there were not something previously repressed ready to assimilate that which is rejected from consciousness.

Under the influence of study of the psychoneuroses, which brings before us the important effects of repression, we are inclined to overestimate their psychological content and to forget too readily that repression does not hinder the instinct-presentation from continuing to exist in the unconscious and from organizing itself further, putting forth derivatives and instituting connections. Really, repression interferes only with the relation of the instinct-presentation to one system of the mind, namely, to consciousness.

Psychoanalysis is able to show us something else which is important for understanding the effects of repression in the psychoneuroses. It shows us, for instance, that the instinct-presentation develops in a more unchecked and luxuriant fashion if it is withdrawn by repression from conscious influence. It ramifies like a fungus, so to speak, in the dark and takes on extreme forms of expression, which when translated and revealed to the neurotic are bound not merely to seem alien to him, but to terrify him by the way in which they reflect an extraordinary and dangerous strength of instinct. This illusory strength of instinct is the result of an uninhibited development of it in fantasy and of the damming-up consequent on lack of real satisfaction. The fact that this last result is bound up with repression points the direction in which we have to look for the true significance of the latter.

In reverting to the contrary aspect, however, let us state definitely that it is not even correct to suppose that repression withholds from consciousness all the derivatives of what was primally repressed. If these derivatives are sufficiently far removed from the repressed instinct-presentation, whether owing to the process of distortion or by reason of the number of intermediate associations, they have free access to consciousness. . . .

We can lay down no general rule concerning the degree of distortion and remoteness necessary before the resistance of consciousness is abrogated. In this matter a delicate balancing takes place, the play of which is hidden from us; its mode of operation, however, leads us to infer that it is a question of a definite degree of intensity in the cathexis of the unconscious—beyond which it would break through for satisfaction. Repression acts, therefore, in a *highly specific* manner in each instance; every single derivative of the repressed may have its peculiar fate—a little more or a little less distortion alters the whole issue. In this connection it becomes comprehensible that those objects to which men give their preference, that is, their ideals, originate in the same perceptions and experiences as those objects of which they have most abhorrence, and that the two originally differed from one another only by slight modifications. Indeed, as we found in the origin of the fetish, it is possible for the original instinct-presentation to be split into two, one part undergoing repression, while the remainder, just on account of its intimate association with the other, undergoes idealization.

The same result as ensues from an increase or a decrease in the degree of distortion may also be achieved at the other end of the apparatus, so to speak, by a modification in the conditions producing pleasure and "pain." Special devices have been evolved, with the object of bringing about such changes in the play of mental forces that what usually gives rise to "pain" may on this occasion result in pleasure, and whenever such a device comes into operation the repression of an instinct-presentation that is ordinarily repudiated is abrogated. The only one of these devices which has till now been studied in any detail is that of joking.[2] Generally the lifting of the repression is only transitory; the repression is immediately re-established.

Observations of this sort, however, suffice to draw our

[2] [See the author's "Wit and its relation to the Unconscious."]

attention to some further characteristics of repression. Not only is it, as we have just explained, *variable* and *specific*, but it is also exceedingly *mobile*. The process of repression is not to be regarded as something which takes place once for all, the results of which are permanent, as when some living thing has been killed and from that time onward is dead; on the contrary, repression demands a constant expenditure of energy, and if this were discontinued the success of the repression would be jeopardized, so that a fresh act of repression would be necessary. We may imagine that what is repressed exercises a continuous straining in the direction of consciousness, so that the balance has to be kept by means of a steady counter-pressure. A constant expenditure of energy, therefore, is entailed in maintaining a repression, and economically its abrogation denotes a saving. The mobility of the repression, incidentally, finds expression also in the mental characteristics of the condition of sleep which alone renders dream-formation possible. With a return to waking life the repressive cathexes which have been called in are once more put forth.

Finally, we must not forget that after all we have said very little about an instinctual impulse when we state it to be repressed. Without prejudice to the repression such an impulse may find itself in widely different conditions; it may be inactive, i.e. cathected with only a low degree of mental energy, or its degree of cathexis (and consequently its capacity for activity) may vary.... It is an everyday occurrence that a derivative [of the repressed] can remain unrepressed so long as it represents only a small amount of energy, although its content is of such a nature as to give rise to a conflict with conscious control. But the quantitative factor is manifestly decisive for this conflict; as soon as an idea which is fundamentally offensive exceeds a certain degree of strength, the conflict takes on actuality, and it is precisely activation of the idea that leads to its repression....

In our discussion hitherto we have dealt with the repression of an instinct-presentation, and by that we understood an idea or group of ideas which is cathected with a definite amount of the mental energy (libido, interest) pertaining to an instinct. Now clinical observation forces us further to dissect something that hitherto we have conceived of as a single entity, for it shows us that beside the idea there is something else, another presentation of the instinct to be considered, and that this other element undergoes a repression which may be quite different from that of the idea. We have adopted the term *charge of affect* for this other element in the mental presentation; it represents that part of the instinct which has become detached from the idea, and finds proportionate expression, according to its quantity, in processes which become observable to perception as affects. From this point on, in describing a case of repression, we must follow up the fate of the idea which undergoes repression separately from that of the instinctual energy attached to the idea. . . . In general, repression of the ideational presentation of an instinct can surely only have the effect of causing it to vanish from consciousness if it had previously been in consciousness, or of holding it back if it is about to enter it. . . .

The fate of the quantitative factor in the instinct-presentation may be one of three, as we see by a cursory survey of the observations made through psychoanalysis: either the instinct is altogether suppressed, so that no trace of it is found, or it appears in the guise of an affect of a particular qualitative tone, or it is transformed into anxiety. With the two last possibilities we are obliged to focus our attention upon the *transformation* into *affects,* and especially into *anxiety,* of the mental energy belonging to the *instincts,* this being a new possible vicissitude undergone by an instinct. . . .

If we confine our observations to the results of its effect on the ideational part of the instinct-presentation, we discover that as a rule repression creates a *substitute-formation.* What then is the mechanism of such a substitute-formation, or must we distinguish several mechanisms here also? Further, we know that repression leaves *symptoms* in its train. May we then regard substitute-formation and symptom-formation as coincident processes, and, if this is on the whole possible, does the mechanism of substitute-formation coincide with that of repression? So far as we know at present, it seems probable that the two are widely divergent, that it is not the repression itself which produces substitute-formations and symptoms, but that these latter constitute indications of a *return of the repressed* and owe their existence to quite other processes. It would also seem advisable to examine the mechanisms of substitute- and symptom-formation before those of repression. . . . I will anticipate by saying: (1) that the mechanism of repression does not in fact coincide with the mechanism or mechanisms of substitute-formation, (2) that there are many different mechanisms of substitute-formation, and (3) that the different mechanisms of repression have at least this one thing in common: *a withdrawal of energic cathexis* (or of *libido*, if it is a question of sexual instincts).

Further, confining myself to the three best-known forms of psychoneurosis, I will show by means of some examples how the conceptions here introduced find application to the study of repression. From *anxiety-hysteria* I will choose an instance which has been subjected to thorough analysis—that of an animal-phobia. The instinctual impulse subjected to repression here is a libidinal attitude towards the father, coupled with dread of him. After repression, this impulse vanishes out of consciousness: the father does not appear in consciousness as an object for the libido. As a substitute for him we find in a corresponding situation some animal which is more or less suited to be an object of dread. The substitute-formation of the ideational element has established itself by way of a displacement along the line of a series of associated ideas which is determined in some particular way. The quantitative element has not vanished, but has been transformed into anxiety. The result is a fear of a wolf, instead of a claim for love from the father. Of course the categories here employed are not enough to supply a complete explanation even of the simplest case of psychoneurosis: there are always other points of view to be taken into account.

Such a repression as that which takes place in an animal-phobia must be described as radically unsuccessful. All that it has done is to remove the idea and set another in its place; it has not succeeded at all in its aim of avoiding "pain." On this account, too, the work of the neurosis, far from ceasing, proceeds into a "second movement," so to speak, which is designed to attain its immediate and more important aim. There follows an attempt at flight, the formation of the *phobia proper*—a number of things have to be *avoided* in order to prevent an outbreak of anxiety. A more particular investigation would enable us to understand the mechanism by which the phobia achieves its aim.

We are led to quite another view of the process of repression when we consider the picture of a true *conversion-hysteria*. Here the salient point is that it is possible to bring about a total disappearance of the charge of affect. The patient then displays towards his symptoms what Charcot called "*la belle indifférence des hystériques*."...

The ideational content of the instinct-presentation is completely withdrawn from consciousness; as a substitute-formation—and concurrently, as a symptom—we have an excessive innervation (in typical cases, a somatic innervation), sometimes of a sensory, sometimes of a motor character, either as an excitation or as an inhibition. The area of over-innervation proves on closer observation to belong to the repressed instinct-presentation itself, and, as if by a process of *condensation*, to have absorbed the whole cathexis. Of course these remarks do not cover the whole mechanism of a conversion-hysteria; the element of *regression* especially, which will be appraised in another connection, has to be taken into account.... In conversion-hysteria the process of repression terminates with the formation of the symptom and does not, as in anxiety-hysteria, need to proceed to a "second movement"—or, strictly speaking, an unlimited number of "movements."

A totally different aspect of repression is shown in the third affection to which we are referring for purposes of this comparison: in the *obsessional neurosis.* Here we are at first in doubt what it is that we have to regard as the repressed instinct-presentation—a libidinal or a hostile trend. This uncertainty arises because the obsessional neurosis rests on the premise of a regression by means of which a sadistic trend has been substituted for a tender one. It is this hostile impulse against a loved person which has undergone repression. The effect at an early phase of the work of repression is quite different from that produced later. At first the repression is completely successful, the ideational content is rejected and the affect made to disappear. As a substitute-formation there arises an alteration in the ego, an increased sensitiveness of conscience, which can hardly be called a symptom. Substitute- and symptom-formation do not coincide here. Here, too, we learn something about the mechanism of repression. Repression, as it invariably does, has brought about a withdrawal of libido, but for this purpose it has made use of a *reaction-formation,* by intensifying an antithesis. So here the substitute-formation has the same mechanism as the repression and at bottom coincides with it, while yet chronologically, as well as in its content, it is distinct from the symptom-formation. It is very probable that the whole process is made possible by the ambivalent relation into which the sadistic impulse destined for repression has been introduced.

But the repression, at first successful, does not hold; in the further course of things its failure becomes increasingly obvious. The ambivalence which has allowed repression to come into being by means of reaction-formation also constitutes the point at which the repressed succeeds in breaking through again. The vanished affect is transformed, without any diminution, into dread of the community, pangs of conscience, or self-reproaches; the rejected idea is replaced by a *displacement-substitute,* often by displacement on to something utterly trivial or indifferent.... The rejection of the idea from consciousness is obstinately maintained, because it ensures abstention from action, preclusion of the motor expression of an impulse. So the final form of the work of repression in the obsessional neurosis is a sterile and never-ending struggle.

SOME CHARACTER-TYPES MET WITH IN PSYCHOANALYTIC WORK [1]

(1915)

WHEN the physician is carrying out psychoanalytic treatment of a neurotic, his interest is by no means primarily directed to the patient's character. He is far more desirous to know what the symptoms signify, what instinctual impulses lurk behind them and are satisfied by them, and by what transitions the mysterious path has led from those impulses to these symptoms. But the technique which he is obliged to follow soon constrains him to direct his immediate curiosity towards other objectives. He observes that his investigation is threatened by resistances set up against him by the patient, and these resistances he may justly attribute to the latter's character, which now acquires the first claim on his interest.

What opposes itself to the physician's labors is not always those traits of character which the patient recognizes in himself and which are attributed to him by those around him. Peculiarities in the patient which he had seemed to possess only in a modest degree are often dis-

[1] *I. iv*, 317-36; *S.k.S.N. iv*, 521-52; *G.S. x*, 287-314; *C.P. iv*, 318-44. Trans. by E. Colburn Mayne, revised by Joan Riviere.

played in surprising intensity, or attitudes reveal themselves in him which in other relations of life would not have been betrayed. The following pages will be devoted to describing and tracing back to their origin some of these astonishing traits of character.

I. *The "Exceptions"*

The psycho-analytic worker is continually confronted with the task of inducing the patient to renounce an immediate and directly attainable source of pleasure. He need not renounce all pleasure.... No, the patient need merely renounce such gratifications as will inevitably be detrimental to him; he need only temporarily abjure, only learn to exchange an immediate source of pleasure for one better assured though longer delayed....

Thus, when one exacts from the patient a provisional renunciation of any source of pleasure, a sacrifice, a readiness to accept some temporary suffering in view of a better end, or even only the resolve to submit to a necessity which applies to all human beings, one will come upon individuals who resist such an appeal on special grounds. They say that they have renounced enough and suffered enough, and have a claim to be spared any further exactions; they will submit no longer to disagreeable necessity, for they are *exceptions* and intend to remain so too. In one patient of the kind this claim had grown into the conviction that a special providence watched over him, which would protect him from any painful sacrifices of the sort....

Now it is surely indubitable that everyone would fain consider himself an "exception" and claim privileges over others. But precisely because of this there must be a particular reason, and one not universally available, if any individual actually proclaims himself an exception and behaves as such. This reason may be of more than one kind; in the cases I investigated I succeeded in tracing it to a common peculiarity in the earlier experiences of these patients' lives. Their neuroses were connected with an event or painful experience from which they had suffered in their earliest childhood, one in respect of which they knew themselves to be guiltless, and which they could look upon as an unjust injury inflicted upon them. The privileges that they claimed as a result of this injustice, and the rebelliousness it engendered, had contributed not a little to intensifying the conflicts leading to the outbreak of neurosis.... The young man who believed himself watched over by a special providence had been in infancy the victim of an accidental infection from his wet-nurse, and had lived his whole later life on the "insurance-dole," as it were, of his claims to compensation, without having any idea on what he based those claims. In his case the analysis, which reconstructed this event out of obscure glimmerings of memory and interpretations of the symptoms, was confirmed objectively by information from the family.

For reasons which will be easily understood I cannot communicate very much about these and other case-histories.... [In place of giving case-histories the author discusses Gloucester's soliloquy in *Richard III*.—ED.]

We will not, however, dismiss the "exceptions" without pointing out that the claim of women to privileges and to exemption from so many of the importunities of existence rests upon the same foundation. As we learn from psycho-analytic work, women regard themselves as wronged from infancy, as undeservedly cut short and set back; and the embitterment of so many daughters against their mothers derives, in the last analysis, from the reproach against her of having brought them into the world as women instead of as men.

II. *Those Wrecked by Success*

Psychoanalytic work has furnished us with the rule that people fall ill of a neurosis as a result of *frustration*. The frustration meant is that of satisfaction for their libidinal desires and a long circumlocution is necessary before the law becomes comprehensible. That is to say, for a neurosis to break out there must be a conflict between the libidinal desires of a person and that part of his being which we call his ego, the expression of his instinct of self-preservation, which also contains his ideals of his own character. A pathogenic conflict of this kind takes place only when the libido is desirous of pursuing paths and aims which the ego has long overcome and despised, and has therefore henceforth proscribed; and this the libido never does until it is deprived of the possibility of an ideal satisfaction consistent with the ego. Hence privation, frustration of a real satisfaction, is the first condition for the outbreak of a neurosis, although, indeed, it is far from being the only one.

So much the more surprising, indeed bewildering, must it appear when as a physician one makes the discovery that people occasionally fall ill precisely because a deeply rooted and long-cherished wish has come to fulfillment. It seems then as though they could not endure their bliss, for the causative connection between this fulfillment and the falling-ill there can be no question. . . .

The contradiction between such experiences and the rule that frustration induces illness is not insoluble. The distinction between an *internal* and an *external* frustration dispels it. When in actuality the object in which the libido can find its satisfaction is withheld, this is an external frustration. In itself it is inoperative, not pathogenic, until an internal frustration has joined hands with it. This must proceed from the ego, and must dispute the right of the libido to the other objects that it then desires to possess. Only then does a conflict arise, and the possibility of neurotic illness, i.e. of a substitutive gratification proceeding circuitously by way of the repressed unconscious. The internal frustration is present, therefore, in every case, only it does not come into operation until the external, actual frustration has prepared the ground for it. In those exceptional cases where illness ensues on success, the internal frustration has operated alone—has indeed only made its appearance when an external frustration has been replaced by fulfillment of the wish. At first sight there remains something astonishing about this; but on closer consideration we shall reflect that it is not so very unusual for the ego to tolerate a wish as harmless so long as this exists in fantasy alone and seems remote from fulfillment, while it will defend itself hotly against such a wish as soon as it approaches fulfillment and threatens to become an actuality. The distinction between this and familiar situations in neurosis-formation is merely that usually it is internal intensifications of the libidinal cathexis which turn the fantasy, that has hitherto been thought little of and tolerated, into a dreaded opponent; while in these cases of ours the signal for the outbreak of conflict is given by an actual external alteration in circumstances.

Analytic work soon shows us that it is forces of conscience which forbid the person to gain the long-hoped-for enjoyment from the fortunate change in reality. It is a difficult task, however, to discover the essence and origin of these censuring and punishing tendencies, which so often surprise us by their presence where we do not expect to find them.... [The author again turns to literature for examples, in this instance Lady Macbeth, and Rebecca in *Rosmersholm.—*Ed.]

III. *Criminality from a Sense of Guilt*

In their narrations about their early years, particularly before puberty, people who have afterwards become very upright and have told me of forbidden actions which they had formerly committed—such as thefts, frauds, and even arson. I was wont to dismiss these statements with the comment that we know the weakness of moral inhibiting influences at that time of life, and I made no attempt to give them an important place in the connected story. But eventually I was constrained to make a more fundamental study of such incidents, by reason of some glaring and more accessible cases in which the transgressions took place while the patients were under my treatment, and were people of riper age. The analytic work then afforded the surprising conclusion that such deeds are done precisely *because* they are forbidden, and because by carrying them out the doer enjoys a sense of mental relief. He suffered from an oppressive feeling of guilt, of which he did not know the origin, and after he had committed a misdeed the oppression was mitigated. The sense of guilt was at least in some way accounted for.

Paradoxical as it may sound, I must maintain that the sense of guilt was present prior to the transgression, that it did not arise from this, but contrariwise—the transgression from the sense of guilt. These persons we might justifiably describe as criminals from a sense of guilt. The pre-existence of the guilty feeling had of course to be demonstrated by a whole succession of other manifestations and effects.

But scientific work is not satisfied with establishing a departure from the norm. There are two further questions to answer: whence derives the obscure sense of guilt before the deed, and whether it is probable that this kind of causation plays a considerable part in the transgressions of mankind. . . .

With children, it is easy to perceive that they are often "naughty" on purpose to provoke punishment, and are quiet and contented after the chastisement. Later analytic investigation can often find a trace of the guilty feeling which bid them seek for punishment. Among adult criminals one must probably except those who transgress without any sense of guilt, who either have developed no moral inhibitions or consider themselves justified in their deed by their conflict with society. But in the majority of other criminals, those for whom punitive measures are really designed, such a motivation towards crime might very well be present, casting light on many obscure points in the psychology of the criminal, and furnishing punishment with a new psychological basis. . . .

ON NARCISSISM: AN INTRODUCTION[1]

(1914)

I. THE word narcissism is taken from clinical terminology and was chosen by P. Näcke[2] in 1899 to denote the attitude of a person who treats his own body in the same way as otherwise the body of a sexual object is treated; that is to say, he experiences sexual pleasure in gazing at, caressing, and fondling his body, till complete gratification ensues upon these activities. Developed to this degree, narcissism has the significance of a perversion, which has absorbed the whole sexual life of the subject; consequently, in dealing with it we may expect to meet with phenomena similar to those for which we look in the study of all perversions.

Now those engaged in psycho-analytic observation were struck by the fact that isolated features of the narcissistic attitude are found in many people who are characterized by other aberrations—for instance, as Sadger states, in homosexuals—and at last it seemed that a disposition of

[1] *Jb. vi*, 1-24; *S.k.S.N. iv*, 78-112; *G.S. vi*, 153-87; *C.P. iv*, 30-59. Trans. by Cecil M. Baines, revised by Joan Riviere.

[2] [In a later paper Professor Freud has corrected this slip and added the name of Havelock Ellis.—ED.]

the libido which must be described as narcissistic might have to be reckoned with in a much wider field, and that it might claim a place in the regular sexual development of human beings.[3] ... Narcissism in this sense would not be a perversion, but the libidinal complement to the egoism of the instinct of self-preservation, a measure of which may justifiably be attributed to every living creature.

A pressing motive for occupying ourselves with the conception of a primary and normal narcissism arose when the attempt was made to bring our knowledge of dementia praecox (Kraepelin), or schizophrenia (Bleuler), into line with the hypothesis upon which the libido-theory is based. Such patients, whom I propose to term paraphrenics, display two fundamental characteristics: they suffer from megalomania and they have withdrawn their interest from the external world (people and things).... A patient suffering from hysteria or obsessional neurosis has also, as far as the influence of his illness goes, abandoned his relation to reality. But analysis shows that he has by no means broken off his erotic relations to persons and things. He still retains them in fantasy; i.e. he has, on the one hand, substituted for actual objects imaginary objects founded on memories, or has blended the two; while, on the other hand, he has ceased to direct his motor activities to the attainment of his aims in connection with real objects. It is only to this condition of the libido that we may legitimately apply the term *introversion* of the libido which is used by Jung indiscriminately. It is otherwise with the paraphrenic. He seems really to have withdrawn his libido from persons and things in the outer world, without replacing them by others in his fantasy. When this does happen, the process seems to be a secondary one, part of an effort towards recovery, designed to lead the libido back towards an object.

The question arises: What is the fate of the libido when withdrawn from external objects in schizophrenia? The megalomania characteristic of these conditions affords a clue here. It has doubtless come into being at the expense

[3] Otto Rank, "Ein Beitrag zum Narzissmus".

of the object-libido. The libido withdrawn from the outer world has been directed on to the ego, giving rise to a state which we may call narcissism. But the megalomania itself is no new phenomenon; on the contrary, it is, as we know, an exaggeration and plainer manifestation of a condition which had already existed previously. . . .

This development of the libido-theory—in my opinion, a legitimate development—receives reinforcement from a third quarter, namely, from the observations we make and the conceptions we form of the mental life of primitive peoples and of children. In the former we find characteristics which, if they occurred singly, might be put down to megalomania: an over-estimation of the power of wishes and mental processes, the "omnipotence of thoughts," a belief in the magical virtue of words, and a method of dealing with the outer world—the art of "magic" —which appears to be a logical application of these grandiose premises.[4] In the child of our own day, whose developments is much more obscure to us, we expect a perfectly analogous attitude towards the external world.[5]

In the complete absence of any theory of the instincts which would help us to find our bearings, we may be permitted, or rather, it is incumbent upon us, in the first place to work out any hypothesis to its logical conclusion, until it either fails or becomes confirmed. There are various points in favor of the hypothesis of a primordial differentiation between sexual instincts and other instincts, ego-instincts, besides the usefulness of such an assumption in the analysis of the transference neuroses. I admit that this latter consideration alone would not be decisive, for it might be a question of an indifferent energy operating in the mind which was converted into libido only by the act of object-cathexis. But, in the first place, this differentiation of concepts corresponds to the distinction between hunger and love, so widely current. And, in the second

---

[4] Cf. the corresponding sections on this subject in my *Totem und Tabu*, 1913.

[5] Cf. Ferenczi, "Stages in the Development of the Sense of Reality".

place, there are biological considerations in its favor. The individual does actually carry on a double existence: one designed to serve his own purposes and another as a link in a chain, in which he serves against, or at any rate without, any volition of his own. The individual himself regards sexuality as one of his own ends; while from another point of view he is only an appendage to his germ-plasm, to which he lends his energies, taking in return his toll of pleasure—the mortal vehicle of a (possibly) immortal substance—like the inheritor of an entailed property who is only the temporary holder of an estate which survives him. The differentiation of the sexual instincts from the ego-instincts would simply reflect this double function of the individual. Thirdly, we must recollect that all our provisional ideas in psychology will someday be based on an organic substructure. This makes it probable that special substances and special chemical processes control the operation of sexuality and provide for the continuation of the individual life in that of the species. We take this probability into account when we substitute special forces in the mind for special chemical substances.

Just because I try in general to keep apart from psychology everything that is not strictly within its scope, even biological thought, I wish at this point expressly to admit that the hypothesis of separate ego-instincts and sexual instincts (that is to say, the libido-theory) rests scarcely at all upon a psychological basis, but is essentially supported upon the facts of biology. So I shall also be consistent enough to drop this hypothesis if psychoanalytic work itself should suggest as more valuable another hypothesis about the instincts. So far, this has not happened. It may then be that—when we penetrate deepest and furthest—sexual energy, the libido, will be found to be only the product of a differentiation in the energy at work generally in the mind. But such a statement is of no importance. It has reference to matters too remote from the problems of our observation and so empty of available knowledge, that to dispute it is as idle as to affirm it; it is possible that this primordial identity has as little to do with our analytical interests as the primordial kinship of all human races has to do with the proof of kinship with a testator required by the Probate Court. All these speculations lead nowhere; since we cannot wait for another science to present us with a theory of the instincts ready-made, it is far more to the purpose that we should try to see what light may be thrown upon this basic problem of biology by a synthesis of psychological phenomena. Let us be fully aware of the possibility of error; but do not let us be deterred from carrying to its logical conclusion the hypothesis we first adopted of an antithesis between ego-instincts and sexual instincts (an hypothesis to which we were impelled by analysis of the transference neuroses), and so from seeing whether it turns out to be consistent and fruitful, and whether it may be applied to other affections also, e.g. to schizophrenia.

[Here follows a technical discussion. The author takes up the point again later on.—ED.]

II. It seems to me that certain peculiar difficulties lie in the way of a direct study of narcissism. Our chief means of access to an understanding of this condition will probably remain the analysis of paraphrenics. As the transference neuroses have enabled us to trace the libidinal instinctual impulses, so dementia praecox and paranoia will give us insight into the psychology of the ego. Once more, in order to arrive at what is normal and apparently so simple, we shall have to study the pathological with its distortions and exaggerations. At the same time, there are other sources from which we may derive a knowledge of narcissism, which I will now mention in their order—namely, the study of organic disease, of hypochondria, and of love between the sexes.

In estimating the influence of organic disease upon the distribution of the libido, I follow a suggestion of S. Ferenczi's, which he made to me in conversation. It is universally known, and seems to us a matter of course, that a perseon suffering organic pain and discomfort relinquishes his interest in the things of the outside world, in so far as they do not concern his suffering. Closer observation teaches us that at the same time he withdraws libidinal interest from his love-objects: so long as he suffers, he ceases to love. The banality of this fact is no reason why we should be deterred from translating it into terms of the libido-theory. We should then say: the sick man withdraws his libidinal cathexes back upon his own ego, and sends them forth again when he recovers. . . . The way in which the readiness to love, however great, is banished by bodily ailments, and suddenly replaced by complete indifference, is a theme which has been sufficiently exploited by comic writers.

The condition of sleep, like illness, implies a narcissistic withdrawal of the libido away from its attachments back to the subject's own person, or, more precisely, to the single desire for sleep. The egoism of dreams fits in very well in this connection. In both states we have, if nothing else, examples of changes in the distribution of the libido which are consequent upon a change in the ego.

Hypochondria, like organic disease, manifests itself in distressing and painful bodily sensations and also concurs with organic disease in its effect upon the distribution of the libido. The hypochondriac withdraws both interest and libido—the latter specially markedly—from the objects of the outer world and concentrates both upon the organ which engages his attention. A differentiation between hypochrondria and organic disease now becomes evident: in the latter, the distressing sensations are based upon demonstrable organic changes; in the former, this is not so. But it would be entirely in keeping with our general conception of the processes of neurosis if we decided to say that hypochrondria must be right; organic changes cannot be absent in it either. Now in what could such changes consist?

Here we may fall back upon our experience, which shows that bodily sensations of a painful nature, comparable to those of hypochrondria, are not lacking in the other neuroses. I have said once before that I am inclined to class hypochrondria with neurasthenia and anxiety-neurosis as a third "actual neurosis." Probably it would not be going too far to put it in this way: that in the other neuroses too there is regularly present some small admixture of hypochrondria. Perhaps we have the best example of this in the anxiety-neurosis and in the hysteria superimposed upon it. Now the familiar prototype of an organ sensitive to pain, in some way changed and yet not diseased in the ordinary sense, is that of the genital organ in a state of excitation. It becomes congested with blood, swollen, moist, and is the seat of manifold sensations. If we apply to that activity of a given bodily area which consists in conveying sexually exciting stimuli to the mind the term *erotogenicity*, and if we reflect that the conclusions of our theory of sexuality have long accustomed us to the notion that certain other areas of the body—the *erotogenic* zones—may act as substitutes for the genitals and behave analogously to them, we then have only one step further to venture here. We can make up our minds to regard erotogenicity as a property common to all organs and are then justified in speaking of an increase or decrease in the degree of it in any given part of the body. It is possible that for every such change in the erotogenicity of the organs there is a parallel change in the libidinal cathexis in the ego. In such factors may lie the explanation of what is at the bottom of hypochrondia and what it is that can have upon the distribution of the libido the same effect as actual organic disease. . . .

I shall try here to penetrate a little further into the mechanism of paraphrenia and put together those conceptions which today seem to me worthy of consideration. The difference between paraphrenic affections and the transference neuroses appears to me to lie in the circumstance that, in the former, the libido that is liberated by frustration does not remain attached to objects in fantasy, but returns to the ego; the megalomania then represents the mastery of this volume of libido, and thus corresponds with the introversion on to the fantasy-creations that is found in the transference neuroses; the hypochrondria of paraphrenia, which is homologous to the anxiety of the transference neuroses, arises from a failure of this effort in the mental apparatus. We know that the anxiety of the neuroses can be relieved by further mental "working-over," e.g. by conversion, reaction-formation or defense-formation (phobia). The corresponding process in paraphrenics is the effort towards recovery, to which the striking phenomena of the disease are due. Since frequently, if not usually, an only partial detachment of the libido from objects accompanies paraphrenia, we can distinguish in the clinical picture three groups of phenomena: (1) those representing such remains as there may be of a normal state or of neuroses (phenomena of a residual nature); (2) those representing the morbid process (the detachment of the libido from its objects and, further, megalomania, hypochondria, affective disturbance and every kind of regression); (3) those representing an attempt at recovery. In (3) the libido is once more attached to objects, after the manner of an hysteria (in dementia praecox or paraphrenia proper), or of an obsessional neurosis (in paranoia). The fresh libidinal cathexis takes place from another level and under other conditions than the primary one. The difference between the transference neuroses arising in this way and the corresponding formations where the ego is normal would afford us the deepest insight into the structure of our mental apparatus.

A third way in which we may study narcissism is by observing the behavior of human beings in love, with its manifold differentiation in man and woman. In much the same way as the object-libido at first concealed from us the ego-libido, so in considering the object-choice of the child (and the adolescent) we first noticed that the sources from which he takes his sexual objects are his experiences of gratification. The first auto-erotic sexual gratifications are experienced in connection with vital functions in the service of self-preservation. The sexual instincts are at the outset supported upon the ego-instincts; only later do they become independent of these, and even then we have an indication of that original dependence in the fact that those persons who have to do with the feeding, care, and protection of the child become his earliest sexual objects: that is to say, in the first instance the mother or her substitute. Side by side with this type and source of object-choice, which may be called the *anaclitic* type, a second type, the existence of which we had not suspected, has been revealed by psychoanalytic investigation. We have found, especially in persons whose libidinal development has suffered some disturbance, as in perverts and homosexuals, that in the choice of their love-object they have taken as their model not the mother but their own selves. They are plainly seeking themselves as a love-object and their type of object-choice may be termed *narcissistic*. . . .

Now this does not mean that human beings are to be divided into two sharply differentiated groups, according as their object-choice conforms to the anaclitic or to the narcissistic type; we rather assume that both kinds of object-choice are open to each individual, though he may show a preference for one or the other. We say that the human being has originally two sexual objects: himself and the woman who tends him, and thereby we postulate a primary narcissism in everyone, which may in the long run manifest itself as dominating his object-choice.

Further, the comparison of man and woman shows that there are fundamental differences between the two in respect of the type of object-choice, although these differences are of course not universal. Complete object-love of the anaclitic type is, properly speaking, characteristic of the man. It displays the marked sexual over-estimation which is doubtless derived from the original narcissism of the child, now transferred to the sexual object. This sexual over-estimation is the origin of the peculiar state of being in love, a state suggestive of a neurotic compulsion, which is thus traceable to an impoverishment of the ego in respect of libido in favor of the love-object. A different course is followed in the type most frequently met with in women, which is probably the purest and truest feminine type. With the development of puberty the maturing of the female sexual organs, which up till then have been in a condition of latency, seems to bring about an intensification of the original narcissim, and this is unfavorable to the development of a true object-love with its accompanying sexual over-estimation; there arises in the woman a certain self-sufficiency (especially when there is a ripening into beauty) which compensates her for the social restrictions upon her object-choice. Strictly speaking, such women love only themselves with an intensity comparable to that of the man's love for them. Nor does their need lie in the direction of loving, but of being loved; and that man finds favor with them who fulfills this condition. The importance of this type of woman for the erotic life of mankind must be recognized as very great. Such women have the greatest fascination for men, not only for aesthetic reasons, since as a rule they are the most beautiful, but also because of certain interesting psychological constellations. It seems very evident that one person's narcissism has a great attraction for those others who have renounced part of their own narcissism and are seeking after object-love; the charm of a child lies to a great extent in his narcissism, his self-sufficiency and inaccessibility, just as does the charm of certain animals which seem not to concern themselves about us, such as cats and the large beasts of prey. In literature, indeed, even the great criminal and the humorist compel our interest by the narcissistic self-importance with which they manage to keep at arm's length everything which would diminish the importance of their ego. It is as if we envied them their power of retaining a blissful state of mind—an unassailable libido-position which we ourselves have since abandoned. The great charm of the narcissistic woman has, however, its reverse side; a large part of the dissatisfaction of the lover, of his doubts of the woman's love, of his complaints of her enigmatic nature, have their root in this incongruity between the types of object-choice.

Perhaps it is not superflous to give an assurance that, in this description of the feminine form of erotic life, no tendency to depreciate woman has any part. Apart from the fact that tendentiousness is alien to me, I also know that these different lines of development correspond to the differentiation of functions in a highly complicated biological connection; further, I am ready to admit that there are countless women who love according to the masculine type and who develop the over-estimation of the sexual object so characteristic of that type.

Even for women whose attitude towards the man remains cool and narcissistic there is a way which leads to complete object-love. In the child to whom they give birth, a part of their own body comes to them as an object other than themselves, upon which they can lavish out of their narcissism complete object-love. Other women again do not need to wait for a child in order to take the step in development from (secondary) narcissism to object-love. Before puberty they have had feelings of a likeness to men and have developed to some extent on masculine lines; after this tendency has been cut short when feminine maturity is reached, they still retain the capacity of longing for a masculine ideal which is really a survival of the boyish nature that they themselves once owned.

We may conclude these suggestions with a short survey of the paths leading to object-choice.

A person may love:

(1) According to the narcissistic type:
    (a) What he is himself (actually himself).
    (b) What he once was.
    (c) What he would like to be.
    (d) Someone who was once part of himself.

(2) According to the anaclitic type:
    (a) The woman who tends.
    (b) The man who protects;

and those substitutes which succeed them one after another. The justification for inserting case (c) of the first type has yet to be demonstrated later on in our discussion.

The significance of narcissistic object-choice for homo-sexuality in men must be appraised in another connection.

The primary narcissism of the child assumed by us, which forms one of the hypotheses in our theories of the libido, is less easy to grasp by direct observation than to confirm by deduction from another consideration. If we look at the attitude of fond parents towards their children, we cannot but perceive it as a revival and re-production of their own, long since abandoned nar-cissism. Their feeling, as is well known, is characterized by over-estimation, that sure indication of a narcissistic feature in object-choice which we have already ap-preciated. Thus they are impelled to ascribe to the child all manner of perfections which sober observation would not confirm, to gloss over and forget all his shortcomings —a tendency with which, indeed, the denial of childish sexuality is connected. Moreover, they are inclined to suspend in the child's favor the operation of all those cultural acquirements which their own narcissism has been forced to respect, and to renew in his person the claims for privileges which were long ago given up by them-selves. The child shall have things better than his parents; he shall not be subject to the necessities which they have recognized as dominating life. Illness, death, renuciation of enjoyment, restrictions on his own will, are not to touch him; the laws of nature, like those of society, are to be abrogated in his favor; he is really to be the center and heart of creation, "His Majesty the Baby," as once we fancied ourselves to be. He is to fulfill those dreams and wishes of his parents which they never carried out, to become a great man and a hero in his father's stead, or to marry a prince as a tardy compensation to the mother. At the weakest point of all in the narcissistic position, the immortality of the ego, which is so relentlessly assailed by reality, security is achieved by fleeing to the child. Parental love, which is so touching and at bottom so childish, is nothing but parental narcissism born again and, trans-formed though it be into object-love, it reveals its former character infallibly. . . .

III ... We have learned that libidinal impulses are fated to undergo pathogenic repression if they come into conflict with the subject's cultural and ethical ideas. By this we do not ever mean: if the individual in question has a merely intellectual knowledge of the existence of these ideas; we always mean: if he recognizes them as constituting a standard for himself and acknowledges the claims they make on him. Regression, as we have said, proceeds from the ego; we might say with greater precision: from the self-respect of the ego. The very impressions, experiences, impulses, and desires that one man indulges or at least consciously elaborates in his mind will be rejected with the utmost indignation by another, or stifled at once even before they enter consciousness. The difference between the two, however—and here we have the conditioning factor in repression—can easily be expressed in terms of the libido-theory. We may say that the one man has set up an *ideal* in himself by which he measures his actual ego, while the other is without this formation of an ideal. From the point of view of the ego this formation of an ideal would be the condition of repression.

To this ideal ego is now directed the self-love which the real ego enjoyed in childhood. The narcissism seems to be now displaced on to this new ideal ego, which, like the infantile ego, deems itself the possessor of all perfections. As always where the libido is concerned, here again man has shown himself incapable of giving up a gratification he has once enjoyed. He is not willing to forgo his narcissistic perfection in his childhood; and if, as he develops, he is disturbed by the admonitions of others and his own critical judgment is awakened, he seeks to recover the early perfection, thus wrested from him, in the form of an ego-ideal. That which he projects ahead of him as his ideal is merely his substitute for the lost narcissism of his childhood—the time when he was his own ideal.

This suggests that we should examine the relation between this forming of ideals and sublimation. Sublima-

tion is a process that concerns the object-libido and consists in the instinct's directing itself towards an aim other
than, and remote from, that of sexual gratification; in this
process the accent falls upon the deflection from the
sexual aim. Idealization is a process that concerns the
object; by it that object, without any alteration in its
nature, is aggrandized and exalted in the mind. Idealization is possible in the sphere of the ego-libido as well as
in that of the object-libido. For example, the sexual over-
estimation of an object is an idealization of it. In so far
as sublimation is a process that concerns the instinct and
idealization one that concerns the object, the two concepts
are to be distinguished one from the other.

The formation of the ego-ideal is often confounded with
sublimation, to the detriment of clear comprehension. A
man who has exchanged his narcissism for the worship of
a high ego-ideal has not necessarily on that account succeeded in sublimating his libidinal instincts. It is true that
the ego-ideal requires such sublimation, but it cannot
enforce it; sublimation remains a special process which
may be prompted by the ideal but the execution of which
is entirely independent of any such incitement. It is just
in neurotics that we find the highest degrees of tension
between the development of their ego-ideal and the
measure of their sublimation of primitive libidinal instincts,
and in general it is far harder to convince the idealist of
the inexpediency of the hiding place found by his libido
than the plain man whose demands in this respect are only
moderate. Further, the formation of an ego-ideal and sublimation are quite differently related to the causation of
neurosis. As we have learned, the formation of the ideal
increases the demands of the ego and is the most powerful
factor favoring repression; sublimation is a way out, a way
by which the claims of the ego can be met without involving repression.

It would not surprise us if we were to find a special institution in the mind which performs the task of seeing
that narcissistic gratification is secured from the ego-ideal
and that, with this end in view, it constantly watches

the real ego and measures it by that ideal. If such an institution does exist, it cannot possibly be something which we have not yet discovered; we only need to recognize it, and we may say that what we call our *conscience* has the required characteristics. Recognition of this institution enables us to understand the so-called "delusions of observation" or, more correctly, of *being watched*, which are such striking symptoms in the paranoid diseases and may perhaps also occur as an isolated form of illness, or intercalated in a transference neurosis. Patients of this sort complain that all their thoughts are known and their actions watched and overlooked; they are informed of the functioning of this mental institution by voices which characteristically speak to them in the third person ("Now she is thinking of that again" ... "now he is going out"). This complaint is justified—it describes the truth; a power of this kind, watching, discovering and criticizing all our intentions, does really exist; indeed, it exists with every one of us in normal life. The delusion of being watched presents it in a regressive form, thereby revealing the genesis of this function and the reason why the patient is in revolt against it.

For that which prompted the person to form an ego-ideal, over which his conscience keeps guard, was the influence of parental criticism (conveyed to him by the medium of the voice), reinforced, as time went on, by those who trained and taught the child and by all the other persons of his environment—an indefinite host, too numerous to reckon (fellow-men, public opinion).

Large quantities of libido which is essentially homosexual are in this way drawn into the formation of the narcissistic ego-ideal and find outlet and gratification in maintaining it. The institution of conscience was at bottom an embodiment, first of parental criticism, and subsequently of that of society; a similar process takes place when a tendency towards repression develops out of a command or prohibition imposed in the first instance from without. The voices, as well as the indefinite number of speakers, are brought into the foreground again by the disease, and so the evolution of conscience is regressively reproduced. But the revolt against this *censorial institution* springs from the person's desire (in accordance with the fundamental character of his illness) to liberate himself from all these influences, beginning with that of his parents, and from his withdrawal of homosexual libido from those influences. His conscience then encounters him in a regressive form as a hostile influence from without.

The lament of the paranoiac shows also that at bottom the self-criticism of conscience is identical with, and based upon, self-observation. That activity of the mind which took over the function of conscience has also enlisted itself in the service of introspection, which furnishes philosophy with the material for its intellectual operations. This must have something to do with the characteristic tendency of paranoiacs to form speculative systems.[6] ...

We may here recall our discovery that dream-formation takes place under the sway of a censorship which compels distortion of the dream-thoughts. We did not picture this censorship as a special force, an entity, but we chose the term to designate a particular aspect of the repressive tendencies which control the ego: namely, their attitude towards the dream-thoughts. Penetrating further into the structure of the ego, we may recognize the *dream-censor* again in the ego-ideal and in the dynamic utterances of conscience. If this censor is to some extent on the alert even during sleep, we can understand that the necessary condition of its activity—self-observation and self-criticism —should contribute to the dream-content some such thoughts as these: "Now he is too sleepy to think ... now he is waking up."

At this point we may enter upon a discussion of the self-regarding attitude in normal persons and in neurotics. First of all, the feeling of self-regard appears to us a

[6] I should like to add, merely by way of suggestion, that the process of development and strengthening of this watching institution might contain within it the genesis later on of (subjective) memory and of the time-factor, the latter of which has no application to unconscious processes.

measure of the ego; what various components go to make up that measure is irrelevant. Everything we possess or achieve, every remnant of the primitive feeling of omnipotence that experience has corroborated, helps to exalt the self-regard.

Applying our distinction between sexual and ego-instincts, we must recognize that the self-regard has a very intimate connection with the narcissistic libido. Here we are supported by two fundamental facts: that in paraphrenics the self-regard is exalted, while in the transference neuroses it is abased, and that where the erotic life is concerned not being loved lowers the self-regarding feelings, while being loved raises them. We have stated that to be loved is the aim and the satisfaction in a narcissistic object-choice.

Further, it is easy to observe that libidinal object-cathexis does not raise the self-regard. The effect of the dependence upon the loved object is to lower that feeling: the lover is humble. He who loves has, so to speak, forfeited a part of his narcissism, which can only be replaced by his being loved. In all these respects the self-regarding feelings seem to remain in a relation to the narcissistic element in the erotic life.

The realization of impotence, of one's own inability to love in consequence of mental or physical disorder, has an exceedingly lowering effect upon the self-regard. Here, as I judge, we shall find one of the sources of the feelings of inferiority of which patients suffering from the transference neuroses so readily complain to us. The main source of these feelings is, however, the impoverishment of the ego, due to the withdrawal from it of extraordinarily large libidinal cathexes—due, that is to say, to the injury sustained by the ego through the sexual trends which are no longer subject to control. . . .

The relations existing between self-regard and erotism (libidinal object-cathexes) may be expressed in the following formula: two cases must be distinguished—in the first, the erotic cathexes are "ego-syntonic," *in accordance with the ego-tendencies;* in the second, on the contrary, those cathexes have suffered repression. In the former case (where the path taken by the libido is acceptable to the ego), love takes its place among all the other activities of the ego. Love in itself, in the form of longing and deprivation, lowers the self-regard; whereas to be loved, to have love returned, and to possess the beloved object, exalts it again. When the libido is repressed the erotic cathexis is felt as a severe depletion of the ego, the satisfaction of love is impossible, and the re-enrichment of the ego can be effected only by a withdrawal of the libido from its objects. The return of the libido from the object to the ego and its transformation into narcissism represents, as it were, the restoration of a happy love, and, conversely, an actual happy love corresponds to the primal condition in which object-libido and ego-libido cannot be distinguished.

Perhaps the importance of the subject, and the difficulty in surveying it, may be my excuse for adding a few remarks that are rather loosely strung together.

The development of the ego consists in a departure from the primary narcissism and results in a vigorous attempt to recover it. This departure is brought about by means of the displacement of libido to an ego-ideal imposed from without, while gratification is derived from the attainment of this ideal.

At the same time the ego has put forth its libidinal object-cathexes. It becomes impoverished in consequence both of these cathexes and of the formation of the ego-ideal, and it enriches itself again both by gratification of its object-love and by fulfilling its ideal.

Part of the self-regard is primary—the residue of childish narcissism; another part arises out of such omnipotence as experience corroborates (the fulfillment of the ego-ideal), while a third part proceeds from gratification of object-libido.

The ego-ideal has imposed several conditions upon the gratification of libido through objects, for, by means of its censorship, it rejects some of them as incompatible with itself. Where no such ideal has been formed, the sexual trend in question makes its appearance unchanged in the personality in the form of a perversion. As in childhood, to be his own ideal once more, also where sexual tendencies are concerned, is the happiness that man strives to attain.

The state of being in love consists in a flowing-over of ego-libido to the object. This state has the power to remove repressions and to restore perversions. It exalts the sexual object to the position of sexual ideal. Since, in cases where the love is of the anaclitic or object type, this state results from the fulfillment of infantile conditions of love, we may say that whatever fulfills this condition of love becomes idealized.

The sexual ideal may enter into an interesting auxiliary relation to the ego-ideal. Where narcissistic gratification encounters actual hindrances, the sexual ideal may be used as a substitutive gratification. In such a case a person loves (in conformity with the narcissistic type of object-choice) someone whom he once was and no longer is, or else someone who possesses excellences which he never had at all (cf. *supra*, (c)). The parallel formula to that given above runs thus: whoever possesses an excellence which the ego lacks for the attainment of its ideal, becomes loved. This expedient is of special importance for the neurotic, whose ego is depleted by his excessive object-cathexes and who on that account is unable to attain to his ego-ideal. He then seeks a way back to narcissism from his prodigal expenditure of libido upon objects, by choosing a sexual ideal after the narcissistic type which shall possess the excellences to which he cannot attain. This is the cure by love, which he generally prefers to cure by analysis. Indeed, he cannot believe in any other curative mechanism; he usually brings expectations of this sort with him to the treatment and then directs them towards the person of the physician. The patient's incapacity for love, an incapacity resulting from his extensive repressions, naturally stands in the way of such a method of cure. When, by means of the treatment, he has been partially freed from his repressions, we are frequently met by the unintended result that he withdraws from further treatment in order to choose a love-object, hoping that life with the beloved person will complete his recovery. We might be satisfied with this result, if it did not bring with it all the dangers of an overwhelming dependence upon this helper in his need.

The ego-ideal is of great importance for the understanding of group psychology. Besides its individual side, this ideal has a social side; it is also the common ideal of a family, a class, or a nation. It not only binds the narcissistic libido, but also a considerable amount of the person's homosexual libido, which in this way becomes turned back into the ego. The dissatisfaction due to the non-fulfillment of this ideal liberates homosexual libido, which is transformed into sense of guilt (dread of the community). Originally this was a fear of punishment by the parents, or, more correctly, the dread of losing their love; later the parents are replaced by an indefinite number of fellow men. This helps us to understand why it is that paranoia is frequently caused by a wounding of the ego, by a frustration of the gratification desired within the sphere of the ego-ideal, and also to understand the coincidence of ideal-formation and sublimation in the ego-ideal, as well as the demolition of sublimations and possible transformation of ideals in paraphrenic disorders.

MOURNING AND MELANCHOLIA [1]

(1917)

Now that dreams have proved of service to us as the normal prototypes of narcissistic mental disorders, we propose to try whether a comparison with the normal emotion of grief, and its expression in mourning, will not throw some light on the nature of melancholia. This time, however, we must make a certain prefatory warning against too great expectations of the result. Even in descriptive psychiatry the definition of melancholia is uncertain; it takes on various clinical forms (some of them suggesting somatic rather than psychogenic affections) that do not seem definitely to warrant reduction to a unity. Apart from those impressions which every observer may gather, our material here is limited to a small number of cases the psychogenic nature of which was indisputable. Any claim to general validity for our conclusions shall be forgone at the outset, therefore, and we will console ourselves by reflecting that, with the means of investigation at our disposal today, we could hardly discover anything that was not typical, at least of a small group if not of a whole class of disorders.

[1] Z. iv, 288-301; S.k.S.N. iv, 356-77; G.S. v, 535-53; C.P. iv, 152-70. Trans. by Joan Riviere.

A correlation of melancholia and mourning seems justified by the general picture of the two conditions.[2] Moreover, wherever it is possible to discern the external influences in life which have brought each of them about, this exciting cause proves to be the same in both. Mourning is regularly the reaction to the loss of a loved person, or to the loss of some abstraction which has taken the place of one, such as fatherland, liberty, an ideal, and so on. As an effect of the same influences, melancholia instead of a state of grief develops in some people, whom we consequently suspect of a morbid pathological disposition. It is also well worth notice that, although grief involves grave departures from the normal attitude to life, it never occurs to us to regard it as a morbid condition and hand the mourner over to medical treatment. We rest assured that after a lapse of time it will be overcome, and we look upon any interference with it as inadvisable or even harmful.

The distinguishing mental features of melancholia are a profoundly painful dejection, abrogation of interest in the outside world, loss of the capacity to love, inhibition of all activity, and a lowering of the self-regarding feelings to a degree that finds utterance in self-reproaches and self-revilings, and culminates in a delusional expectation of punishment. This picture becomes a little more intelligible when we consider that, with one exception, the same traits are met with in grief. The fall in self-esteem is absent in grief; but otherwise the features are the same. Profound mourning, the reaction to the loss of a loved person, contains the same feeling of pain, loss of interest in the outside world—in so far as it does not recall the dead one—loss of capacity to adopt any new object of love, which would mean a replacing of the one mourned, the same turning from every active effort that is not connected with thoughts of the dead. It is easy to see that this inhibition and circumscription in the ego is the ex-

[2] Abraham, to whom we owe the most important of the few analytic studies on this subject, also took this comparison as his starting point.

ʌ of an exclusive devotion to its mourning, which
ʌs nothing over for other purposes or other interests.
ʌ ʌs really only because we know so well how to explain
it that this attitude does not seem to us pathological.

We should regard it as a just comparison, too, to call
the temper of grief "painful." The justification for this
comparison will probably prove illuminating when we
are in a position to define pain in terms of the economics
of the mind.[3]

Now in what consists the work which mourning performs? I do not think there is anything farfetched in the
following representation of it. The testing of reality, having shown that the loved object no longer exists, requires
forthwith that all the libido shall be withdrawn from its
attachments to this object. Against this demand a struggle
of course arises—it may be universally observed that man
never willingly abandons a libido-position, not even when
a substitute is already beckoning to him. This struggle
can be so intense that a turning away from reality ensues,
the object being clung to through the medium of a hallucinatory wish-psychosis. The normal outcome is that
deference for reality gains the day. Nevertheless its behest
cannot be at once obeyed. The task is now carried through
bit by bit, under great expense of time and cathectic
energy, while all the time the existence of the lost object
is continued in the mind. Each single one of the memories
and hopes which bound the libido to the object is brought
up and hyper-cathected, and the detachment of the libido
from it accomplished. Why this process of carrying out
the behest of reality bit by bit, which is in the nature of
a compromise, should be extraordinarily painful is not
at all easy to explain in terms of mental economics. It
is worth noting that this pain [4] seems natural to us. The

[3] [The words "painful" and "pain" in this paragraph represent
the German *Schmerz* (i.e. the ordinary connotation of *pain* in
English) and not *Unlust*, the mental antithesis of pleasure, also
technically translated "pain." —*Translator*.]

[4] [The German here is *Schmerz-Unlust*, a combination of the
two words for *pain*.—*Translator*.]

fact is, however, that when the work of mourning is completed the ego becomes free and uninhibited again.

Now let us apply to melancholia what we have learned about grief. In one class of cases it is evident that melancholia too may be the reaction to the loss of a loved object; where this is not the exciting cause one can perceive that there is a loss of a more ideal kind. The object has not perhaps actually died, but has become lost as an object of love (e.g. the case of a deserted bride). In yet other cases one feels justified in concluding that a loss of the kind has been experienced, but one cannot see clearly what has been lost, and may the more readily suppose that the patient too cannot consciously perceive what it is he has lost. This, indeed, might be so even when the patient was aware of the loss giving rise to the melancholia, that is, when he knows whom he has lost but not *what* it is he has lost in them. This would suggest that melancholia is in some way related to an unconscious loss of a love-object, in contradistinction to mourning, in which there is nothing unconscious about the loss.

In grief we found that the ego's inhibited condition and loss of interest was fully accounted for by the absorbing work of mourning. The unknown loss in melancholia would also result in an inner labor of the same kind and hence would be responsible for the melancholic inhibition. Only, the inhibition of the melancholiac seems puzzling to us because we cannot see what it is that absorbs him so entirely. Now the melancholiac displays something else which is lacking in grief—an extraordinary fall in his self-esteem, an impoverishment of his ego on a grand scale. In grief the world becomes poor and empty; in melancholia it is the ego itself [which becomes poor and empty]. The patient represents his ego to us as worthless, incapable of any effort, and morally despicable; he reproaches himself, vilifies himself, and expects to be cast out and chastised. He abases himself before everyone and commiserates his own relatives for being connected with someone so unworthy. He does not realize that any change has taken place in him, but extends his self-criticism back over the past and declares that he was never any better. This picture of delusional belittling—which is predominantly moral—is completed by sleeplessness and refusal of nourishment, and by an overthrow, psychologically very remarkable, of that instinct which constrains every living thing to cling to life.

Both scientifically and therapeutically it would be fruitless to contradict the patient who brings these accusations against himself. He must surely be right in some way and be describing something that corresponds to what he thinks. Some of his statements, indeed, we are at once obliged to confirm without reservation. He really is as lacking in interest, as incapable of love and of any achievement as he says. But that, as we know, is secondary, the effect of the inner travail consuming his ego, of which we know nothing but which we compare with the work of mourning. In certain other self-accusations he also seems to us justified, only that he has a keener eye for the truth than others who are not melancholic. When in his exacerbation of self-criticism he describes himself as petty, egoistic, dishonest, lacking in independence, one whose sole aim has been to hide the weaknesses of his own nature, for all we know it may be that he has come very near to self-knowledge; we only wonder why a man must become ill before he can discover truth of this kind. For there can be no doubt that whoever holds and expresses to others such an opinion of himself—one that Hamlet harbored of himself and all men [5]—that man is ill, whether he speaks the truth or is more or less unfair to himself. Nor is it difficult to see that there is no correspondence, so far as we can judge, between the degree of self-abasement and its real justification. A good, capable, conscientious woman will speak no better of herself after she develops melancholia than one who is actually worthless; indeed, the first is more likely to fall ill of the disease than the other, of whom we too should have nothing good to say. Finally, it must strike us that after all the melan-

[5] "Use every man after his desert, and who should 'scape whipping?" (Act II, Sc. 2).

choliac's behavior is not in every way the same as that of
one who is normally devoured by remorse and self-re-
proach. Shame before others, which would characterize
this condition above everything, is lacking in him, or at
least there is little sign of it. One could almost say that
the opposite trait of insistent talking about himself and
pleasure in the consequent exposure of himself predomi-
nates in the melancholiac.

The essential thing, therefore, is not whether the melancholiac's distressing self-abasement is justified in the
opinion of others. The point must be rather that he is correctly describing his psychological situation in his lamenta-
tions. He has lost his self-respect and must have some
good reason for having done so. It is true that we are then
faced with a contradiction which presents a very difficult
problem. From the analogy with grief we should have
to conclude that the loss suffered by the melancholiac is
that of an object; according to what he says the loss is
one in himself.

Before going into this contradiction, let us dwell for
a moment on the view melancholia affords of the constitution of the ego. We see how in this condition one
part of the ego sets itself over against the other, judges it
critically, and, as it were, looks upon it as an object. Our
suspicion that the critical institution in the mind which is
here split off from the ego might also demonstrate its independence in other circumstances will be confirmed by
all further observations. We shall really find justification
for distinguishing this institution from the rest of the ego.
It is the mental faculty commonly called conscience that
we are thus recognizing; we shall ... find evidence elsewhere showing that it can become diseased independently.
In the clinical picture of melancholia dissatisfaction with
the self on moral grounds is far the most outstanding feature; the self-criticism much less frequently concerns itself
with bodily infirmity, ugliness, weakness, social inferiority;
among these latter ills that the patient dreads or asseverates
the thought of poverty alone has a favored position.

There is one observation, not at all difficult to make,

which supplies an explanation of the contradiction mentioned above. If one listens patiently to the many and various self-accusations of the melancholiac, one cannot in the end avoid the impression that often the most violent of them are hardly at all applicable to the patient himself, but that with insignificant modifications they do fit someone else, some person whom the patient loves, has loved or ought to love. This conjecture is confirmed every time one examines the facts. So we get the key to the clinical picture—by perceiving that the self-reproaches are reproaches against a loved object which has been shifted on to the patient's own ego.

The woman who loudly pities her husband for being bound to such a poor creature as herself is really accusing her husband of being a poor creature in some sense or other. There is no need to be greatly surprised that among those transferred from him some genuine self-reproaches are mingled: they are allowed to obtrude themselves since they help to mask the others and make recognition of the true state of affairs impossible; indeed, they derive from the "for" and "against" contained in the conflict that has led to the loss of the loved object. The behavior of the patients too becomes now much more comprehensible. Their complaints are really "plaints" in the legal sense of the word; it is because everything derogatory that they say of themselves at bottom relates to someone else that they are not ashamed and do not hide their heads. Moreover, they are far from evincing towards those around them the attitude of humility and submission that alone would befit such worthless persons; on the contrary, they give a great deal of trouble, perpetually taking offense and behaving as if they had been treated with great injustice. All this is possible only because the reactions expressed in their behavior still proceed from an attitude of revolt, a mental constellation which by a certain process has become transformed into melancholic contrition.

Once this is recognized there is no difficulty in reconstructing this process. First there existed an object-choice, the libido had attached itself to a certain person; then, owing to a real injury or disappointment concerned with the loved person, this object-relationship was undetermined. The result was not the normal one of withdrawal of the libido from this object and transference of it to a new one, but something different for which various conditions seem to be necessary. The object-cathexis proved to have little power of resistance, and was abandoned; but the free libido was withdrawn into the ego and not directed to another object. It did not find application there, however, in any one of several possible ways, but served simply to establish an *identification* of the ego with the abandoned object. Thus the shadow of the object fell upon the ego, so that the latter could henceforth be criticized by a special mental faculty like an object, like the forsaken object. In this way the loss of the object became transformed into a loss in the ego, and the conflict between the ego and the loved person transformed into a cleavage between the criticizing faculty of the ego and the ego as altered by the identification.

Certain things may be directly inferred with regard to the necessary conditions and effects of such a process. On the one hand, a strong fixation to the love-object must have been present; on the other hand, in contradiction to this, the object-cathexis can have had little power of resistance. . . .

We have elsewhere described how object-choice develops from a preliminary stage of identification, the way in which the ego first adopts an object and the ambivalence in which this is expressed. The ego wishes to incorporate this object into itself, and the method by which it would do so, in this oral and cannibalistic stage, is by devouring it. Abraham is undoubtedly right in referring to this connection the refusal of nourishment met with in severe forms of melancholia. . . .

In the opening remarks of this paper I admitted that the empirical material upon which this study is founded does not supply all we could wish. . . . On the one hand, like mourning, melancholia is the reaction to a real loss of a loved object; but, over and above this, it is bound to a condition which is absent in normal grief or which, if it supervenes, transforms the latter into a pathological variety. The loss of a love-object constitutes an excellent opportunity for the ambivalence in love-relationships to make itself felt and come to the fore. Consequently where there is a disposition to obsessional neurosis the conflict of ambivalence casts a pathological shade on the grief, forcing it to express itself in the form of self-reproaches, to the effect that the mourner himself is to blame for the loss of the loved one, i.e. desired it. These obsessional states of depression following upon the death of loved persons show us what the conflict of ambivalence by itself can achieve, when there is no regressive withdrawal of libido as well. The occasions giving rise to melancholia for the most part extend beyond the clear case of a loss by death, and include all those situations of being wounded, hurt, neglected, out of favor, or disappointed, which can import opposite feelings of love and hate into the relationship or reinforce an already existing ambivalence. This conflict of ambivalence, the origin of which lies now more in actual experience, now more in constitution, must not be neglected among the conditioning factors in melancholia. If the object-love, which cannot be given up, takes refuge in narcissistic identification, while the object itself is abandoned, then hate is expanded upon this new substitute-object, railing at it, depreciating it, making it suffer and deriving sadistic gratification from its suffering. The self-torments of melancholiacs, which are without doubt pleasurable, signify, just like the corresponding phenomenon in the obsessional neurosis, a gratification of sadistic tendencies and of hate,[6] both of which relate to an object and in this way have both been turned round upon the self. In both disorders the sufferers usually succeed in the end in taking revenge, by the circuitous path of self-punishment, on the original objects and in tormenting them by means of the illness, having de-

[6] For the distinction between the two, see the paper entitled "Instincts and their Vicissitudes."

veloped the latter so as to avoid the necessity of openly expressing their hostility against the loved ones. After all, the person who has occasioned the injury to the patient's feelings, and against whom his illness is aimed, is usually to be found among those in his near neighborhood. The melancholiac's erotic cathexis of his object thus undergoes a twofold fate: part of it regresses to identification, but the other part, under the influence of the conflict of ambivalence, is reduced to the stage of sadism, which is near to this conflict.

It is this sadism, and only this, that solves the riddle of the tendency to suicide which makes melancholia so interesting—and so dangerous. As the primal condition from which instinct-life proceeds we have come to recognize a self-love of the ego which is so immense, in the fear that rises up at the menace of death we see liberated a volume of narcissistic libido which is so vast, that we cannot conceive how this ego can conceive at its own destruction. It is true we have long known that no neurotic harbors thoughts of suicide which are not murderous impulses against others redirected upon himself, but we have never been able to explain what interplay of forces could carry such a purpose through to execution. Now the analysis of melancholia shows that the ego can kill itself only when, the object-cathexis having been withdrawn upon it, it can treat itself as an object, when it is able to launch against itself the animosity relating to an object—that primordial reaction on the part of the ego to all objects in the outer world.[7] Thus in the regression from narcissistic object-choice the object is indeed abolished, but in spite of all it proves itself stronger than the ego's self. In the two contrasting situations of intense love and of suicide the ego is overwhelmed by the object, though in totally different ways.

We may expect to find the derivation of that one striking feature of melancholia, the manifestations of dread of poverty, in anal erotism, torn out of its context and altered by regression.

[7] Cf. "Instincts and their Vicissitudes."

Melancholia confronts us with yet other problems, the answer to which in part eludes us. The way in which it passes off after a certain time has elapsed without leaving traces of any gross change is a feature it shares with grief. It appeared that in grief this period of time is necessary for detailed carrying out of the behest imposed by the testing of reality, and that by accomplishing this labor the ego succeeds in freeing its libido from the lost object. We may imagine that the ego is occupied with some analogous task during the course of a melancholia; in neither case have we any insight into the economic processes going forward. The sleeplessness characteristic of melancholia evidently testifies to the inflexibility of the condition, the impossibility of effecting the general withdrawal of cathexes necessary for sleep. The complex of melancholia behaves like an open wound, drawing to itself cathectic energy from all sides (which we have called in the transference-neuroses "anti-cathexes") and draining the ego until it is utterly depleted; it proves easily able to withstand the ego's wish to sleep. The amelioration in the condition that is regularly noticeable towards evening is probably due to a somatic factor and not explicable psychologically. These questions link up with the further one, whether a loss in the ego apart from any object (a purely narcissistic wound to the ego) would suffice to produce the clinical picture of melancholia and whether an impoverishment of ego-libido directly due to toxins would not result in certain forms of the disease.

The most remarkable peculiarity of melancholia, and one most in need of explanation, is the tendency it displays to turn into mania accompanied by a completely opposite symptomatology. Not every melancholia has this fate, as we know. Many cases run their course in intermittent periods, in the intervals of which signs of mania may be entirely absent or only very slight. Others show that regular alternation of melancholic and manic phases which has been classified as circular insanity. One would be tempted to exclude these cases from among those of psychogenic origin, if the psychoanalytic method had not succeeded in effecting an explanation and therapeutic improvement of several cases of the kind. It is not merely permissible, therefore, but incumbent upon us to extend the analytic explanation of melancholia to mania.

I cannot promise that this attempt will prove entirely satisfying; it is much more in the nature of a first sounding and hardly goes beyond that. There are two points from which one may start: the first is a psychoanalytic point of view, and the second one may probably call a matter of general observation in mental economics. The psychoanalytic point is one which several analytic investigators have already formulated in so many words, namely, that the content of mania is no different from that of melancholia, that both the disorders are wrestling with the same "complex," and that in melancholia the ego has succumbed to it, whereas in mania it has mastered the complex or thrust it aside. The other point of view is founded on the observation that all states such as joy, triumph, exultation, which form the normal counterparts of mania, are economically conditioned in the same way. First, there is always a long-sustained condition of great mental expenditure, or one established by long force of habit, upon which at last some influence supervenes making it superfluous, so that a volume of energy becomes available for manifold possible applications and ways of discharge—for instance, when some poor devil, by winning a large sum of money, is suddenly relieved from perpetual anxiety about his daily bread, when any long and arduous struggle is finally crowned with success, when a man finds himself in a position to throw off at one blow some heavy burden, some false position he had long endured, and so on. All such situations are characterized by high spirits, by the signs of discharge of joyful emotion, and by increased readiness to all kinds of action, just like mania, and in complete contrast to the dejection and inhibition of melancholia. One may venture to assert that mania is nothing other than a triumph of this sort, only that here again what the ego has surmounted and is triumphing over remains hidden from it. Alcoholic intoxication, which belongs to the same group of conditions, may be explained in the same way—in so far as it consists in a state of elation; here there is probably a relaxation produced by toxins of the expenditure of energy in repression. The popular view readily takes for granted that a person in a maniacal state finds such delight in movement and action because he is so "cheery." This piece of false logic must of course be exploded. What has happened is that the economic condition described above has been fulfilled, and this is the reason why the maniac is in such high spirits on the one hand and is so uninhibited in actions on the other.

If we put together the two suggestions reached, we have the following result. When mania supervenes, the ego must have surmounted the loss of the object (or the mourning over the loss, or perhaps the object itself), whereupon the whole amount of anti-cathexis which the painful suffering of melancholia drew from the ego and "bound" has become available. Besides this, the maniac plainly shows us that he has become free from the object by whom his suffering was caused, for he runs after new object-cathexes like a starving man after bread.

This explanation certainly sounds plausible, but in the first place it is too indefinite, and, secondly, it gives rise to more new problems and doubts than we can answer. We will not evade a discussion of them, even though we cannot expect it to lead us to clear understanding.

First, then: in normal grief too the loss of the object is undoubtedly surmounted, and this process too absorbs all the energies of the ego while it lasts. Why then does it not set up the economic condition for a phase of triumph after it has run its course or at least produce some slight indication of such a state? I find it impossible to answer this objection offhand. It reminds us again that we do not even know by what economic measures the work of mourning is carried through; possibly, however, a conjecture may help us here. Reality passes its verdict—that the object no longer exists—upon each single one of the memories and hopes through which the libido was attached to the lost object, and the ego, confronted as it were with the decision whether it will share this fate, is persuaded by the sum of its narcissistic satisfactions in being alive to sever its attachment to the non-existent object. We may imagine that, because of the slowness and the gradual way in which this severance is achieved, the expenditure of energy necessary for it becomes somehow dissipated by the time the task is carried through.[8]

It is tempting to essay a formulation of the work performed during melancholia on the lines of this conjecture concerning the work of mourning. Here we are met at the outset by an uncertainty. So far we have hardly considered the topographical situation in melancholia, nor put the question in what systems or between what systems in the mind the work of melancholia goes on. How much of the mental processes of the disease is still occupied with the unconscious object-cathexes that have been given up and how much with their substitute, by identification, in the ego?

Now, it is easy to say and to write that "the unconscious (thing-)presentation of the object has been abandoned by the libido." In reality, however, this presentation is made up of innumerable single impressions (unconscious traces of them), so that this withdrawl of libido is not a process that can be accomplished in a moment, but must certainly be, like grief, one in which progress is slow and gradual. Whether it begins simultaneously at several points or follows some sort of definite sequence is not at all easy to decide; in analyses it often becomes evident that first one, then another memory is activated and that the laments which are perpetually the same and wearisome in their monotony nevertheless each time take their rise in some different unconscious source. If

[8] The economic point of view has up till now received little attention in psychoanalytic researches. I would mention as an exception a paper by Viktor Tausk (1913), "Compensation as a Means of Discounting the Motive of Repression," *International Journal of Psychoanalysis*, vol. v.

the object had not this great significance, strengthened by a thousand links, to the ego, the loss of it would be no meet cause for either mourning or melancholia. This character of withdrawing the libido bit by bit is therefore to be ascribed alike to mourning and to melancholia; it is probably sustained by the same economic arrangements and serves the same purposes in both.

As we have seen, however, there is more in the content of melancholia than in that of normal grief. In melancholia the relation to the object is no simple one; it is complicated by the conflict of ambivalence. This latter is either constitutional, i.e. it is an element of every love-relation formed by this particular ego, or else it proceeds from precisely those experiences that involved a threat of losing the object. For this reason the exciting causes of melancholia are of a much wider range than those of grief, which is for the most part occasioned only by a real loss of the object, by its death. In melancholia, that is, countless single conflicts in which love and hate wrestle together are fought for the object; the one seeks to detach the libido from the object, the other to uphold this libido-position against assault. These single conflicts cannot be located in any system but the Ucs, the region of memory-traces of things (as contrasted with word-cathexes). The efforts to detach the libido are made in this system also during mourning; but in the latter nothing hinders these processes from proceeding in the normal way through the Pcs to consciousness. For the work of melancholia this way is blocked, owing perhaps to a number of causes or to their combined operation. Constitutional ambivalence belongs by nature to what is repressed, while traumatic experiences with the object may have stirred to activity something else that has been repressed. Thus everything to do with these conflicts of ambivalence remains excluded from consciousness, until the outcome characteristic of melancholia sets in. This, as we know, consists in the libidinal cathexis that is being menaced at last abandoning the object, only, however, to resume its occupation of that place in the ego whence it came. So by taking flight into the ego love escapes annihilation. After this regression of the libido the process can become conscious; it appears in consciousness as a conflict between one part of the ego and its self-criticizing faculty.

That which consciousness is aware of in the work of melancholia is thus not the essential part of it, nor is it even the part which we may credit with an influence in bringing the suffering to an end. We see that the ego debases itself and rages against itself, and as little as the patient do we understand what this can lead to and how it can change. We can more readily credit such an achievement to the unconscious part of the work, because it is not difficult to perceive an essential analogy between the work performed in melancholia and in mourning. Just as the work of grief, by declaring the object to be dead and offering the ego the benefit of continuing to live, impels the ego to give up the object, so each single conflict of ambivalence, by disparaging the object, denigrating it, even as it were by slaying it, loosens the fixation of the libido to it. It is possible, therefore, for the process in the Ucs to come to an end, whether it be that the fury has spent itself or that the object is abandoned as no longer of value. We cannot tell which of these two possibilities is the regular or more usual one in bringing melancholia to an end, nor what influence this termination has on the future condition of the case. The ego may enjoy here the satisfaction of acknowledging itself as the better of the two, as superior to the object.

Even if we accept this view of the work of melancholia, it still does not supply an explanation of the one point upon which we hoped for light. By analogy with various other situations we expected to discover in the ambivalence prevailing in melancholia the economic condition for the appearance of mania when the melancholia has run its course. But there is one fact to which our expectations must bow. Of the three conditioning factors in melancholia —loss of the object, ambivalence, and regression of libido into the ego—the first two are found also in the obsessional reproaches arising after the death of loved persons. In these it is indubitably the ambivalence that motivates the conflict, and observation shows that after it has run its course nothing in the nature of a triumph or a manic state of mind is left. We are thus directed to the third factor as the only one that can have this effect. That accumulation of cathexis which is first of all "bound" and then, after termination of the work of melancholia, becomes free and makes mania possible must be connected with the regression of the libido into narcissism. The conflict in the ego, which in melancholia is substituted for the struggle surging round the object, must act like a painful wound which calls out unusually strong anti-cathexes. Here again, however, it will be well to call a halt and postpone further investigations into mania until we have gained some insight into the economic conditions, first, of bodily pain, and then of the mental pain which is its analogue. For we know already that, owing to the inter-dependence of the complicated problems of the mind, we are forced to break off every investigation at some point until such time as the results of another attempt elsewhere can come to its aid.

> [*For the further discussion of this problem see "Group Psychology and the Analysis of the Ego": 1921.—Ed.*]

BEYOND THE PLEASURE-PRINCIPLE [1]

(1920)

I. IN the psychoanalytical theory of the mind we take it for granted that the course of mental processes is automatically regulated by "the pleasure-principle": that is to say, we believe that any given process originates in an unpleasant state of tension and thereupon determines for itself such a path that its ultimate issue coincides with a relaxation of this tension, i.e. with avoidance of "pain" or with production of pleasure. When we consider the psychic processes under observation in reference to such a sequence we are introducing into our work the *economic* point of view. In our opinion a presentation which seeks to estimate, not only the *topographical* and *dynamic,* but also the economic element is the most complete that we can at present imagine, and deserves to be distinguished by the term *metapsychological.*

We are not interested in examining how far in our assertion of the pleasure-principle we have approached to or adopted any given philosophical system historically established. Our approach to such speculative hypotheses

[1] *Jenseits der Lustprinzips.* Wein, 1920. *G.S. vi,* 189-257; LIB. 4. Trans. by C. J. M. Hubback.

is by way of our endeavor to describe and account for the facts falling within our daily sphere of observation. Priority and originality are not among the aims which psychoanalysis sets itself. . . .

We have decided to consider pleasure and "pain" in relation to the quantity of excitation present in the psychic life—and not confined in any way—along such lines that "pain" corresponds with an increase and pleasure with a decrease in this quantity. We do not thereby commit ourselves to a simple relationship between the strength of the feelings and the changes corresponding with them, least of all, judging from psychophysiological experiences, to any view of the direct proportion existing between them. . .

The facts that have led us to believe in the supremacy of the pleasure-principle in psychic life also find expression in the hypothesis that there is an attempt on the part of the psychic apparatus to keep the quantity of excitation present as low as possible, or at least constant . . . . The pleasure-principle is deduced from the principle of constancy; in reality the principle of constancy was inferred from the facts that necessitated our assumption of the pleasure-principle. On more detailed discussion we shall find further that this tendency on the part of the psychic apparatus postulated by us may be classified as a special case of Fechner's principle of the *tendency towards stability* to which he has related the pleasure-pain feelings. . . .

The first case of . . . a check on the pleasure-principle is perfectly familiar to us in the regularity of its occurrence. We know that the pleasure-principle is adjusted to a primary mode of operation on the part of the psychic apparatus, and that for the preservation of the organism amid the difficulties of the external world it is ab initio useless and indeed extremely dangerous. Under the influence of the instinct of the ego for self-preservation it is replaced by the "reality-principle," which without giving up the intention of ultimately attaining pleasure yet demands and enforces the postponement of satisfaction, the renunciation of manifold possibilities of it, and the temporary endurance of "pain" on the long and circuitous road to pleasure. The pleasure-principle however remains for a long time the method of operation of the sex impulses, which are not so easily educable, and it happens over and over again that, whether acting through these impulses or operating in the ego itself, it prevails over the reality-principle to the detriment of the whole organism.

It is at the same time indubitable that the replacement of the pleasure-principle by the reality-principle can account only for a small part, and that not the most intense, of painful experiences. Another and no less regular source of "pain" proceeds from the conflicts and dissociations in the psychic apparatus during the development of the ego towards a more highly co-ordinated organization. Nearly all the energy with which the apparatus is charged comes from the inborn instincts, but not all of these are allowed to develop to the same stage. On the way it over and again happens that particular instincts, or portions of them, prove irreconcilable in their aims or demands with others which can be welded into the comprehensive unity of the ego. They are thereupon split off from this unity by the process of repression, retained on lower stages of psychic development, and for the time being cut off from all possibility of gratification. If they then succeed, as so easily happens with the repressed sex-impulses, in fighting their way through—along circuitous routes—to a direct or a substitutive gratification, this success, which might otherwise have brought pleasure, is experienced by the ego as "pain." . . .

The two sources of "pain" here indicated still do not nearly cover the majority of our painful experiences, but as to the rest one may say with a fair show of reason that their presence does not impugn the supremacy of the pleasure-principle. Most of the "pain" we experience is of a perceptual order, perception either of the urge of unsatisfied instincts or of something in the external world which may be painful in itself or may arouse painful anticipations in the psychic apparatus and is recognized by it as "danger." The reaction to these claims of impulse and these threats of danger, a reaction in which the real activity of the psychic apparatus is manifested, may be guided correctly by the pleasure-principle or by the reality-principle which modifies this. It seems thus unnecessary to recognize a still more far-reaching limitation of the pleasure-principle, and nevertheless it is precisely the investigation of the psychic reaction to external danger that may supply new material and new questions in regard to the problem here treated.

II. After severe shock of a mechanical nature, railway collision, or other accident in which danger to life is involved, a condition may arise which has long been recognized and to which the name "traumatic neurosis" is attached.... The clinical picture of traumatic neurosis approaches that of hysteria in its wealth of similar motor symptoms, but usually surpasses it in its strongly marked signs of subjective suffering—in this resembling rather hypochondria or melancholia—and in the evidences of a far more comprehensive general weakening and shattering of the mental functions....

Fright, fear, apprehension are incorrectly used as synonymous expressions: in their relation to danger they admit of quite clear distinction. Apprehension (*Angst*) denotes a certain condition as of expectation of danger and preparation for it, even though it be an unknown one; fear (*Furcht*) requires a definite object of which one is afraid; fright (*Schreck*) is the name of the condition to which one is reduced if one encounters a danger without being prepared for it; it lays stress on the element of surprise. In my opinion apprehension cannot produce a traumatic neurosis; in apprehension there is something which protects against fright and therefore against the fright-neurosis....

The study of dreams may be regarded as the most

trustworthy approach to the exploration of the deeper psychic processes. Now in the traumatic neuroses the dream life has this peculiarity: it continually takes the patient back to the situation of his disaster, from which he awakens in renewed terror. . . . The patient has so to speak undergone a physical fixation as to the trauma. . . .

I propose now to leave the obscure and gloomy theme of the traumatic neuroses and to study the way in which the psychic apparatus works in one of its earliest normal activities. I refer to the play of children. . . . Without the intention of making a comprehensive study of these phenomena I availed myself of an opportunity which offered of elucidating the first game invented by himself of a boy eighteen months old. It was more than a casual observation, for I lived for some weeks under the same roof as the child and his parents, and it was a considerable time before the meaning of his puzzling and continually repeated performance became clear to me.

The child was in no respect forward in his intellectual development; . . . but he made himself understood by his parents and the maidservant, and had a good reputation for behaving "properly." He did not disturb his parents at night; he scrupulously obeyed orders about not touching various objects and not going into certain rooms; and above all he never cried when his mother went out and left him for hours together, although the tie to his mother was a very close one: she had not only nourished him herself, but had cared for him and brought him up without any outside help. Occasionally, however, this well-behaved child evinced the troublesome habit of flinging into the corner of the room or under the bed all the little things he could lay his hands on, so that to gather up his toys was often no light task. He accompanied this by an expression of interest and gratification, emitting a loud long-drawn-out "o-o-o-oh" which in the judgment of the mother (one that coincided with my own) was not an interjection but meant "go away" (*fort*). I saw at last that this was a game, and that the child used all his toys only to play "being gone" (*forstein*) with them. One day I made an observation that confirmed my view. The child had a wooden reel with a piece of string wound round it. It never occurred to him, for example, to drag this after him on the floor and so play horse and cart with it, but he kept throwing it with considerable skill, held by the string, over the side of his little draped cot, so that the reel disappeared into it, then said his significant "o-o-o-oh" and drew the reel by the string out of the cot again, greeting its reappearance with a joyful *"Da"* (there). This was therefore the complete game, disappearance and return, the first act being the only one generally observed by the onlookers, and the one untiringly repeated by the child as a game for its own sake, although the greater pleasure unquestionably attached to the second act.[2]

The meaning of the game was then not far to seek. It was connected with the child's remarkable cultural achievement—the forgoing of the satisfaction of an instinct—as the result of which he could let his mother go away without making any fuss. He made it right with himself, so to speak, by dramatizing the same disappearance and return with the objects he had at hand. It is of course of no importance for the affective value of this game whether the child invented it himself or adopted it from the suggestion from outside. Our interest will attach itself to another point. The departure of the mother cannot possibly have been pleasant for the child, nor merely a matter of indifference. How then does it accord with the pleasure-principle that he repeats this painful experience as a game? The answer will perhaps be forthcoming that the departure must be played as the necessary prelude to the joyful return, and that in this latter lay the true purpose of the game. As against this, however, there is the ob-

[2] This interpretation was fully established by a further observation. One day when the mother had been out for some hours she was greeted on her return by the information "Baby o-o-o-o" which at first remained unintelligible. It soon proved that during his long lonely hours he had found a method of bringing about his own disappearance. He had discovered his reflection in the long mirror which nearly reached to the ground and had then crouched down in front of it, so that the reflection was *"fort."*

servation that the first act, the going away, was played by itself as a game and far more frequently than the whole drama with its joyful conclusion.

The analysis of a single case of this kind yields no sure conclusion: on impartial consideration one gains the impression that it is from another motive that the child has turned the experience into a game. He was in the first place passive, was overtaken by the experience, but now brings himself in as playing an active part, by repeating the experience as a game in spite of its unpleasing nature. This effort might be ascribed to the impulse to obtain the mastery of a situation (the "power" instinct), which remains independent of any question of whether the recollection was a pleasant one or not. But another interpretation may be attempted. The flinging away of the object so that it is gone might be the gratification of an impulse of revenge suppressed in real life but directed against the mother for going away, and would then have the defiant meaning: "Yes, you can go, I don't want you, I am sending you away myself." . . .

It is known of other children also that they can give vent to similar hostile feelings by throwing objects away in place of people.[3] Thus one is left in doubt whether the compulsion to work over in psychic life what has made a deep impression, to make oneself fully master of it, can express itself primarily and independently of the pleasure-principle. In the case discussed here, however, the child might have repeated a disagreeable impression in play only because with the repetition was bound up a pleasure gain of a different kind but more direct. . . .

We see that children repeat in their play everything that has made a great impression on them in actual life, that they thereby abreact the strength of the impression and so to speak make themselves masters of the situation. But on the other hand it is clear enough that all their

[3] [The author analyzes a similar case from Goethe's childhood in "A Childhood Recollection from 'Dichtung und Wahrheit.'" —ED.]

play is influenced by the dominant wish of their time of life: viz. to be grown-up and to be able to do what grown-up people do.... If a doctor examines a child's throat, or performs a small operation on him, the alarming experience will quite certainly be made the subject of the next game, but in this the pleasure gain from another source is not to be overlooked. In passing from the passivity of experience to the activity of play the child applies to his playfellow the unpleasant occurrence that befell himself and so avenges himself on the person of this proxy.

From this discussion it is at all events evident that it is unnecessary to assume a particular imitation impulse as the motive of play. We may add the reminder that the dramatic and imitative art of adults, which differs from the behavior of children in being directed towards the spectator, does not however spare the latter the most painful impressions, e.g. in tragedy, and yet can be felt by him as highly enjoyable. This convinces us that even under the domination of the pleasure-principle there are ways and means enough of making what is in itself disagreeable the object of memory and of psychic preoccupation. A theory of aesthetics with an economic point of view should deal with these cases and situations ending in final pleasure gain....

III. Five-and-twenty years of intensive work have brought about a complete change in the more immediate aims of psychoanalytic technique. At first the endeavors of the analytic physician were confined to divining the unconscious of which his patient was unaware, effecting a synthesis of its various components and communicating it at the right time. Psychoanalysis was above all an art of interpretation. Since the therapeutic task was not thereby accomplished, the next aim was to compel the patient to confirm the reconstruction through his own memory. In this endeavor the chief emphasis was on the resistances of the patient; the art now lay in unveiling these as soon as possible, in calling the patient's attention to them, and by human influence—here came in suggestion acting as "transference"—teaching him to abandon the resistances.

It then became increasingly clear, however, that the aim in view, the bringing into consciousness of the unconscious, was not fully attainable by this method either. The patient cannot recall all of what lies repressed, perhaps not even the essential part of it, and so gains no conviction that the conclusion presented to him is correct. He is obliged rather to *repeat* as a current experience what is repressed, instead of, as the physician would prefer to see him do, *recollecting* it as a fragment of the past. This reproduction appearing with unwelcome fidelity always contains a fragment of the infantile sex life, therefore of the Oedipus complex and its offshoots, and is played regularly in the sphere of transference, i.e. the relationship to the physician. When this point in the treatment is reached, it may be said that the earlier neurosis is now replaced by a fresh one, viz. the transference-neurosis. The physician makes it his concern to limit the scope of this transference-neurosis as much as he can, to force into memory as much as possible, and to leave as little as possible to repetition. . . .

[The "repetition-compulsion"] which psychoanalysis reveals in the transference phenomena with neurotics can also be observed in the life of normal persons. It here gives the impression of a pursuing fate, a daemonic trait in their destiny, and psychoanalysis has from the outset regarded such a life history as in a large measure self-imposed and determined by infantile influences. . . . Thus one knows people with whom every human relationship ends in the same way: benefactors whose protégés, however different they may otherwise have been, invariably after a time desert them in ill will, so that they are apparently condemned to drain to the dregs all the bitterness of ingratitude; men with whom every friendship ends in the friend's treachery; others who indefinitely often in their lives invest some other person with authority either in their own eyes or generally, and themselves overthrow such authority after a given time, only to replace it by a new one; lovers whose tender relationships with woman each and all run through the same phases and come to the same end, and so on. We are less astonished at this "endless repetition of the same" if there is involved a question of active behavior on the part of the person concerned, and if we detect in his character an unalterable trait which must always manifest itself in the repetition of identical experiences. Far more striking are those cases where the person seems to be experiencing something passively, without exerting any influence of his own, and yet always meets with the same fate over and over again. . . .

In the light of such observations . . . drawn from the behavior during transference and from the fate of human beings, we may venture to make the assumption that there really exists in psychic life a repetition-compulsion, which goes beyond the pleasure-principle. We shall now also feel disposed to relate to this compelling force the dreams of shock-patients and the play-impulse in children. We must of course remind ourselves that only in rare cases can we recognize the workings of this repetition-compulsion in a pure form, without the co-operation of other motives. . . .

IV. What follows now is speculation, speculation often farfetched, which each will according to his particular attitude acknowledge or neglect. Or one may call it the exploitation of an idea out of curiosity to see whither it will lead.

Psychoanalytic speculation starts from the impression gained on investigating unconscious processes that consciousness cannot be the most general characteristic of psychic processes, but merely a special function of them; . . . it asserts that consciousness is the functioning of a particular system which may be called *Cs*. Since consciousness essentially yields perceptions of excitations coming from without and feelings (*Empfindungen*) of pleasure and "pain" which can only be derived from within the psychic apparatus, we may allot the system *Pcpt-Cs*.

(= perceptual consciousness) a position in space. It must lie on the boundary between outer and inner, must face towards the outer world, and must envelop the other psychic systems. . . .

Consciousness is not the only peculiar feature that we ascribe to the processes in [the system *Pcpt-Cs.*]. . . . All excitation processes in the other systems leave in them permanent traces forming the foundations of memory-records which have nothing to do with the question of becoming conscious. They are often strongest and most enduring when the process that left them behind never reached consciousness at all. But we find it difficult to believe that such lasting traces of excitation are formed also in the system *Pcpt-Cs.* itself. If they remained permanently in consciousness they would very soon limit the fitness of the system for registration of new excitations;[4] on the other hand, if they became unconscious we should be confronted with the task of explaining the existence of unconscious processes in a system whose functioning is otherwise accompanied by the phenomenon of consciousness. . . . If one reflects how little we know from other sources about the origin of consciousness the pronouncement that *consciousness arises in the place of the memory-trace* must be conceded at least the importance of a statement which is to some extent definite.

The system *Cs.* would thus be characterized by the peculiarity that the excitation process does not leave in it, as it does in all other psychic systems, a permanent alteration of its elements, but is as it were discharged in the phenomenon of becoming conscious and vanishes. Such a departure from the general rule requires an explanation on the ground of a factor which comes into account in this one system only: this factor which is absent from all other systems might well be the exposed situation of the *Cs.* system—its immediate contact with the outer world.

[4] Here I follow throughout J. Breuer's exposition in the theoretical section of the *Studien über Hysterie,* 1895.

Let us imagine the living organism in the simplest possible form as an undifferentiated vesicle of sensitive substance: then its surface, exposed as it is to the outer world, is by its very position differentiated and serves as an organ for receiving stimuli. ... It would then be easily conceivable that, owing to the constant impact of external stimuli on the superficies of the vesicle, its substance would undergo lasting alteration to a certain depth, so that its excitation process takes a different course from that taken in the deeper layers. ... Applying this idea to the system $Cs.$, this would mean that its elements are not susceptible of any further lasting alteration from the passage of the excitation, because they are already modified to the uttermost in that respect. But they are then capable of giving rise to consciousness. In what exactly these modifications of the substance and of the excitation process in it consist many views may be held which as yet cannot be tested. It may be assumed that the excitation has, in its transmission from one element to another, to overcome a resistance, and that this diminution of the resistance itself lays down the permanent trace of the excitation (a path): in system $Cs.$ there would no longer exist any such resistance to transmission from one element to another. We may associate with this conception Breuer's distinction between quiescent (bound) and free-moving "investment-energy" in the elements of the psychic systems;[5] the elements of the system $Cs.$ would then convey no "bound" energy, only free energy capable of discharge. In my opinion, however, it is better for the present to express oneself as to these conditions in the least committal way. At any rate by these speculations we should have brought the origin of consciousness into a certain connection with the position of the system $Cs.$ and with the peculiarities of the excitation process to be ascribed to this.

We have more to say about the living vesicle with its receptive outer layer. This ... operates as a special integu-

[5] J. Breuer and S. Freud: *Studien über Hysterie.*

ment or membrane that keeps off the stimuli, i.e. makes it impossible for the energies of the outer world to act with more than a fragment of their intensity on the layers immediately below [it] which have preserved their vitality. . . . For the living organism protection against stimuli is almost a more important task than reception of stimuli; the protective barrier is equipped with its own store of energy and must above all endeavor to protect the special forms of energy-transformations going on within itself from the equalizing and therefore destructive influence of the enormous energies at work in the outer world. The reception of stimuli serves above all the purpose of collecting information about the direction and nature of the external stimuli, and for that it must suffice to take little samples of the outer world, to taste it, so to speak, in small quantities. In highly developed organisms the receptive external layer of what was once a vesicle has long been withdrawn into the depths of the body, but portions of it have been left on the surface immediately beneath the common protective barrier. These portions form the sense organs, . . . and . . . it is characteristic of them that they assimilate only very small quantities of the outer stimulus, and take in only samples of the outer world; one might compare them to antennae which touch at the outer world and then constantly withdraw from it again.

At this point I shall permit myself to touch cursorily upon a theme which would deserve the most thorough treatment. The Kantian proposition that time and space are necessary modes of thought may be submitted to discussion today in the light of certain knowledge reached through psychoanalysis. We have found by experience that unconscious mental processes are in themselves "timeless." That is to say to begin with: they are not arranged chronologically, time alters nothing in them, nor can the idea of time be applied to them. These are negative characteristics, which can be made plain only by instituting a comparison with conscious psychic processes. Our abstract conception of time seems rather to be derived wholly from the mode of functioning of the system *Pcpt-*

Cs., and to correspond with a self-perception of it. In this mode of functioning of the system another form of protection against stimulation probably comes into play. I know that these statements sound very obscure, but I must confine myself to these few hints.

So far we have got to the point that the living vesicle is equipped with a protection against stimuli from the outer world. Before that, we had decided that the cortical layer next to it must be differentiated as the organ for reception of external stimuli. But this sensitive layer (what is later the system *Cs.*) also receives excitations from within: the position of the system between outer and inner and the difference in the conditions under which this receptivity operates on the two sides become deciding factors for the functioning of the system and of the whole psychic apparatus. Towards the outer world there is a barrier against stimuli, and the mass of excitations coming up against it will take effect only on a reduced scale; towards what is within no protection against stimuli is possible, the excitations of the deeper layers pursue their way direct and in undiminished mass into the system, while certain characteristics of their discharge produce the series of pleasure-pain feelings. Naturally the excitations coming from within will, in conformity with their intensity and other qualitative characteristics (or possibly their amplitude), be more proportionate to the mode of operation of the system than the stimuli streaming in from the outer world. Two things are, however, decisively determined by these conditions: first the preponderance over all outer stimuli of the pleasure and "pain" feelings, which are an index for processes within the mechanism; and secondly a shaping of behavior towards such inner excitations as bring with them an overplus of "pain." There will be a tendency to treat them as though they were acting not from within but from without, in order for it to be possible to apply against them the defensive measures of the barrier against stimuli (*Reizschutz*). This is the origin of projection, for which so important a part is reserved in the production of pathological states. . . .

Let us go a step further. Such external excitations as are strong enough to break through the barrier against stimuli we call traumatic. In my opinion the concept of trauma involves such a relationship to an otherwise efficacious barrier. An occurrence such as an external trauma will undoubtedly provoke a very extensive disturbance in the workings of the energy of the organism, and will set in motion every kind of protective measure. But the pleasure-principle is to begin with put out of action here. The flooding of the psychic apparatus with large masses of stimuli can no longer be prevented: on the contrary, another task presents itself—to bring the stimulus under control, to "bind" in the psyche the stimulus mass that has broken its way in, so as to bring about a discharge of it.

Probably the specific discomfort of bodily pain is the result of some local breaking through of the barrier against stimuli. From this point in the periphery there stream to the central psychic apparatus continual excitations such as would otherwise come only from within.[6] What are we to expect as the reaction of the psychic life to this invasion? From all sides the "charging energy" is called on in order to create all round the breach correspondingly high "charges" of energy. An immense "counter-charge" is set up, in favor of which all the other psychic systems are improverished, so that a wide spread paralysis or diminution of other psychic activity follows.

The indefinite nature of all the discussions that we term metapsychological naturally comes from the fact that we know nothing about the nature of the excitation process in the elements of the psychic systems and do not feel justified in making any assumption about it. Thus we are all the time operating with a large X, which we carry over into every new formula. . . .

I think one may venture (tentatively) to regard the ordinary traumatic neurosis as the result of an extensive rupture of the barrier against stimuli. In this way the old

[6] Cf. "Instincts and their Vicissitudes."

naïve doctrine of "shock" would come into its own again, apparently in opposition to a later and psychologically more pretentious view which ascribes etiological significance not to the effect of the mechanical force, but to the fright and the menace to life. But these opposing views are not irreconcilable, and the psychoanalytic conception of the traumatic neurosis is far from being identical with the crudest form of the "shock" theory. While the latter takes the essential nature of the shock as residing in the direct injury to the molecular structure, or even to the histological structure, of the nervous elements, we seek to understand the effect of the shock by considering the breaking through of the barrier with which the psychic organ is provided against stimuli, and from the tasks with which this is thereby faced. Fright retains its meaning for us too. What conditions it is the failure of the mechanism of apprehension to make the proper preparation, including the over-charging of the systems first receiving the stimulus. In consequence of this lower degree of charging these systems are hardly in a position to bind the oncoming masses of excitation, and the consequences of the breaking through of the protective barrier appear all the more easily. We thus find that the apprehensive preparation, together with the over-charging of the receptive systems, represents the last line of defense against stimuli. . . . When the dreams of patients suffering from traumatic neuroses so regularly take them back to the situation of the disaster, they do not thereby, it is true, serve the purpose of wish-fulfillment, . . . but we may assume that they thereby subserve another purpose, which must be fulfilled before the pleasure-principle can begin its sway. These dreams are attempts at restoring control of the stimuli by developing apprehension, the pretermission of which caused the traumatic neurosis. They thus afford us an insight into a function of the psychic apparatus, which without contradicting the pleasure-principle is nevertheless independent of it, and appears to be of earlier origin than the aim of attaining pleasure and avoiding "pain."

This is therefore the moment to concede for the first

time an exception to the principle that the dream is a
wish-fulfillment. Anxiety dreams are no such exception,
as I have repeatedly and in detail shown; nor are the
"punishment dreams," for they merely put in the place of
the interdicted wish fulfillment the punishment appropriate to it, and are thus the wish-fulfillment of the sense
of guilt reacting on the contemned impulse. But the dreams
mentioned above of patients suffering from traumatic
neuroses do not permit of classification under the category
of wish-fulfillment, nor do the dreams occurring during
psychoanalysis that bring back the recollection of the
psychic traumata of childhood. They obey rather the repetition-compulsion, which in analysis, it is true, is supported
by the (not unconscious) wish to conjure up again what
has been forgotten and repressed. . . .

V. The fact that the sensitive cortical layer has no
protective barrier against excitations emanating from
within will have one inevitable consequence: viz. that these
transmissions of stimuli acquire increased economic significance and frequently give rise to economic disturbances
comparable to the traumatic neuroses. The most prolific
sources of such inner excitations are the so-called instincts
of the organism, the representatives of all forces arising
within the body and transmitted to the psychic apparatus—
the most important and most obscure element in psychological research.

Perhaps we shall not find it too rash an assumption
that the excitations proceeding from the instincts do not
conform to the type of the "bound" but of the free-moving
nerve processes that are striving for discharge. The most
trustworthy knowledge we have of these processes comes
from the study of dreams. There we found that the
processes in the unconscious systems are fundamentally
different from those in the (pre)conscious; that in the
unconscious "charges" may easily be completely transferred, displaced, or condensed, while if this happened
with preconscious material only defective results would be
obtained. This is the reason for the well-known peculiari-

ties of the manifest dream, after the preconscious residues of the day before have undergone elaboration according to the laws of the unconscious. I termed this kind of process in the unconscious the psychic "primary process" in contradistinction to the secondary process valid in our normal waking life. Since the excitations of instincts all affect the unconscious systems, it is scarcely an innovation to say that they follow the lines of the primary process, and little more so to identify the psychic primary process with the freely mobile charge, the secondary process with changes in Breuer's bound or tonic charge.[7] . . .

The expressions of a repetition-compulsion which we have described, both in the early activities of infantile psychic life and in the experiences of psychoanalytic treatment, show in a high degree an instinctive character, and, where they come into contrast with the pleasure-principle, a daemonic character. . . . Here there is no contradiction of the pleasure-principle: it is evident that the repetition, the rediscovery of the identity, is itself a source of pleasure. . . .

In what way is the instinctive connected with the compulsion to repetition? At this point the idea is forced upon us that we have stumbled on the trace of a general and hitherto not clearly recognized—or at least not expressly emphasized—characteristic of instinct, perhaps of all organic life. According to this, *an instinct would be a tendency innate in living organic matter impelling it towards the reinstatement of an earlier condition,* one which it had to abandon under the influence of external disturbing forces—a kind of organic elasticity, or, to put it another way, the manifestation of inertia in organic life.[8]

This conception of instinct strikes us as strange, since we are accustomed to see in instinct the factor urging towards change and development, and now we find ourselves required to recognize in it the very opposite, viz.

[7] Cp. Section VII, "Psychology of the Dream-Processes" in my *Interpretation of Dreams.*

[8] I have little doubt that similar conjectures about the nature of instinct have been already repeatedly put forward.

the expression of the conservative nature of living beings. On the other hand, we soon think of those examples in animal life which appear to confirm the idea of instinct having been historically conditioned. When certain fish undertake arduous journeys at spawning time ... they are only seeking the earlier homes of their kind; ... the same is said to be true of the migratory flights of birds of passage, but the search for further examples becomes superfluous when we remember that in the phenomena of heredity and in the facts of embryology we have the most imposing proofs of the organic compulsion to repetition. We see that the germ cell of a living animal is obliged to repeat in its development—although in a fleeting and curtailed fashion—the structures of all the forms from which the animal is descended, instead of hastening along the shortest path to its own final shape. A mechanical explanation of this except in some trifling particulars is impossible, and the historical explanation cannot be disregarded. ...

The obvious objection, that it may well be that besides the conservative instincts compelling repetition there are others which press towards new formation and progress, should certainly not be left unnoticed; it will be considered at a later stage of our discussion. ...

If then all organic instincts are conservative, historically acquired, and are directed towards regression, towards reinstatement of something earlier, we are obliged to place all the results of organic development to the credit of external, disturbing, and distracting influences. The rudimentary creature would from its very beginning not have wanted to change, would, if circumstances had remained the same, have always merely repeated the same course of existence. But in the last resort it must have been the evolution of our earth, and its relation to the sun, that has left its imprint on the development of organisms. The conservative organic instincts have absorbed every one of these enforced alterations in the course of life and have stored them for repetition; they thus present the delusive appearance of forces striving after change and progress, while they are merely endeavoring to reach an old goal by ways both old and new. This final goal of all organic striving can be stated too. It would be counter to the conservative nature of instinct if the goal of life were a state never hitherto reached. It must rather be an ancient starting point, which the living being left long ago, and to which it harks back again by all the circuitous paths of development. If we may assume as an experience admitting of no exception that everything living dies from causes within itself, and returns to the inorganic, we can only say *"The goal of all life is death,"* and, casting back, *"The inanimate was there before the animate."* ...

If these conclusions sound strangely in our ears, equally so will those we are led to make concerning the great groups of instincts which we regard as lying behind the vital phenomena of organisms. The postulate of the self-preservative instincts we ascribe to every living being stands in remarkable contrast to the supposition that the whole life of instinct serves the one end of bringing about death. The theoretic significance of the instincts of self-preservation, power, and self-assertion, shrinks to nothing, seen in this light; they are part-instincts designed to secure the path to death peculiar to the organism and to ward off possibilities of return to the inorganic other than the immanent ones, but the enigmatic struggle of the organism to maintain itself in spite of all the world, a struggle that cannot be brought into connection with anything else, disappears. It remains to be added that the organism is resolved to die only in its own way; even these watchmen of life were originally the myrmidons of death. Hence the paradox comes about that the living organism resists with all its energy influences (dangers) which could help it to reach its life-goal by a short way (a short circuit, so to speak); but this is just the behavior that characterizes a pure instinct as contrasted with an intelligent striving.[9]

But we must bethink ourselves: this cannot be the whole truth. The sexual instincts, for which the theory of the neuroses claims a position apart, lead us to quite another

[9] Compare the subsequent criticism of this extreme view of the self-preservative instincts.

point of view. Not all organisms have yielded to the external compulsion driving them to an even further development. Many have succeeded in maintaining themselves on their low level up to the present time: there are in existence today, if not all, at all events many forms of life that must resemble the primitive stages of the higher animals and plants. And, similarly, not all the elementary organisms that make up the complicated body of a higher form of life take part in the whole path of evolution to the natural end, i.e. death. Some among them, the reproductive cells, probably retain the original structure of the living substance and, after a given time, detach themselves from the parent organism, charged as they are with all the inherited and newly acquired instinctive dispositions. Possibly it is just those two features that make their independent existence possible. If brought under favorable conditions they begin to develop, that is, to repeat the same cycle to which they owe their origin, the end being that again one portion of the substance carries through its development to a finish, while another part, as a new germinal core, again harks back to the beginning of the development. Thus these reproductive cells operate against the death of the living substance and are able to win for it what must seem to us to be potential immortality, although perhaps it only means a lengthening of the path to death. Of the highest significance is the fact that the reproductive cell is fortified for this function, or only becomes capable of it, by the mingling with another like it and yet different from it.

There is a group of instincts that care for the destinies of these elementary organisms which survive the individual being, that concern themselves with the safe sheltering of these organisms as long as they are defenseless against the stimuli of the outer world, and finally bring about their conjunction with other reproductive cells. These are collectively the sexual instincts. They are conservative in the same sense as the others are, in that they reproduce earlier conditions of the living substance, but they are so in a higher degree in that they show themselves specially resistant to external influences, and they are more conservative in a wider sense still, since they preserve life itself for a longer time. They are the actual life-instincts; the fact that they run counter to the trend of the other instincts which lead towards death indicates a contradiction between them and the rest, one which the theory of neuroses has recognized as full of significance. There is as it were an oscillating rhythm in the life of organisms: the one group of instincts presses forward to reach the final goal of life as quickly as possible, the other flies back at a certain point on the way only to traverse the same stretch once more from a given spot and thus to prolong the duration of the journey.

Let us now retrace our steps for the first time, to ask whether all these speculations are not after all without foundation. Are there really, *apart from the sexual instincts,* no other instincts than those which have as their object the reinstatement of an earlier condition, none that strive towards a condition never yet attained? I am not aware of any satisfactory example in the organic world running counter to the characteristic I have suggested. The existence of a general impulse towards higher development in the plant and animal world can certainly not be established, though some such line of development is as a fact unquestionable. But, on the one hand, it is often merely a question of our own valuation when we pronounce one stage of development to be higher than another, and, on the other hand, biology makes clear to us that a higher development in one particular is often purchased with, or balanced by, retrogression in another....

Many of us will also find it hard to abandon our belief that in man himself there dwells an impulse towards perfection, which has brought him to his present heights of intellectual prowess and ethical sublimation, and from which it might be expected that his development into superman will be ensured. But I do not believe in the existence of such an inner impulse, and I see no way of preserving this pleasing illusion. The development of man up to now does not seem to me to need any explanation

differing from that of animal development, and the rest-
less striving towards further perfection which may be
observed in a minority of human beings is easily explicable as the result of that repression of instinct upon
which what is most valuable in human culture is built.
The repressed instinct never ceases to strive after its complete satisfaction which would consist in the repetition
of a primary experience of satisfaction: all substitution-
or reaction-formations and sublimations avail nothing towards relaxing the continual tension; and out of the excess
of the satisfaction demanded over that found is born the
driving momentum which allows of no abiding in any
situation presented to it, but in the poet's words "urges
ever forward, ever unsubdued." The path in the other
direction, back to complete satisfaction, is as a rule barred
by the resistances that maintain the repressions, and thus
there remains nothing for it but to proceed in the other,
still unobstructed direction, that of development, without,
however, any prospect of being able to bring the process
to a conclusion or to attain the goal. What occurs in the
development of a neurotic phobia, which is really nothing
but an attempt at flight from the satisfaction of an in-
sible "impulse towards perfection" which, however, we
stinct, gives us the prototype for the origin of his osten-
cannot possibly ascribe to all human beings. The dynamic
conditions are, it is true, quite generally present, but the
economic relations seem only in rare cases to favor the
phenomenon.

VI. ... Let us turn back ... to one of the assumptions
we interpolated, in the expectation that it will permit
of exact refutation. We built up further conclusions on
the basis of the assumption that all life must die from
internal causes. We made this assumption so lightheartedly
because it does not seem to us to be one. We are accustomed so to think, and every poet encourages us in
the idea. Perhaps we have resolved so to think because
there lies a certain consolation in this belief. If man must
himself die, after first losing his most beloved ones by

death, he would prefer that his life be forfeit to an inexorable law of nature, the sublime 'Aνάγχή, than to a mere accident which perhaps could have been in some way avoided. But perhaps this belief in the incidence of death as the necessary consequence of an inner law of being is also only one of those illusions that we have fashioned for ourselves so as to endure the burden of existence." It is certainly not a primordial belief: the idea of a "natural death" is alien to primitive races; they ascribe every death occurring among themselves to the influence of an enemy or an evil spirit. So let us not neglect to turn to biological science to test the belief.

If we do so, we may be astonished to find how little agreement exists among biologists on the question of natural death, that indeed the very conception of death altogether eludes them. . . .

[At this point the author enters into a lengthy biological discussion, which does not lend itself readily to abridgement.—Ed.]

I think this is the point at which to break off. But not without a few words of critical reflection in conclusion. I might be asked whether I am myself convinced of the views here set forward, and if so how far. My answer would be that I am neither convinced myself, nor am I seeking to arouse conviction in others. More accurately: I do not know how far I believe in them. It seems to me that the affective feature "conviction" need not come into consideration at all here. One may surely give oneself up to a line of thought, and follow it up as far as it leads, simply out of scientific curiosity, or—if you prefer—as advocatus diaboli, without, however, making a pact with the devil about it. . . . At all events there is no way of working out this idea except by combining facts with pure imagination many times in succession, and thereby departing far from observation. We know that the final result becomes the more untrustworthy the oftener one does this in the course of building up a theory, but the precise degree of uncertainty is not ascertainable. One may have gone ignominiously astray. In such work I trust little to so-called intuition: what I have seen of it seems to me to be the result of a certain impartiality of the intellect— only that people unfortunately are seldom impartial where they are concerned with the ultimate things, the great problems of science and of life. My belief is that there everyone is under the sway of preferences deeply rooted within, into the hands of which he unwittingly plays as he pursues his speculation. Where there are such good grounds for distrust, only a tepid feeling of indulgence is possible towards the results of one's own mental labors. But I hasten to add that such self-criticism does not render obligatory any special tolerance of divergent opinions. One may inexorably reject theories that are contradicted by the very first steps in the analysis of observation and yet at the same time be aware that those one holds oneself have only a tentative validity. Were we to appraise our speculations upon the life and death-instincts it would disturb us but little that so many processes go on which are surprising and hard to picture, such as one instinct being expelled by others, or turning from the ego to an object, and so on. This comes only from our being obliged to operate with scientific terms, i.e. with the metaphorical expressions peculiar to psychology (or more correctly: psychology of the deeper layers). Otherwise we should not be able to describe the corresponding processes at all, nor in fact even to have remarked them. The shortcomings of our description would probably disappear if for the psychological terms we could substitute physiological or chemical ones. These too only constitute a metaphorical language, but one familiar to us for a much longer time and perhaps also simpler.

On the other hand we wish to make it quite clear that the uncertainty of our speculation is enhanced in a high degree by the necessity of borrowing from biological science. Biology is truly a realm of limitless possibilities; we have the most surprising revelations to expect from it, and cannot conjecture what answers it will offer in some decades to the questions we have put to it. Perhaps they may be such as to overthrow the whole artificial structure of hypotheses. If that is so, someone may ask why does one undertake such work as the one set out in this article, and why should it be communicated to the world? Well, I cannot deny that some of the analogies, relations, and connections therein traced appeared to me worthy of consideration. ...

VII. ... Let us distinguish function and tendency more sharply than we have hitherto done. The pleasure-principle is then a tendency which subserves a certain function—namely, that of rendering the psychic apparatus as a whole free from any excitation, or to keep the amount of excitation constant or as low as possible. We cannot yet decide with certainty for either of these conceptions, but we note that the function so defined would partake of the most universal tendency of all living matter—to return to the peace of the inorganic world. We all know by experience that the greatest pleasure it is possible for us to attain, that of the sexual act, is bound up with the temporary quenching of a greatly heightened state of excitation. The "binding" of instinct-excitation, however, would be a preparatory function, which would direct the excitation towards its ultimate adjustment in the pleasure of discharge.

In the same connection, the question arises whether the sensations of pleasure and "pain" can emanate as well from the bound as from the "unbound" excitation-processes. It appears quite beyond doubt that the "unbond," the primary, processes give rise to much more intense sensations in both directions than the bound ones, those of the "secondary processes." The primary processes are also the earlier in point of time; at the beginning of mental life there are no others, and we may conclude that if the pleasure-principle were not already in action in respect to them, it would not establish itself in regard to the later processes. We thus arrive at the result which at bottom is not a simple one, that the search for pleasure manifests itself with far greater intensity at the beginning of psychic life than later on, but less unrestrictedly: it has to put up with repeated breaches. At a maturer age the dominance of the pleasure-principle is very much more assured, though this principle as little escapes limitations as all the other instincts. In any case, whatever it is in the process of excitation that engenders the sensations of pleasure and "pain" must be equally in existence when the secondary process is at work as with the primary process.

This would seem to be the place to institute further studies. Our consciousness conveys to us from within not only the sensations of pleasure and "pain," but also those of a peculiar tension, which again may be either pleasurable or painful in itself. Now is it the "bound" and "unbound" energy processes that we have to distinguish from each other by the help of these sensations, or is the sensation of tension to be related to the absolute quantity, perhaps to the level of the charge, while the pleasure-pain series refers to the changes in the quantity of charge in the unit of time? We must also be struck with the fact that the life-instincts have much more to do with our inner perception, since they make their appearance as disturbers of the peace, and continually bring along with them states of tension the resolution of which is experienced as pleasure; while the death-instincts, on the other hand, seem to fulfill their function unostentatiously. The pleasure-principle seems directly to subserve the death-instincts; it keeps guard, of course, also over the external stimuli, which are regarded as dangers by both kinds of instincts, but in particular over the inner increases in stimulation which have for their aim the complication of the task of living. At this point innumerable other questions arise to which no answer can yet be given. We must be patient and wait for other means and opportunities for investigation. We must hold ourselves too in readiness to abandon the path we have followed for a time, if it should seem to lead to no good result. Only such "true believers" as expect from science a substitute for the creed they have relinquished will take it amiss if the investigator develops his views further or even transforms them.

For the rest we may find consolation in the words of a poet for the slow rate of progress in scientific knowledge:

> Whither we cannot fly, we must go limping . . .
> The Scripture saith that limping is no sin.

GROUP PSYCHOLOGY AND THE ANALYSIS
OF THE EGO [1]

(1921)

1. *Introduction*

THE contrast between Individual Psychology and Social
or Group [2] Psychology, which at a first glance may seem
to be full of significance, loses a great deal of its sharp-
ness when it is examined more closely. It is true that
Individual Psychology [3] is concerned with the individual
man and explores the paths by which he seeks to find
satisfaction for his instincts; but only rarely and under
certain exceptional conditions is Individual Psychology

[1] *Massenpsychologie und Ich-Analyse.* Wien: 1921. *G.S. vi,*
259-349. LIB. 6. Trans. by James Strachey.

[2] ["Group" is used throughout this translation as equivalent
to the rather more comprehensive German *"Masse."* The author
uses this latter word to render both McDougall's "group," and
also Le Bon's *"foule,"* which would more naturally be translated
"crowd" in English. For the sake of uniformity, however,
"group" has been preferred in this case as well, and has been
substituted for "crowd" even in the extracts from the English
translation of Le Bon.—*Translator.*]

[3] ["Individual Psychology" is here used literally in contrast to
"Group Psychology." The late Dr. Alfred Adler (Vienna) used
the term as a name for his school of thought.—ED.]

in a position to disregard the relations of this individual to others. In the individual's mental life someone else is invariably involved, as a model, as an object, as a helper, as an opponent, and so from the very first Individual Psychology is at the same time Social Psychology as well —in this extended but entirely justifiable sense of the words. . . .

The individual in [his] relation . . . to his parents and to his brothers and sisters, to the person he is in love with, to his friend, and to his physician, comes under the influence of only a single person, or of a very small number of persons, each one of whom has become enormously important to him. Now in speaking of Social or Group Psychology it has become usual to leave these relations on one side and to isolate as the subject of inquiry the influencing of an individual by a large number of people simultaneously, people with whom he is connected by something, though otherwise they may in many respects be strangers to him. Group Psychology is therefore concerned with the individual man as a member of a race, of a nation, of a caste, of a profession, of an institution, or as a component part of a crowd of people who have been organized into a group at some particular time for some definite purpose. When once natural continuity has been severed in this way, it is easy to regard the phenomena that appear under these special conditions as being expressions of a special instinct that is not further reducible, the social instinct ("herd instinct," "group mind"), which does not come to light in any other situations. But we may perhaps venture to object that it seems difficult to attribute to the factor of number a significance so great as to make it capable by itself of arousing in our mental life a new instinct that is otherwise not brought into play. Our expectation is therefore directed towards two other possibilities: that the social instinct may not be a primitive one and insusceptible of dissection, and that it may be possible to discover the beginnings of its development in a narrower circle, such as that of the family.

Although Group Psychology is only in its infancy, it embraces an immense number of separate issues and offers to investigators countless problems which have hitherto not even been properly distinguished from one another. . . . Anyone who compares the narrow dimensions of this little book with the extent of Group Psychology will at once be able to guess that only a few points chosen from the whole material are to be dealt with here. And they will in fact only be a few questions with which the depth-psychology of psychoanalysis is specially concerned.

II. *Le Bon's Description of the Group Mind*[4]

Instead of starting from a definition, it seems more useful to begin with some indication of the range of the phenomena under review, and to select from among them a few specially striking and characteristic facts to which our inquiry can be attached. . . .

What is a "group"? How does it acquire the capacity for exercising such a decisive influence over the mental life of the individual? And what is the nature of the mental change which it forces upon the individual? It is the task of a theoretical Group Psychology to answer these three questions. The best way of approaching them is evidently to start with the third. . . .

Le Bon explains the condition of an individual in a group as being actually hypnotic, and does not merely make a comparison between the two states. We have no intention of raising any objection at this point, but wish only to emphasize the fact that two [of the] causes [he mentions] of an individual becoming altered in a group (the contagion and the heightened suggestibility) are evidently not on a par, since the contagion seems actually to be a manifestation of the suggestibility. . . . We cannot avoid being struck with a sense of deficiency when we notice that one of the chief elements of the comparison,

---

[4] [The author discusses Le Bon's *The Crowd: A Study of the Popular Mind* (1920) much more fully than can be gathered from these short extracts.—ED.]

namely the person who is to replace the hypnotist in the case of the group, is not mentioned in Le Bon's exposition. . . .

Let us now leave the individual, and turn to the group mind, as it has been outlined by Le Bon. It shows not a single feature which a psychoanalyst would find any difficulty in placing or in deriving from its source. . . . A group is extraordinarily credulous and open to influence, it has no critical faculty, and the improbable does not exist for it. It thinks in images, which call one another up by association (just as they arise with individuals in states of free imagination), and whose agreement with reality is never checked by any reasonable function. The feelings of a group are always very simple and very exaggerated. So that a group knows neither doubt nor uncertainty.[5] It goes directly to extremes; if a suspicion is expressed, it is instantly changed into an incontrovertible certainty; a trace of antipathy is turned into furious hatred.[6] Inclined as it itself is to all extremes, a group can only be excited by an excessive stimulus. Anyone who wishes to produce an effect upon it needs no logical adjustment in his arguments; he must paint in the most forcible colors, he must exaggerate, and he must repeat the same thing again and again.

Since a group is in no doubt as to what constitutes truth or error, and is conscious, moreover, of its own great strength, it is as intolerant as it is obedient to authority. It respects force and can only be slightly influenced by kindness, which it regards merely as a form of weakness.

[5] In the interpretation of dreams, to which, indeed, we owe our best knowledge of unconscious mental life, we follow a technical rule of disregarding doubt and uncertainty in the narrative of the dream, and of treating every element of the manifest dream as being quite certain. We attribute doubt and uncertainty to the influence of the censorship to which the dream-work is subjected, and we assume that the primary dream-thoughts are not acquainted with doubt and uncertainty as critical processes. . . .

[6] The same extreme and unmeasured intensification of every emotion is also a feature of the affective life of children, and it is present as well in dream life . . .

What it demands of its heroes is strength, or even violence. It wants to be ruled and oppressed and to fear its masters. Fundamentally it is entirely conservative, and it has a deep aversion from all innovations and advances and an unbounded respect for tradition.

In order to make a correct judgment upon the morals of groups, one must take into consideration the fact that when individuals come together in a group all their individual inhibitions fall away and all the cruel, brutal, and destructive instincts, which lie dormant in individuals as relics of a primitive epoch, are stirred up to find free gratification. But under the influence of suggestion, groups are also capable of high achievements in the shape of abnegation, unselfishness, and devotion to an ideal. . . . Whereas the intellectual capacity of a group is always far below that of an individual, its ethical conduct may rise as high above his as it may sink deep below it. . . .

And, finally, groups have never thirsted after truth. They demand illusions, and cannot do without them. They constantly give what is unreal precedence over what is real; they are almost as strongly influenced by what is untrue as by what is true. They have an evident tendency not to distinguish between the two.

We have pointed out that this predominance of the life of fantasy and of the illusion born of an unfulfilled wish is the ruling factor in the psychology of neuroses. We have found that what neurotics are guided by is not ordinary objective reality but psychological reality. A hysterical symptom is based upon fantasy instead of upon the repetition of real experience, and the sense of guilt in an obsessional neurosis is based upon the fact of an evil intention which was never carried out. . . .

[Le Bon] ascribes both to the ideas and to the leaders a mysterious and irresistible power, which he calls "prestige." Prestige is a sort of domination exercised over us by an individual, a work or an idea. It entirely paralyzes our critical faculty, and fills us with astonishment and respect. It would seem to arouse a feeling like that of fascination in hypnosis. . . . [But] we cannot feel that Le Bon has brought the function of the leader and the importance of prestige completely into harmony with his brilliantly executed picture of the group mind.

III. *Other Accounts of Collective Mental Life*

We have made use of Le Bon's description by way of introduction, because it fits in so well with our own Psychology in the emphasis which it lays upon unconscious mental life. But we must now add that as a matter of fact none of that author's statements bring forward anything new. Everything that he says to the detriment and depreciation of the manifestations of the group mind had already been said ... [others note that it is only society which prescribes any standards at all for the individual, and that enthusiasm may arise making the most splendid group achievements possible]. ...[7]

McDougall, in his book on *The Group Mind* [1920], starts out from the same contradiction that has just been mentioned, and finds a solution for it in the factor of organization. ... The most remarkable and also the most important result of the formation of a group is the "exaltation or intensification of emotion" produced in every member of it. In McDougall's opinion men's emotions are stirred in a group to a pitch that they seldom or never attain under other conditions; and it is a pleasurable experience for those who are concerned to surrender themselves so unreservedly to their passions and thus to become merged in the group and to lose the sense of the limits of their individuality. The manner in which individuals are thus carried away by a common impulse is explained by McDougall by means of what he calls the "principle of direct induction of emotion by way of the primitive sympathetic response," that is, by means of the emotional contagion with which we are already familiar. ...

[7] B. Kraškovič jun.: *Die Psychologie der Kollektivitäten.* Translated [into German] from the Croatian by Siegmund von Posavec. Vukovar, 1915. See the body of the work as well as the bibliography.

The judgment with which McDougall sums up the psychological behavior of a simple "unorganized" group is no more friendly than that of Le Bon. Such a group "is excessively emotional, impulsive, violent, fickle, inconsistent, irresolute, and extreme in action, displaying only the coarser emotions and the less refined sentiments; extremely suggestible, careless in deliberation, hasty in judgment, incapable of any but the simpler and imperfect forms of reasoning; easily swayed and led, lacking in self-consciousness, devoid of self-respect and of sense of responsibility, and apt to be carried away by the consciousness of its own force, so that it tends to produce all the manifestations we have learned to expect of any irresponsible and absolute power. Hence its behavior is like that of an unruly child or an untutored passionate savage in a strange situation, rather than like that of its average member, and in the worst cases it is like that of a wild beast, rather than like that of human beings."

... [Here are McDougall's] five "principal conditions" for raising collective mental life to a higher level. The *first* and fundamental condition is that there should be some degree of continuity of existence in the group.... The *second* condition is that in the individual member of the group some definite idea should be formed of the nature, composition, functions, and capacities of the group, so that from this he may develop an emotional relation to the group as a whole. The *third* is that the group should be brought into interaction (perhaps in the form of rivalry) with other groups similar to it but differing from it in many respects. The *fourth* is that the group should possess traditions, customs, and habits, and especially such as determine the relations of its members to one another. The *fifth* is that the group should have a definite structure, expressed in the specialization and differentiation of the functions of its constituents.

According to McDougall, if these conditions are fulfilled, the psychological disadvantages of the group formation are removed. The collective lowering of intellectual ability is avoided by withdrawing the performance of intellectual tasks from the group and reserving them for individual members of it.

It seems to us that the condition which McDougall designates as the "organization" of a group can with more justification be described in another way. The problem consists in how to procure for the group precisely those features which were characteristic of the individual and which are extinguished in him by the formation of the group. For the individual, outside the primitive group, possessed his own continuity, his self-consciousness, his traditions and customs, his own particular functions and position, and kept apart from his rivals. Owing to his entry into an "unorganized" group he had lost this distinctiveness for a time. If we thus recognize that the aim is to equip the group with the attributes of the individual, we shall be reminded of a valuable remark of Trotter's,[8] to the effect that the tendency towards the formation of groups is biologically a continuation of the multicellular character of all the higher organisms.

IV. *Suggestion and Libido*

We started from the fundamental fact that an individual in a group is subjected through its influence to what is often a profound alteration in his mental activity. His emotions became extraordinarily intensified, while his intellectual ability becomes markedly reduced ... [though] these often unwelcome consequences are to some extent at least prevented by a higher "organization" of the group; but this does not contradict the fundamental fact of Group Psychology—the two theses as to the intensification of the emotions and the inhibition of the intellect in primitive groups. Our interest is now directed to discovering the psychological explanation of this mental change which is experienced by the individual in a group....

There is no doubt that something exists in us which, when we become aware of signs of an emotion in someone else, tends to make us fall into the same emotion; but

[8] *Instincts of the Herd in Peace and War* (1916).

how often do we not successfully oppose it, resist the emotion, and react in quite an opposite way? Why, therefore,
do we invariably give way to this contagion when we are
in a group? ... We shall be prepared for the statement
that suggestion (or more correctly suggestibility) is actually an irreducible, primitive phenomenon, a fundamental fact in the mental life of man. Such, too, was the
opinion of Bernheim, of whose astonishing arts I was a
witness in the year 1889.... (Now that I once more
approach the riddle of suggestion after having kept away
from it for some thirty years, I find there is no change in
the situation.) ...

I shall [now] make an attempt at using the concept of
libido for the purpose of throwing light upon Group Psychology, a concept which has done us such good service
in the study of psycho-neuroses. Libido is an expression
taken from the theory of the emotions. We call by that
name the energy (regarded as a quantitative magnitude,
though not at present actually mensurable) of those instincts which have to do with all that may be comprised
under the word "love." The nucleus of what we mean by
love naturally consists (and this is what is commonly
called love, and what the poets sing of) in sexual love
with sexual union as its aim. But we do not separate from
this—what in any case has a share in the name "love"—on
the one hand, self-love, and on the other, love for parents
and children, friendship, and love for humanity in general,
and also devotion to concrete objects and to abstract ideas.
Our justification lies in the fact that psychoanalytic research has taught us that all these tendencies are an expression of the same instinctive activities; in relations
between the sexes these instincts force their way towards
sexual union, but in other circumstances they are diverted
from this aim or are prevented from reaching it, though
always preserving enough of their original nature to keep
their identity recognizable (as in such features as the longing for proximity, and self-sacrifice). We are of opinion,
then, that language has carried out an entirely justifiable

piece of unification in creating the word "love" with its numerous uses, and that we cannot do better than take it as the basis of our scientific discussions and expositions as well. . . .

We will try our fortune, then, with the supposition that love relationships (or, to use a more neutral expression, emotional ties) also constitute the essence of the group mind. . . .

V. *Two Artificial Groups: The Church and the Army*

We may recall from what we know of the morphology of groups that it is possible to distinguish very different kinds of groups and opposing lines in their development. There are very fleeting groups and extremely lasting ones; homogeneous ones, made up of the same sorts of individuals, and unhomogeneous ones; natural groups, and artificial ones, requiring an external force to keep them together; primitive groups, and highly organized ones with a definite structure. But for reasons which have yet to be explained we should like to lay particular stress upon a distinction to which the authorities have rather given too little attention; I refer to that between leaderless groups and those with leaders. . . .

The most interesting example of [highly organized, lasting and artificial groups] are churches—communities of believers—and armies. A church and an army are artificial groups, that is, a certain external force is employed to prevent them from disintegrating and to check alterations in their structure. . . . In a church (and we may with advantage take the Catholic Church as a type) as well as in an army, however different the two may be in other respects, the same illusion holds good of there being a head—in the Catholic Church, Christ, in an army its commander in chief—who loves all the individuals in the group with an equal love. Everything depends upon this illusion; if it were to be dropped, then both Church and army would dissolve, so far as the external force permitted them to. This equal love was expressly enunciated by Christ: "Inasmuch as ye have done it unto one of the least of these my brethren, ye have done it unto me." He stands to the individual members of the group of believers in the relation of a kind elder brother; he is their father surrogate. All the demands that are made upon the individual are derived from this love of Christ's. (A democratic character runs through the Church, for the very reason that before Christ everyone is equal, and everyone has an equal share in his love.) . . . The like holds good of an army. The commander in chief is a father who loves all his soldiers equally, and for that reason they are comrades among themselves. The army differs structually from the church in being built up of a series of such groups. Every captain is, as it were, the commander in chief and the father of his company, and so is every noncommissioned officer of his section. . . .

It is to be noticed that in these two artificial groups each individual is bound by libidinal[9] ties on the one hand

[9] An objection will justly be raised against this conception of the libidinal structure of an army on the ground that no place has been found in it for such ideas as those of one's country, of national glory, etc., which are of such importance in holding an army together. The answer is that that is a different instance of a group tie, and no longer such a simple one; for the examples of great generals, like Caesar, Wallenstein, or Napoleon, show that such ideas are not indispensable to the existence of an army. We shall presently touch upon the possibility of a leading idea being substituted for a leader and upon the relations between the two. The neglect of this libidinal factor in an army, even when it is not the only factor operative, seems to be not merely a theoretical omission but also a practical danger. Prussian militarism, which was just as unpsychological as German science, may have had to suffer the consequences of this in the Great War. We know that the war neuroses which ravaged the German army have been recognized as being a protest of the individual against the part he was expected to play in the army; and according to the communication of E. Simmel (*Kriegsneurosen und "Psychisches Trauma"*. Munich, 1918), the hard treatment of the men by their superiors may be considered as foremost among the motive forces of the disease. If the importance of the libido's claims on this score had been better appreciated, the fantastic promises of the American President's fourteen points would probably not have been believed so easily, and the splendid instrument would not have been broken in the hands of the German leaders.

to the leader (Christ, the commander in chief) and on the other hand to the other members of the group.... If each individual is bound in two directions by such an intense emotional tie, we shall find no difficulty in attributing to that circumstance the alteration and limitation which have been observed in his personality. A hint to the same effect, that the essence of a group lies in the libidinal ties existing in it, is also to be found in the phenomenon of panic, which is best studied in military groups. A panic arises if a group of that kind becomes disintegrated. Its characteristics are that none of the orders given by superiors are any longer listened to, and that each individual is only solicitous on his own account, and without any consideration for the rest. The mutual ties have ceased to exist, and a gigantic and senseless dread [*Angst*] is set free.... The contention that dread in a group is increased to enormous proportions by means of induction (contagion) is not in the least contradicted by these remarks.... But the really instructive case and the one which can be best employed for our purposes is that in which a body of troops breaks into a panic although the danger has not increased beyond a degree that is usual and has often been previously faced.... Dread in an individual is provoked either by the greatness of a danger or by the cessation of emotional ties (libidinal cathexes[10]); the latter is the case of neurotic dread. In just the same way panic arises either owing to an increase of the com-

[10] ["Cathexis", from the Greek "$\kappa\alpha\tau\acute{\epsilon}\omega$," "I occupy." The German word "*Besetzung*" has become of fundamental importance in the exposition of psycho-analytical theory. Any attempt at a short definition or description is likely to be misleading, but speaking very loosely, we may say that "cathexis" is used on the analogy of an electric charge, and that it means the concentration or accumulation of mental energy in some particular channel. Thus, when we speak of the existence in someone of a libidinal cathexis of an object, or, more shortly, of an object-cathexis, we mean that his libidinal energy is directed towards, or rather infused into, the idea (*Vorstellung*) of some object in the outer world. Readers who desire to obtain a more precise knowledge of the term are referred to the discussions in "On Narcissism: An Introduction" and the essays on metapsychology.—*Translator*.]

mon danger or owing to the disappearance of the emotional ties which hold the group together; and the latter case is analogous to that of neurotic dread. Anyone who, like McDougall, describes a panic as one of the plainest functions of the "group mind" arrives at the paradoxical position that this group mind does away with itself in one of its most striking manifestations. It is impossible to doubt that panic means the disintegration of a group; it involves the cessation of all the feelings of consideration which the members of the group otherwise show one another. . . .

The dissolution of a religious group is not so easy to observe. A short time ago there came into my hands an English novel of Catholic origin, recommended by the Bishop of London, with the title *When It Was Dark*. It gave a clever and, as it seems to me, a convincing picture of such a possibility and its consequences. The novel, which is supposed to relate to the present day, tells how a conspiracy of enemies of the figure of Christ and of the Christian faith succeed in arranging for a sepulcher to be discovered in Jerusalem. In this sepulcher is an inscription, in which Joseph of Arimathaea confesses that for reasons of piety he secretly removed the body of Christ from its grave on the third day after its entombment and buried it in this spot. The resurrection of Christ and his divine nature are by this means disposed of, and the result of this archaeological discovery is a convulsion in European civilization and an extraordinary increase in all crimes and acts of violence, which only ceases when the forgers' plot has been revealed.

The phenomenon which accompanies the dissolution that is here supposed to overtake a religious group is not dread, for which the occasion is wanting. Instead of it ruthless and hostile impulses towards other people make their appearance, which, owing to the equal love of Christ, they had previously been unable to do.[11] But even during

[11] Compare the explanation of similar phenomena after the abolition of the paternal authority of the sovereign given in P. Federn's *Zur Psychologie der Revolution: die vaterlose Gesellschaft*. (Vienna, 1919.)

the kingdom of Christ those people who do not belong to the community of believers, who do not love him, and whom he does not love, stand outside this tie. Therefore a religion, even if it calls itself the religion of love, must be hard and unloving to those who do not belong to it. Fundamentally indeed every religion is in this same way a religion of love for all those whom it embraces; while cruelty and intolerance towards those who do not belong to it are natural to every religion. However difficult we may find it personally we ought not to reproach believers too severely on this account; people who are unbelieving or indifferent are so much better off psychologically in this respect. If today that intolerance no longer shows itself so violent and cruel as in former centuries, we can scarcely conclude that there has been a softening in human manners. The cause is rather to be found in the undeniable weakening of religious feelings and the libinal ties which depend upon them. If another group tie takes the place of the religious one—and the socialistic tie seems to be succeeding in doing so—then there will be the same intolerance towards outsiders as in the age of the Wars of Religion; and if differences between scientific opinions could ever attain a similar significance for groups, the same result would again be repeated with this new motivation.

VI. *Further Problems and Lines of Work*

... Now much else remains to be examined and described in the morphology of groups. We should have to start from the ascertained fact that a mere collection of people is not a group, so long as these ties have not been established in it; but we should have to admit that in any collection of people the tendency to form a psychological group may very easily become prominent. ... We should above all be concerned with the distinction between groups which have a leader and leaderless groups. We should consider whether groups with leaders may not be the more primitive and complete, whether in the others an idea, an abstraction, may not be substituted for the leader (a state of things to which religious groups, with their invisible head, form a transition stage), and whether a common tendency, a wish in which a number of people can have a share, may not in the same way serve as a substitute. This abstraction, again, might be more or less completely embodied in the figure of what we might call a secondary leader, and interesting varieties would arise from the relation between the idea and the leader. The leader or the leading idea might also, so to speak, be negative; hatred against a particular person or institution might operate in just the same unifying way, and might call up the same kind of emotional ties as positive attachment. Then the question would also arise whether a leader is really indispensable to the essence of a group—and other questions besides.

But all these questions ... will not succeed in diverting our interest from the fundamental psychological problems that confront us in the structure of a group.... Let us keep before our eyes the nature of the emotional relations which hold between men in general....

The evidence of psychoanalysis shows that almost every intimate emotional relation between two people which lasts for some time—marriage, friendship, the relations between parents and children—leaves a sediment of feelings of aversion and hostility, which have first to be eliminated by repression.... The same thing happens when men come together in larger units. Every time two families become connected by a marriage, each of them thinks itself superior to or of better birth than the other. Of two neighboring towns each is the other's most jealous rival; every little canton looks down upon the others with contempt. Closely related races keep one another at arm's length; the South German cannot endure the North German, the Englishman casts every kind of aspersion upon the Scotsman, the Spaniard despises the Portuguese. We are no longer astonished that greater differences should lead to an almost insuperable repugnance, such as the Gallic people feel for the German, the Aryan for the Semite, and the white races for the colored. When this hostility is directed against people who are otherwise loved we describe it as ambivalence of feeling; and we explain the fact, in what is probably far too rational a manner, by means of the numerous occasions for conflicts of interest which arise precisely in such intimate relations. In the undisguised antipathies and aversions which people feel towards strangers with whom they have to do we may recognize the expression of self-love—of narcissism. This self-love works for the self-assertion of the individual, and behaves as though the occurrence of any divergence from his own particular lines of development involved a criticism of them and the demand for their alteration. . . .

But the whole of this intolerance vanishes, temporarily or permanently, as the result of the formation of a group, and in a group. So long as a group formation persists or so far as it extends, individuals behave as though they were uniform, tolerate other people's peculiarities, put themselves on an equal level with them, and have no feeling of aversion towards them. Such a limitation of narcissism can, according to our theoretical views, only be produced by one factor, a libidinal tie with other people. Love for oneself knows only one barrier—love for others, love for objects[12]. . . . And in the development of mankind as a whole, just as in individuals, love alone acts as the civilizing factor in the sense that it brings a change from egoism to altruism. And this is true both of the sexual love for women, with all the obligations which it involves of sparing what women are fond of, and also of the de-sexualized, sublimated homosexual love for other men, which springs from work in common. If therefore in groups narcissistic self-love is subject to limitations which do not operate outside them, that is cogent evidence that the essence of a group formation consists in a new kind of libidinal ties among the members of the group.

But our interest now leads us on to the pressing question as to what may be the nature of these ties which exist in groups. In the psychoanalytic study of neuroses we have hitherto been occupied almost exclusively with ties

[12] See "On Narcissism: an Introduction."

that unite with their objects those love instincts which still pursue directly sexual aims. In groups there can evidently be no question of sexual aims of that kind. We are concerned here with love instincts which have been diverted from their original aims, though they do not operate with less energy on that account.... As a matter of fact we learn from psychoanalysis that there do exist other mechanisms for emotional ties, the so-called *identifications*, insufficiently-known processes and hard to describe, the investigation of which will for some time keep us away from the subject of Group Psychology.

VII. *Identification*

Identification is known to psychoanalysis as the earliest expression of an emotional tie with another person.... A little boy will exhibit a special interest in his father; he would like to grow like him and be like him, and take his place everywhere. We may say simply that he takes his father as his ideal. This behavior has nothing to do with a passive or feminine attitude towards his father (and towards males in general); it is on the contrary typically masculine. . . . It is easy to state in a formula the distinction between an identification with the father and the choice of the father as an object. In the first case one's father is what one would like to *be*, and in the second he is what one would like to *have*. The distinction, that is, depends upon whether the tie attaches to the subject or to the object of the ego....

What we have learned [from our clinical work] may be summarized as follows. First, identification is the original form of emotional tie with an object; secondly, in a regressive way it [may] become a substitute for a libidnal object tie, as it were by means of the introjection of the object into the ego; and thirdly, it may arise with every new perception of a common quality shared with some other person who is not an object of the sexual instinct. The more important this common quality is, the more successful may this partial identification become, and it may thus represent the beginning of a new tie.

We already begin to divine that the mutual tie between members of a group is in the nature of an identification of this kind, based upon an important emotional common quality; and we may suspect that this common quality lies in the nature of the tie with the leader. Another suspicion may tell us that we are far from having exhausted the problem of identification, and that we are faced by the process which psychology calls "empathy" and which plays the largest part in our understanding of what is inherently foreign to our ego in other people. But we shall here limit ourselves to the immediate emotional effects of identification, and shall leave on one side its significance for our intellectual life.

Psychoanalytic research, which has already occasionally attacked the more difficult problems of the psychoses, has also been able to exhibit identification to us in some other cases which are not immediately comprehensible. I shall treat two of these cases in detail as material for our further consideration.

The genesis of male homosexuality in a large class of cases is as follows. A young man has been unusually long and intensely fixated upon his mother in the sense of the Oedipus complex. But at last, after the end of his puberty, the time comes for exchanging his mother for some other sexual object. Things take a sudden turn: the young man does not abandon his mother, but identifies himself with her; he transforms himself into her, and now looks about for objects which can replace his ego for him, and on which he can bestow such love and care as he has experienced from his mother. This is a frequent process, which can be confirmed as often as one likes, and which is naturally quite independent of any hypothesis that may be made as to the organic driving force and the motives of the sudden transformation. A striking thing about this identification is its ample scale; it remolds the ego in one of its important features—in its sexual character—upon the model of what has hitherto been the object. In this process the object itself is renounced—

whether entirely or in the sense of being preserved only in the unconscious is a question outside the present discussion. Identification with an object that is renounced or lost as a substitute for it, introjection of this object into the ego, is indeed no longer a novelty to us. A process of the kind may sometimes be directly observed in small children. A short time ago an observation of this sort was published in the *Internationale Zeitschrift für Psychoanalyse*. A child who was unhappy over the loss of a kitten declared straight out that now he himself was the kitten, and accordingly crawled about on all fours, would not eat at table, etc.

Another such instance of introjection of the object has been provided by the analysis of melancholia, an affection which counts among the most remarkable of its exciting causes the real or emotional loss of a loved object. A leading characteristic of these cases is a cruel self-depreciation of the ego combined with relentless self-criticism and bitter self-reproaches. Analyses have shown that this disparagement and these reproaches apply at bottom to the object and represent the ego's revenge upon it. The shadow of the object has fallen upon the ego, as I have said elsewhere.[13] The introjection of the object is here unmistakably clear.

But these melancholias also show us something else, which may be of importance for our later discussions. They show us the ego divided, fallen into two pieces, one of which rages against the second. This second piece is the one which has been altered by introjection and which contains the lost object. But the piece which behaves so cruelly is not unknown to us either. It comprises the conscience, a critical faculty within the ego, which even in normal times takes up a critical attitude towards the ego, though never so relentlessly and so unjustifiably. On previous occasions we have been driven to the hypothesis[14] that some such faculty develops in our ego which may cut itself off from the rest of the ego and come into conflict

[13] "Mourning and Melancholia."

[14] "On Narcissism: an Introduction" and "Mourning and Melancholia."

with it. We have called it the "ego ideal," and by way of functions we have ascribed to it self-observation, the moral conscience, the censorship of dreams, and the chief influence in repression. We have said that it is the heir to the original narcissism in which the childish ego found its self-sufficiency; it gradually gathers up from the influences of the environment the demands which the environment makes upon the ego and which the ego cannot always rise to; so that a man, when he cannot be satisfied with his ego itself, may nevertheless be able to find satisfaction in the ego ideal which has been differentiated out of the ego. In delusions of observation, as we have further shown, the disintegration of this faculty has become patent, and has thus revealed its origin in the influence of superior powers, and above all of parents. But we have not forgotten to add that the amount of distance between this ego ideal and the real ego is very variable from one individual to another, and that with many people this differentiation within the ego does not go further than with children.

But before we can employ this material for understanding the libidinal organizations of groups, we must take into account some other examples of the mutual relations between the object and the ego.[15]

[15] We are very well aware that we have not exhausted the nature of identification with these examples taken from pathology, and that we have consequently left part of the riddle of group formations untouched. . . . A path leads from identification by way of imitation to empathy, that is, to the comprehension of the mechanism by means of which we are enabled to take up any attitude at all towards another mental life. Moreover there is still much to be explained in the manifestations of existing identifications. These result among other things in a person limiting his aggressiveness towards those with whom he has identified himself, and in his sparing them and giving them help. The study of such identifications, for instance, which lie at the root of clan feeling, led Robertson Smith to the surprising result that they rest upon the recognition of a common substance (*Kinship and Marriage*, 1885), and may even therefore be brought about by a meal eaten in common. This feature makes it possible to connect this kind of identification with the early history of the human family which I constructed in *Totem und Tabu*.

VIII. *Being in Love and Hypnosis*

Even in its caprices the usage of language remains true to some kind of reality. Thus it gives the name of "love" to a great many kinds of emotional relationship which we too group together theoretically as love; but then again it feels a doubt whether this love is real, true, actual love, and so hints at a whole scale of possibilities within the range of the phenomena of love. We shall have no difficulty in making the same discovery empirically.

In one class of cases being in love is nothing more than object-cathexis on the part of the sexual instincts with a view to directly sexual satisfaction, a cathexis which expires, moreover, when this aim has been reached; this is what is called common, sensual love. But, as we know, the libidinal situation rarely remains so simple. It was possible to calculate with certainty upon the revival of the need which had just expired; and this must no doubt have been the first motive for directing a lasting cathexis upon the sexual object and for "loving" it in the passionless intervals as well.

To this must be added another factor derived from the astonishing course of development which is pursued by the erotic life of man. In his first phase, which has usually come to an end by the time he is five years old, a child has found the first object for his love in one or other of his parents, and all of his sexual instincts with their demand for satisfaction have been united upon this object. The repression which then sets in compels him to renounce the greater number of these infantile sexual aims, and leaves behind a profound modification in his relation to his parents. The child still remains tied to his parents, but by instincts which must be described as being "inhibited in their aim." The emotions which he feels henceforward towards these objects of his love are characterized as "tender." It is well known that the earlier "sensual" tendencies remain more or less strongly preserved in the unconscious, so that in a certain sense the whole of the original current continues to exist.

At puberty, as we know, there set in new and very

strong tendencies with directly sexual aims. In unfavorable cases they remain separate, in the form of a sensual current, from the "tender" emotional trends which persist. We are then faced by a picture the two aspects of which certain movements in literature take such delight in idealizing. A man of this kind will show a sentimental enthusiasm for women whom he deeply respects but who do not excite him to sexual activities, and he will only be potent with other women whom he does not "love" but thinks little of or even despises.[16] More often, however, the adolescent succeeds in bringing about a certain degree of synthesis between the unsensual, heavenly love and the sensual, earthly love, and his relation to his sexual object is characterized by the interaction of uninhibited instincts and of instincts inhibited in their aim. The depth to which anyone is in love, as contrasted with his purely sensual desire, may be measured by the size of the share taken by the inhibited instincts of tenderness.

In connection with this question of being in love we have always been struck by the phenomenon of sexual over-estimation—the fact that the loved object enjoys a certain amount of freedom from criticism, and that all its characteristics are valued more highly than those of people who are not loved, or than its own were at a time when it itself was not loved. If the sensual tendencies are somewhat more effectively repressed or set aside, the illusion is produced that the object has come to be sensually loved on account of its spiritual merits, whereas on the contrary these merits may really only have been lent to it by its sensual charm.

The tendency which falsifies judgment in this respect is that of *idealization*. But this makes it easier for us to find our way about. We see that the object is being treated in the same way as our own ego, so that when we are in love a considerable amount of narcissistic libido overflows on the object. It is even obvious, in many forms of love choice, that the object serves as a substitute for some unattained ego ideal of our own. We love it on account

[16] See "Contributions to the Psychology of Love."

of the perfections which we have striven to reach for our own ego, and which we should now like to procure in this roundabout way as a means of satisfying our narcissism.

If the sexual over-estimation and the being in love increase even further, then the interpretation of the picture becomes still more unmistakable. The tendencies whose trend is towards directly sexual satisfaction may now be pushed back entirely, as regularly happens, for instance, with the young man's sentimental passion; the ego becomes more and more unassuming and modest, and the object more and more sublime and precious, until at last it gets possession of the entire self-love of the ego, whose self-sacrifice thus follows as a natural consequence. . . .

This happens especially easily with love that is unhappy and cannot be satisfied; for in spite of everything each sexual satisfaction always involves a reduction in sexual over-estimation. Contemporaneously with this "devotion" of the ego to the object, which is no longer to be distinguished from a sublimated devotion to an abstract idea, the functions allotted to the ego ideal entirely cease to operate. The criticism exercised by that faculty is silent; everything that the object does and asks for is right and blameless. Conscience has no application to anything that is done for the sake of the object; in the blindness of love remorselessness is carried to the pitch of crime. The whole situation can be completely summarized in a formula: *The object has taken the place of the ego ideal.*

It is now easy to define the distinction between identification and such extreme developments of being in love as may be described as fascination or infatuation. In the former case the ego has enriched itself with the properties of the object, it has "introjected" the object into itself, as Ferenczi expresses it. In the second case it is impoverished, it has surrendered itself to the object, it has substituted the object for its most important constituent. . . . In the case [of infatuation] the object is retained, and there is a hyper-cathexis of it by the ego and at the ego's expense. But here again a difficulty presents itself. Is it quite certain that identification presupposes that object-cathexis has been given up? Can there be no identification with the object retained? And before we embark upon a discussion of this delicate question, the perception may already be beginning to dawn on us that yet another alternative embraces the real essence of the matter, namely, *whether the object is put in the place of the ego or of the ego ideal.*

From being in love to hypnosis is evidently only a short step. The respects in which the two agree are obvious. There is the same humble subjection, the same compliance, the same absence of criticism towards the hypnotist just as towards the loved object. There is the same absorption of one's own initiative; no one can doubt that the hypnotist has stepped into the place of the ego ideal. . . . The hypnotic relation is the devotion of someone in love to an unlimited degree but with sexual satisfaction excluded; whereas in the case of being in love this kind of satisfaction is only temporarily kept back, and remains in the background as a possible aim at some later time.

But on the other hand we may also say that the hypnotic relation is (if the expression is permissible) a group formation with two members. Hypnosis is not a good object for comparison with a group formation, because it is truer to say that it is identical with it. Out of the complicated fabric of the group it isolates one element for us—the behavior of the individual to the leader. Hypnosis is distinguished from a group formation by this limitation of number, just as it is distinguished from being in love by the absence of directly sexual tendencies. In this respect it occupies a middle position between the two.

It is interesting to see that it is precisely those sexual tendencies that are inhibited in their aims which achieve such lasting ties between men. But this can easily be understood from the fact that they are not capable of complete satisfaction, while sexual tendencies which are uninhibited in their aims suffer an extraordinary reduction through the discharge of energy every time the sexual aim is attained. It is the fate of sensual love to become extinguished when it is satisfied; for it to be able to last, it must from the first be mixed with purely tender components—with such, that is, as are inhibited in their aims—or it must itself undergo a transformation of this kind.

Hypnosis would solve the riddle of the libidinal constitution of groups for us straightaway, if it were not that it itself exhibits some features which are not met by the rational explanation we have hitherto given of it as a state of being in love with the directly sexual tendencies excluded. There is still a great deal in it which we must recognize as unexplained and mystical. It contains an additional element of paralysis derived from the relation between someone with superior power and someone who is without power and helpless—which may afford a transition to the hypnosis of terror which occurs in animals. . . . It is noticeable that, even when there is complete suggestive compliance in other respects, the moral conscience of the person hypnotized may show resistance. But this may be due to the fact that in hypnosis as it is usually practiced some knowledge may be retained that what is happening is only a game, an untrue reproduction of another situation of far more importance to life.

But after the preceding discussions we are quite in a position to give the formula for the libidinal constitution of groups: or at least of such groups as we have hitherto considered, namely, those that have a leader and have not been able by means of too much "organization" to acquire secondarily the characteristics of an individual. *A primary group of this kind is a number of individuals who have substituted one and the same object for their ego ideal and have consequently identified themselves with one another in their ego.* . . .

IX. *The Herd Instinct*

We cannot for long enjoy the illusion that we have solved the riddle of the group with this formula. . . .

It might be said that the intense emotional ties which we observe in groups are quite sufficient to explain one of their characteristics—the lack of independence and initiative in their members, the similarity in the reactions of all of them, their reduction, so to speak, to the level of group individuals. But if we look at it as a whole, a group shows us more than this. Some of its features—the weakness of intellectual ability, the lack of emotional restraint, the incapacity for moderation and delay, the inclination to exceed every limit in the expression of emotion and to work it off completely in the form of action—these and similar features ... show an unmistakable picture of a regression of mental activity to an earlier stage such as we are not surprised to find among savages or children. A regression of this sort is in particular an essential characteristic of common groups, while, as we have heard, in organized and artificial groups it can to a large extent be checked. ... We are reminded of how many of these phenomena of dependence are part of the normal constitution of human society, of how little originality and personal courage are to be found in it, of how much every individual is ruled by those attitudes of the group mind which exhibit themselves in such forms as racial characteristics, class prejudices, public opinon, etc. The influence of suggestion becomes a greater riddle for us when we admit that it is not exercised only by the leader, but by every individual upon every other individual; and we must reproach ourselves with having unfairly emphasized the relation to the leader and with having kept the other factor of mutual suggestion too much in the background.

After this encouragement to modesty, we shall be inclined to listen to another voice, which promises us an explanation based upon simpler grounds. ... Trotter derives the mental phenomena that are described as occurring in groups from a herd instinct ("gregariousness"), which is innate in human beings just as in other species of animals. ... The individual feels "incomplete" if he is alone. The dread shown by small children would seem already to be an expression of this herd instinct. Opposition to the herd is as good as separation from it, and is therefore anxiously avoided. But the herd turns away from anything that is new or unusual. The herd instinct would appear to be something primary, something "which cannot be split up." . . . But Trotter's exposition, with even more justice than the others', is open to the objection that it takes too little account of the leader's part in a group, while we incline rather to the opposite judgment, that it is impossible to grasp the nature of a group if the leader is disregarded. The herd instinct leaves no room at all for the leader; he is merely thrown in along with the herd, almost by chance; it follows, too, that no path leads from this instinct to the need for a God; the herd is without a herdsman. . . .

It is naturally no easy matter to trace the ontogenesis of the herd instinct. The dread which is shown by small children when they are left alone, and which Trotter claims as being already a manifestation of the instinct, nevertheless suggests more readily another interpretation. The dread relates to the child's mother, and later to other familiar persons, and it is the expression of an unfulfilled desire, which the child does not yet know how to deal with in any way except by turning it into dread.[17] Nor is the child's dread when it is alone pacified by the sight of any haphazard "member of the herd," but on the contrary it is only brought into existence by the approach of a "stranger" of this sort. Then for a long time nothing in the nature of herd instinct or group feeling is to be observed in children. Something like it grows up first of all, in a nursery containing many children, out of the children's relation to their parents, and it does so as a reaction to the initial envy with which the elder child would certainly like to put its successor jealously aside, to keep it away from the parents, and to rob it of all its privileges; but in face of the fact that this child (like all that come later) is loved by the parents in just the same way, and in consequence of the impossibility of maintaining its hostile attitude without damaging itself, it is forced into identifying itself with the other children. So there grows up in the troop of children a communal or group

[17] See remarks on Dread in "The Introductory Lectures" (1915-16).

feeling, which is then further developed at school. The first demand made by this reaction-formation is for justice, for equal treatment by all.... This transformation—the replacing of jealousy by a group feeling in the nursery and classroom—might be considered improbable, if the same process could not later on be observed again in other circumstances....

What appears later on in society in the shape of *Gemeingeist, esprit de corps,* "group spirit," etc., does not belie its derivation from what was originally envy. No one must want to put himself forward, every one must be the same and have the same. Social justice means that we deny ourselves many things so that others may have to do without them as well, or, what is the same thing, may not be able to ask for them. This demand for equality is the root of social conscience and the sense of duty....

Thus social feeling is based upon the reversal of what was first a hostile feeling into a positively toned tie of the nature of an identification. So far as we have hitherto been able to follow the course of events, this reversal appears to be effected under the influence of a common tender tie with a person outside the group. We do not ourselves regard our analysis of identification as exhaustive, but it is enough for our present purpose that we should revert to this one feature—its demand that equalization shall be consistently carried through. We have already heard in the discussion of the two artificial groups, church and army, that their preliminary condition is that all their members should be loved in the same way by one person, the leader. Do not let us forget, however, that the demand for equality in a group applies only to its members and not to the leader.... Let us venture, then, to correct Trotter's pronouncement that a man is a herd animal and assert that he is rather a *horde* animal, an individual creature in a horde led by a chief.

X. *The Group and the Primal Horde*

In 1912 I took up a conjecture of Darwin's to the

effect that the primitive form of human society was that
of a horde ruled over despotically by a powerful male. I
attempted to show that the fortunes of this horde have
left indestructible traces upon the history of human de-
scent; and, especially, that the development of totemism,
which comprises in itself the beginnings of religion,
morality, and social organization, is connected with the
killing of the chief by violence and the transformation of
the paternal horde into a community of brothers.[18] To be
sure, this is only a hypothesis, like so many others with
which archaeologists endeavor to lighten the darkness of
prehistoric times—a "Just-So Story," as it was amusingly
called by a not unkind critic (Kroeber)....

Human groups exhibit once again the familiar picture
of an individual of superior strength among a troop of
similar companions, a picture which is also contained in
our idea of the primal horde. The psychology of such a
group, as we know it from the descriptions to which we
have so often referred—the dwindling of the conscious
individual personality, the focusing of thoughts and feelings into a common direction, the predominance of the
emotions and of the unconscious mental life, the tendency to the immediate carrying out of intensions as they
emerge—all this corresponds to a state of regression to a
primitive mental activity, of just such a sort as we should
be inclined to ascribe to the primal horde.

Thus the group appears to us as a revival of the primal
horde. Just as primitive man virtually survives in every
individual, so the primal horde may arise once more out
of any random crowd; in so far as men are habitually
under the sway of group formation we recognize in it
the survival of the primal horde. We must conclude that
the psychology of the group is the oldest human psychology; what we have isolated as individual psychology,
by neglecting all traces of the group, has only since come
into prominence out of the old group psychology, by a
gradual process which may still, perhaps, be described

[18] *Totem und Tabu.*

as incomplete. We shall later venture upon an attempt at specifying the point of departure of this development.

Further reflection will show us in what respect this statement requires correction. Individual psychology must, on the contrary, be just as old as group psychology, for from the first there were two kinds of psychologies, that of the individual members of the group and that of the father, chief, or leader. . . . He, at the very beginning of the history of mankind, was the *Superman* whom Nietzsche only expected from the future. . . .

The uncanny and coercive characteristics of group formations, which are shown in their suggestion phenomena, may with justice be traced back to the fact of their origin from the primal horde. The leader of the group is still the dreaded primal father; the group still wishes to be governed by unrestricted force; it has an extreme passion for authority . . . a thirst for obedience. The primal father is the group ideal, which governs the ego in the place of the ego ideal. Hypnosis has a good claim to being described as a group of two; there remains as a definition for suggestion—a conviction which is not based upon perception and reasoning but upon an erotic tie.

XI. *A Differentiating Grade in the Ego*

. . . We are aware that what we have been able to contribute towards the explanation of the libidinal structure of groups leads back to the distinction between the ego and the ego ideal and to the double kind of tie which this makes possible—identification, and substitution of the object for the ego ideal. . . . Let us reflect that the ego now appears in the relation of an object to the ego ideal which has been developed out of it, and that all the interplay between an outer object and the ego as a whole, with which our study of the neuroses has made us acquainted, may possibly be repeated upon this new scene of action inside the ego.[19]

[19] [See "Mourning and Melancholia" (1917) for a further discussion; also *The Ego and the Id* (1923) for amplifications of this point.—Ed.]

In this place I shall only follow up one of the consequences which seem possible from this point of view, thus resuming the discussion of a problem which I was obliged to leave unsolved elsewhere. Each of the mental differentiations that we have become acquainted with represents a fresh aggravation of the difficulties of mental functioning, increases its instability, and may become the starting point for its breakdown, that is, for the onset of a disease. Thus, by being born we have made the step from an absolutely self-sufficient narcissism to the perception of a changing outer world and to the beginnings of the discovery of objects. And with this is associated the fact that we cannot endure the new state of things for long, that we periodically revert from it, in our sleep, to our former condition of absence of stimulation and avoidance of objects. It is true, however, that in this we are following a hint from the outer world, which, by means of the periodical change of day and night, temporarily withdraws the greater part of the stimuli that affect us. The second example, which is pathologically more important, is not subject to any such qualification. In the course of our development we have effected a separation of our mental existence into a coherent ego and into an unconscious and repressed portion which is left outside it; and we know that the stability of this new acquisition is exposed to constant shocks. In dreams and in neuroses what is thus excluded knocks for admission at the gates, guarded though they are by resistances; and in our waking health we make use of special artifices for allowing what is repressed to circumvent the resistances and for receiving it temporarily into our ego to the increase of our pleasure. Wit and humor, and to some extent the comic in general, may be regarded in this light. Everyone acquainted with the psychology of the neuroses will think of similar examples of less importance; but I hasten on to the application I have in view.

It is quite conceivable that the separation of the ego ideal from the ego cannot be borne for long either, and has to be temporarily undone. In all renunciations and limitations imposed upon the ego a periodical infringement of the prohibition is the rule; this indeed is shown by the institution of festivals, which in origin are nothing more nor less than excesses provided by law and which owe their cheerful character to the release which they bring. The Saturnalia of the Romans and our modern carnival agree in this essential feature with the festivals of primitive people, which usually end in debaucheries of every kind and the transgression of what are at other times the most sacred commandments. But the ego ideal comprises the sum of all the limitations in which the ego has to acquiesce, and for that reason the abrogation of the ideal would necessarily be a magnificent festival for the ego, which might then once again feel satisfied with itself.[20]

There is always a feeling of triumph when something in the ego coincides with the ego ideal. And the sense of guilt (as well as the sense of inferiority) can also be understood as an expression of tension between the ego and the ego ideal.

It is well known that there are people the general color of whose mood oscillates periodically from an excessive depression through some kind of intermediate state to an exalted sense of well-being. . . . The foundation of these spontaneous oscillations of mood is unknown; we are without insight into the mechanism of the displacement of a melancholia by a mania. So we are free to suppose that these patients are people in whom our conjecture might find an actual application—their ego ideal might be temporarily resolved into their ego after having previously ruled it with especial strictness.

Let us keep to what is clear: On the basis of our analysis of the ego it cannot be doubted that in cases of mania the ego and the ego ideal have fused together, so that the person, in a mood of triumph and self-satisfaction, disturbed by no self-criticism, can enjoy the abolition of his inhibitions, his feelings of consideration for others, and his self-reproaches. It is not so obvious, but nevertheless

[20] *Totem und Tabu.*

very probable, that the misery of the melancholiac is the expression of a sharp conflict between the two faculties of his ego, a conflict in which the ideal, in an excess of sensitiveness, relentlessly exhibits its condemnation of the ego in delusions of inferiority and in self-depreciation. . . .

A change into mania is not an indispensable feature of the symptomatology of melancholic depression. There are simple melancholias, some in single and some in recurring attacks, which never show this development. On the other hand there are melancholias in which the exciting cause clearly plays an etiological part. They are those which occur after the loss of a loved object, whether by death or as a result of circumstances which have necessitated the withdrawal of the libido from the object. A psychogenic melancholia of this sort can end in mania, and this cycle can be repeated several times, just as easily as in a case which appears to be spontaneous. Thus the state of things is somewhat obscure, especially as only a few forms and cases of melancholia have been submitted to psychoanalytical investigation. So far we only understand those cases in which the object is given up because it has shown itself unworthy of love. It is then set up again inside the ego, by means of identification, and severely condemned by the ego ideal. The reproaches and attacks directed towards the object come to light in the shape of melancholic self-reproaches.[21] . . .

XII. *Postscript*

In the course of the inquiry which has just been brought to a provisional end we came across a number of side paths which we avoided pursuing in the first instance but in which there was much that offered us promises of insight. We propose now to take up a few

[21] To speak more accurately, they conceal themselves behind the reproaches directed towards the person's own ego, and lend them the fixity, tenacity, and imperativeness which characterize the self-reproaches of a melancholiac.

of the points that have been left on one side in this way.

A. The distinction between identification of the ego with an object and replacement of the ego ideal by an object finds an interesting illustration in the two great artificial groups which we began by studying, the army and the Christian Church.

It is obvious that a soldier takes his superior, that is, really, the leader of the army, as his ideal, while he identifies himself with his equals, and derives from this community of their egos the obligations for giving mutual help and for sharing possessions which comradeship implies. But he becomes ridiculous if he tries to identify himself with the general. . . . It is otherwise in the Catholic Church. Every Christian loves Christ as his ideal and feels himself united with all other Christians by the tie of identification. But the Church requires more of him. He has also to identify himself with Christ and love all other Christians as Christ loved them. At both points, therefore, the Church requires that the position of the libido which is given by a group formation should be supplemented. Identification has to be added where object-choice has taken place, and object-love where there is identification. This addition evidently goes beyond the constitution of the group. One can be a good Christian and yet be far from the idea of putting oneself in Christ's place and of having like him an all-embracing love for mankind. One need not think oneself capable, weak mortal that one is, of the Saviour's largeness of soul and strength of love. But this further development in the distribution of libido in the group is probably the factor upon which Christianity bases its claim to have reached a higher ethical level.

B. We have said that it would be possible to specify the point in the mental development of man at which the advance from group to individual psychology was also achieved by the individual members of the group.[22]

For this purpose we must return for a moment to the scientific myth of the father of the primal horde. He was

[22] What follows at this point was written under the influence of an exchange of ideas with Otto Rank.

later on exalted into the creator of the world, and with justice, for he had produced all the sons who composed the first group. He was the ideal of each one of them, at once feared and honored, a fact which led later to the idea of taboo. These many individuals eventually banded themselves together, killed him, and cut him in pieces. None of the group of victors could take his place, or, if one of them did, the battles began afresh, until they understood that they must renounce their father's heritage. They then formed the totemistic community of brothers, all with equal rights and united by the totem prohibitions which were to preserve and to expiate the memory of the murder. But the dissatisfaction with what had been achieved still remained, and it became the source of new developments. . . .

It was then, perhaps, that some individual, in the exigency of his longing, may have been moved to free himself from the group and take over the father's part. He who did this was the first epic poet; and the advance was achieved in his imagination. This poet disguised the truth with lies in accordance with his longing. He invented the heroic myth. The hero was a man who by himself had slain the father—the father who still appeared in the myth as a totemistic monster. Just as the father had been the boy's first ideal, so in the hero who aspires to the father's place the poet now created the first ego ideal. The transition to the hero was probably afforded by the youngest son, the mother's favorite, whom she had protected from paternal jealousy, and who, in the era of the primal horde, had been the father's successor. In the lying poetic fancies of prehistoric times the woman, who had been the prize of battle and the allurement to murder, was probably turned into the seducer and instigator to the crime.

The hero claims to have acted alone in accomplishing the deed, which certainly only the horde as a whole would have ventured upon. But, as Rank has observed, fairy tales have preserved clear traces of the facts which were disavowed. For we often find in them that the hero who has to carry out some difficult task (usually a youngest son, and not infrequently one who has represented himself to the father surrogate as being stupid, that is to say, harmless)—we often find, then, that this hero can carry out his task only by the help of a crowd of small animals, such as bees or ants. These would be the brothers in the primal horde, just as in the same way in dream symbolism insects or vermin signify brothers and sisters (contemptuously, considered as babies). Moreover every one of the tasks in myths and fairy tales is easily recognizable as a substitute for the heroic deed.

The myth, then, is the step by which the individual emerges from group psychology. The first myth was certainly the psychological, the hero myth; the explanatory nature myth must have followed much later. The poet who had taken this step and had in this way set himself free from the group in his imagination is nevertheless able (as Rank has further observed) to find his way back to it in reality. For he goes and relates to the group his hero's deeds which he has invented. At bottom this hero is no one but himself. Thus he lowers himself to the level of reality, and raises his hearers to the level of imagination. But his hearers understand the poet, and, in virtue of their having the same relation of longing towards the primal father, they can identify themselves with the hero.[23]

The lie of the heroic myth culminates in the deification of the hero. Perhaps the deified hero may have been earlier than the Father God and may have been a precursor to the return of the primal father as a deity. The series of gods, then, would run chronologically: Mother Goddess—Hero—Father God. But it is only with the elevation of the never-forgotten primal father that the deity acquires the features that we will still recognize in him today.[24]

C. A great deal has been said in this paper about di-

[23] Cf. Hanns Sachs: "Day-Dreams in Common." *International Journal of Psychoanalysis*, 1920, Vol. I.

[24] In this brief exposition I have made no attempt to bring forward any of the material existing in legends, myths, fairy tales, the history of manners, etc., in support of the construction.

rectly sexual instincts and those that are inhibited in their aims, and it may be hoped that this distinction will not meet with too much resistance. . . . A psychology, which will not or cannot penetrate the depths of what is repressed, regards tender emotional ties as being invariably the expression of tendencies which have no sexual aim, even though they are derived from tendencies which have such an aim.[25] We are justified in saying that they have been diverted from these sexual aims, even though there is some difficulty in giving a representation of such a diversion . . . moreover, those instincts which are inhibited in their aims always preserve some few of their original sexual aims; even an effectionate devotee, even a friend or an admirer desires the physical proximity and the sight of the person who is now loved only in the "Pauline" sense. If we choose, we may recognize in this diversion of aim a beginning of the *sublimation* of the sexual instincts, or on the other hand we may fix the limits of sublimation at some more distant point. Those sexual instincts which are inhibited in their aims have a great functional advantage over those which are uninhibited. Since they are not capable of really complete satisfaction, they are especially adapted to create permanent ties; while those instincts which are directly sexual incur a loss of energy each time they are satisfied, and must wait to be renewed by a fresh accumulation of sexual libido, so that meanwhile the object may have been changed. The inhibited instincts are capable of any degree of admixture with the uninhibited; they can be transformed back into them, just as they arose out of them. It is well known how easily erotic wishes develop out of emotional relations of a friendly character, based upon appreciation and admiration (compare Molière's "Embrassez-moi pour l'amour du grec"), between a master and a pupil, between a performer and a delighted listener, and especially in the case of women. In fact the growth of emotional ties of this kind, with their purposeless beginnings, provides a much frequented path-

[25] Hostile feelings, which are a little more complicated in their construction, offer no exception to this rule.

way to sexual object-choice.... On the other hand it is also very usual for directly sexual tendencies, short-lived in themselves, to be transformed into a lasting and purely tender tie; and the consolidation of a passionate love marriage rests to a large extent upon this process.

We shall naturally not be surprised to hear that the sexual tendencies that are inhibited in their aims arise out of the directly sexual ones when inner or outer obstacles make the sexual aims unattainable. The repression during the period of latency is an inner obstacle of this kind—or rather one which has become inner.... Here we approach the discussion of a new subject, which deals with the relation between directly sexual instincts and the formation of groups....

D. Directly sexual tendencies are unfavorable to the formation of groups. In the history of the development of the family there have also, it is true, been group relations of sexual love (group marriages); but the more important sexual love became for the ego, and the more it developed the characteristics of being in love, the more urgently it required to be limited to two people—*una cum uno*—as is prescribed by the nature of the genital aim. Polygamous inclinations had to be content to find satisfaction in a succession of changing objects.

Two people coming together for the purpose of sexual satisfaction, in so far as they seek for solitude, are making a demonstration against the herd instinct, the group feeling. The more they are in love, the more completely they suffice for each other. The rejection of the group's influence is manifested in the shape of a sense of shame. The extremely violent feelings of jealousy are summoned up in order to protect the sexual object-choice from being encroached upon by a group tie. It is only when the tender, that is, the personal, factor of a love relation gives place entirely to the sensual one that it is possible for two people to have sexual intercourse in the presence of others or for there to be simultaneous sexual acts in a group as occurs at an orgy....

There are abundant indications that being in love

only made its appearance late on in the sexual relations between men and women; so that the opposition between sexual love and group ties is also a late development.... In the great artificial groups, the church and the army, there is no room for women as a sexual object. The love relation between men and women remains outside these organizations. Even where groups are formed which are composed of both men and women the distinction between the sexes plays no part. There is scarcely any sense in asking whether the libido which keeps groups together is of a homosexual or of a heterosexual nature, for it is not differentiated according to the sexes, and particularly shows a complete disregard for the aims of the genital organization of the libido.

Even in a person who has in other respects become absorbed in a group the directly sexual tendencies preserve a little of his individual activity. If they become too strong they disintegrate every group formation. The Catholic Church had the best of motives for recommending its followers to remain unmarried and for imposing celibacy upon its priests; but falling in love has often driven even priests to leave the church. In the same way love for women breaks through the group ties of race, of national separation, and of the social class system, and it thus produces important effects as a factor in civilization. It seems certain that homosexual love is far more compatible with group ties, even when it takes the shape of uninhibited sexual tendencies—a remarkable fact, the explanation of which might carry us far.

The psychoanalytic investigation of the psychoneuroses has taught us that their symptoms are to be traced back to directly sexual tendencies which are repressed but still remain active. We can complete this formula by adding to it: or, to tendencies inhibited in their aims, whose inhibition has not been entirely successful or has made room for a return to the repressed sexual aim. It is in accordance with this that a neurosis should make its victim asocial and should remove him from the usual group formations. It may be said that a neurosis has the same disintegrating effect upon a group as being in love. On the other hand it appears that where a powerful impetus has been given to group formation neuroses may diminish and at all events temporarily disappear. Justifiable attempts have also been made to turn this antagonism between neuroses and group formation to therapeutic account. Even those who do not regret the disappearance of religious illusions from the civilized world of today will admit that so long as they were in force they offered those who were bound by them the most powerful protection against the danger of neurosis. Nor is it hard to discern in all the ties with mystico-religious or philosophico-religious sects and communities the manifestation of distorted cures of all kinds of neuroses. All of this is bound up with the contrast between directly sexual tendencies and those which are inhibited in their aims.

If he is left to himself, a neurotic is obliged to replace by his own symptom formations the great group formations from which he is excluded. He creates his own world of imagination for himself, his own religion, his own system of delusions, and thus recapitulates the institutions of humanity in a distorted way which is clear evidence of the dominating part played by the directly sexual tendencies.[26]

E. In conclusion, we will add a comparative estimate, from the standpoint of the libido theory, of the states with which we have been concerned, of being in love, of hypnosis, of group formation, and of the neurosis.

Being in love is based upon the simultaneous presence of directly sexual tendencies and of sexual tendencies that are inhibited in their aims, so that the object draws a part of the narcissistic ego-libido to itself. It is a condition in which there is only room for the ego and the object.

Hypnosis resembles being in love in being limited to these two persons, but it is based entirely upon sexual tendencies that are inhibited in their aims and substitutes the object for the ego ideal.

[26] See *Totem und Tabu.*

The group multiplies this process; it agrees with hypnosis in the nature of the instincts which hold it together, and in the replacement of the ego ideal by the object; but to this it adds identification with other individuals, which was perhaps originally made possible by their having the same relation to the object. . . .

The neurosis stands outside this series. It also is based upon a peculiarity in the development of the human libido—the twice-repeated start made by the directly sexual function, with an intervening period of latency.[27] To this extent it resembles hypnosis and group formation in having the character of a regression, which is absent from being in love. It makes its appearance wherever the advance from directly sexual instincts to those that are inhibited in their aims has not been completely successful; and it represents a *conflict* between those instincts which have been received into the ego after having passed through this development and those portions of the same instincts which, like other instinctive desires that have been completely repressed, strive, from the repressed unconscious, to attain direct satisfaction. The neurosis is extraordinarily rich in content, for it embraces all possible relations between the ego and the object—both those in which the object is retained and others in which it is abandoned or erected inside the ego itself—and also the conflicting relations between the ego and its ego ideal.

[27] See *Three Contributions to the Theory of Sexuality.*

THE EGO AND THE ID [1]

(1923)

I. *Consciousness and the Unconscious*

IN this preliminary chapter there is nothing new to be said and it will not be possible to avoid repeating what has often been said before. . . .

We obtain[ed] our concept of the unconscious from the theory of repression. The repressed serves us as a prototype of the unconscious. We see, however, that we have two kinds of unconscious—that which is latent but capable of becoming conscious, and that which is repressed and not capable of becoming conscious in the ordinary way. This piece of insight into mental dynamics cannot fail to affect terminology and description. That which is latent, and only unconscious in the descriptive and not in the dynamic sense, we call *preconscious;* the term unconscious we reserve for the dynamically unconscious repressed, so that we now have three terms, conscious (Cs), preconscious (Pcs), and unconscious (Ucs), which are no longer purely descriptive in sense. The Pcs is presumably a great deal closer to the Cs than is the Ucs,

[1] *Das Ich und das Es.* Wein: 1923. G.S. *vi*, 353-405; LIB. 12. Trans. by Joan Riviere.

and since we have called the Ucs mental we shall with even less hesitation call the latent Pcs mental. ... We can now set to work comfortably with our three terms, Cs, Pcs, and Ucs, so long as we do not forget that, while in the descriptive sense there are two kinds of unconscious, in the dynamic sense there is only one. For purposes of exposition this distinction can in many cases be ignored, but in others it is of course indispensable. ...

We have here formulated the idea that in every individual there is a coherent organization of mental processes, which we call his *ego*. This ego includes consciousness and it controls the approaches to motility, i.e to the discharge of excitations into the external world; it is this institution in the mind which regulates all its own constituent processes, and which goes to sleep at night, though even then it continues to exercise a censorship upon dreams. From this ego proceed the repressions, too, by means of which an attempt is made to cut off certain trends in the mind not merely from consciousness but also from their other forms of manifestation and activity. In analysis these trends which have been shut out stand in opposition to the ego and the analysis is faced with the task of removing the resistances which the ego displays against concerning itself with the repressed. Now we find that during analysis, when we put certain tasks before the patient, he gets into difficulties; his associations fail when they ought to be getting near to the repressed. We then tell him that he is dominated by a resistance; but he is quite unaware of the fact, and, even if he guesses from his feelings of discomfort that a resistance is now at work in him, he does not know what it is nor how to describe it. Since, however, there can be no question but that this resistance emanates from his ego and belongs to it, we find ourselves in an unforeseen situation. We have come upon something in the ego itself which is also unconscious, which behaves exactly like the repressed, that is, which produces powerful effects without itself being conscious and which requires special work before it can be made conscious. From the point of view of analytic practice the consequence of this piece of observation is that we land in endless confusion and difficulty if we cling to our former way of expressing ourselves and try, for instance, to derive neuroses from a conflict between the conscious and the unconscious. We shall have to substitute for this antithesis another, taken from our understanding of the structural conditions of the mind, namely, the antithesis between the organized ego and what is repressed and dissociated from it.[2]

For our conception of the unconscious, however, the consequences of our new observation are even more important. Dynamic considerations caused us to make our first correction; our knowledge of the structure of the mind leads to the second. We recognize that the Ucs does not coincide with what is repressed; it is still true that all that is repressed is Ucs, but not that the whole Ucs is repressed. A part of the ego, too—and heaven knows how important a part—may be Ucs, undoubtedly is Ucs. And this Ucs belonging to the ego is not latent like the Pcs; for if it were, it could not be activated without becoming Cs, and the process of making it conscious would not encounter such great difficulties. When we find ourselves thus confronted by the necessity of postulating a third Ucs which is not repressed, we must admit that the property of being unconscious begins to lose significance for us. It becomes a quality which can have many implications, so that we are unable to make it, as we should have hoped to do, the basis of far-reaching and inevitable conclusions. Nevertheless, we must beware of ignoring this property, for in the last resort the quality of being conscious or not is the single ray of light that penetrates the obscurity of depth-psychology.

II. *The Ego and the Id*

Pathological research has centered our interest too exclusively on the repressed. We wish to know more about the ego, now that we know that it, too, can be

[2] Cf. *Beyond the Pleasure Principle.*

unconscious in the proper sense of the word. Hitherto the only guide we have had while pursuing our investigations has been the distinguishing mark of being conscious or unconscious; and in the end we have come to see that this quality itself is ambiguous. . . .

I have already, in another place,[3] suggested that the real difference between a Ucs and a Pcs idea (thought) consists in this: that the former is worked out upon some sort of material which remains unrecognized, whereas the latter (the Pcs) has in addition been brought into connection with verbal images. This is the first attempt to find a distinguishing mark for the two systems, the Pcs and the Ucs, other than their relation to consciousness. It would seem, then, that the question, "How does a thing become conscious?" could be put more advantageously thus: "How does a thing become preconscious?" And the answer would be: "By coming into connection with the verbal images that correspond to it." . . .

We must not be led away, in the interests of simplification perhaps, into forgetting the importance of optical memory-residues—those of *things* (as opposed to *words*)—or to deny that it is possible for thought-processes to become conscious through a reversion to visual residues, and that in many people this seems to be a favorite method. . . . Thinking in pictures is, therefore, only a very incomplete form of becoming conscious. In some way, too, it approximates more closely to unconscious processes than does thinking in words, and it is unquestionably older than the latter both ontogenetically and phylogenetically. . . .

Whereas the relation between external perceptions and the ego is quite perspicuous, that between internal perceptions and the ego requires special investigation. It gives rise once more to a doubt whether we are really justified in referring the whole of consciousness to the single superficial system Pcpt-Cs. Internal perceptions yield sensations of processes arising in the most diverse and certainly also in the deepest strata of the mental

[3] "The Unconscious" (1915).

apparatus. Very little is known about these sensations and feelings; the best examples we have of them are still those belonging to the pleasure-pain series.... Sensations of a pleasurable nature are not characterized by any inherently impelling quality, whereas "painful" ones possess this quality in a high degree. The latter impel towards change, towards discharge, and that is why we interpret "pain" as implying a heightening and pleasure a lowering of energetic cathexis. Suppose we describe what becomes conscious in the shape of pleasure and "pain" as an undetermined quantitative and qualitative element in the mind; the question then is whether that element can become conscious where it actually is, or whether it must first be transmitted into the system Pcpt. Clinical experience decides for the latter.... Actually the difference is that, whereas with Ucs *ideas* connecting links must be forged before they can be brought into the Cs, with *feelings*, which are themselves transmitted directly, there is no necessity for this. In other words: the distinction between Cs and Pcs has no meaning where feelings are concerned; the Pcs here falls out of account, and feelings are either conscious or unconscious. Even when they are connected with verbal images, their becoming conscious is not due to that circumstance, but they become so directly....

After this clarifying of the relations between external and internal perception and the superficial system Pcpt-Cs, we can go on to work out our conception of the ego. It clearly starts out from its nucleus, the system Pcpt, and begins by embracing the Pcs, which is adjacent to the memory-residues. But the ego, as we have learned, is also unconscious.

Now I think we shall gain a great deal by following the suggestion of ...Georg Groddeck [who pointed] out that the conduct through life of what we call our ego is essentially passive, and that, as he expresses it, we are "lived" by unknown and uncontrollable forces.... I propose to take [this] into account by calling the entity which starts out from the system Pcpt and begins by being Pcs the *ego,* and by following Groddeck in giving to the other part of the mind, into which this entity extends and which behaves as though it were Ucs, the name of *Id.* We shall soon see whether this conception affords us any gain in understanding or any advantage for purposes of description. We shall now look upon the mind of an individual as an unknown and unconscious id, upon whose surface rests the ego, developed from its nucleus the Pcpt-system. . . .

It is easy to see that the ego is that part of the id which has been modified by the direct influence of the external world acting through the Pcpt-Cs: in a sense it is an extension of the surface-differentiation. Moreover, the ego has the task of bringing the influence of the external world to bear upon the id and its tendencies, and endeavors to substitute the reality-principle for the pleasure-principle which reigns supreme in the id. In the ego perception plays the part which in the id devolves upon instinct. The ego represents what we call reason and sanity, in contrast to the id which contains the passions. All this falls into line with popular distinctions which we are all familiar with; at the same time, however, it is only to be regarded as holding good in an average or "ideal" case.

The functional importance of the ego is manifested in the fact that normally control over the approaches to motility devolves upon it. Thus in its relation to the id it is like a man on horseback, who has to hold in check the superior strength of the horse; with this difference, that the rider seeks to do so with his own strength while the ego uses borrowed forces. . . .

It seems that another factor, besides the influence of the system Pcpt, has been at work in bringing about the formation of the ego and its differentiation from the id. The body itself, and above all its surface, is a place from which both external and internal perceptions may spring. It is seen in the same way as any other object, but to the touch it yields two kinds of sensations, one of which is equivalent to an internal perception. . . . The ego is first and foremost a body-ego; it is not merely a surface entity, but it is itself the projection of a surface.[4] . . .

The relation of the ego to consciousness has been gone into repeatedly; yet there are still some important facts in this connection which remain to be described. Accustomed as we are to taking our social or ethical standard of values along with us wherever we go, we feel no surprise at hearing that the scene of the activities of the lower passions is in the unconscious; we expect, moreover, that the higher any mental function ranks in our scale of values the more easily it will find access to consciousness assured to it. Here, however, psychoanalytic experience disappoints us. On the one hand, we have evidence that even subtle and intricate intellectual operations which ordinarily require strenuous concentration can equally be carried out preconsciously and without coming into consciousness. Instances of this are quite incontestable; they may occur, for instance, during sleep, as is shown when someone finds, immediately after waking that he knows the solution of a difficult mathematical or other problem with which he had been wrestling in vain the day before.

There is another phenomenon, however, which is far stranger. In our analyses we discover that there are people in whom the faculties of self-criticism and conscience —mental activities, that is, that rank as exceptionally high ones—are unconscious and unconsciously produce effects of the greatest importance; the example of resistances remaining unconscious during analysis is therefore by no means unique. But this new discovery, which compels us, in spite of our critical faculties, to speak of an "unconscious sense of guilt," bewilders us far more than the other and sets us fresh problems, especially when we gradually come to see that in a great number of neuroses this unconscious

[4] [*I.e.* the ego is ultimately derived from bodily sensations, chiefly from those springing from the surface of the body. It may thus be regarded as a mental projection of the surface of the body, besides, as we have seen above, representing the superficies of the mental apparatus.—Authorized note by the Translator.]

sense of guilt plays a decisive economic part and puts the most powerful obstacles in the way of recovery. If we come back once more to our scale of values, we shall have to say that not only what is lowest but also what is highest in the ego can be unconscious. It is as if we were thus supplied with a proof of what we have just asserted of the conscious ego: that it is first and foremost a body-ego.

III. *The Ego and the Super-Ego* (*Ego-Ideal*)

If the ego were merely the part of the id that is modified by the influence of the perceptual system, the representative in the mind of the real external world, we should have a simple state of things to deal with. But there is a further complication. The considerations that led us to assume the existence of a differentiating grade within the ego, which may be called the ego-ideal or super-ego, have been set forth elsewhere.[5] ... The new proposition which must now be gone into is that this part of the ego is less closely connected with consciousness than the rest.

At this point we must widen our range a little. We succeeded in explaining the painful disorder of melancholia by supposing that, in those suffering from it, an object which was lost has been reinstated within the ego; that is, that an object-cathexis has been replaced by an identification.[6] When this explanation was first proposed, however, we did not appreciate the full significance of the process and did not know how common and how typical it is. Since then we have come to understand that this kind of substitution has a great share in determining the form taken on by the ego and that it contributes materially towards building up what is called its "character."

At the very beginning, in the primitive oral phase of the individual's existence, object-cathexis and identification are hardly to be distinguished from each other. We can

[5] "On Narcissism: an Introduction" (1914), and *Group Psychology and the Analysis of the Ego* (1921).

[6] "Mourning and Melancholia" (1917).

only suppose that later on object-cathexes proceed from the id, in which erotic trends are felt as needs. The ego, which at its inception is still far from robust, becomes aware of the object-cathexes, and either acquiesces in them or tries to defend itself against them by the process of repression.[7]

When it happens that a person has to give up a sexual object, there quite often ensues a modification in his ego which can only be described as a reinstatement of the object within the ego, as it occurs in melancholia; the exact nature of this substitution is as yet unknown to us. It may be that, by undertaking this introjection, which is a kind of regression to the mechanism of the oral phase, the ego makes it easier for an object to be given up or renders that process possible. It may even be that this identification is the sole condition under which the id can give up its objects. At any rate the process, especially in the early phases of development, is a very frequent one, and it points to the conclusion that the character of the ego is a precipitate of abandoned object-cathexes and that it contains a record of past object-choices. . . . From another point of view it may be said that this transformation of an erotic object-choice into a modification of the ego is also a method by which the ego can obtain control over the id and deepen its relations with it—at the cost, it is true, of acquiescing to a large extent in the id's experiences. . . . The transformation of object-libido into narcissistic libido which thus takes place obviously implies an abandonment of sexual aims, a process of desexualization; it is consequently a kind of sublimation. . . .

[7] An interesting parallel to the replacement of object-choice by identification is to be found in the belief of primitive peoples, and in the taboos based upon it, that the attributes of animals which are assimilated as nourishment survive as part of the character of the persons who eat them. As is well known, this belief is one of the roots of cannibalism and its effects can be traced throughout the series of customs derived from the totem feast down to the Holy Communion. The consequences ascribed by this belief to oral mastery of the object do in fact follow in the case of the later sexual object-choice.

But, whatever the character's capacity for resisting the influences of abandoned object-cathexes may turn out to be in after years, the effects of the first identifications in earliest childhood will be profound and lasting. This leads us back to the origin of the ego-ideal; for behind the latter there lies hidden the first and most important identification of all, the identification with the father,[8] which takes place in the prehistory of every person. This is apparently not in the first instance the consequence or outcome of an object-cathexis; it is a direct and immediate identification and takes place earlier than any object-cathexis. But the object-choices belonging to the earliest sexual period and relating to the father and mother seem normally to find their outcome in an identification of the kind discussed, which would thus reinforce the primary one. . . .

In its simplified form the case of the male child may be described as follows. At a very early age the little boy develops an object-cathexis of his *mother*, which originally related to the mother's breast and is the earliest instance of an object-choice on the anaclitic model; his *father* the boy deals with by identifying himself with him. For a time these two relationships exist side by side, until the sexual wishes in regard to the mother become more intense and the father is perceived as an obstacle to them; this gives rise to the Oedipus complex.[9] The identification with the father then takes on a hostile coloring and changes into a wish to get rid of the father in order to take his place with the mother. Henceforward the relation to the father is ambivalent; it seems as if the ambivalence inherent in the identification from the beginning had become manifest. An ambivalent attitude to the father and an object-relation of a purely affectionate kind to the mother make up the content of the simple positive Oedipus complex in the boy.

[8] Perhaps it would be safer to say "with the parents;" . . . in order to simplify my presentment I shall discuss only identification with the father.

[9] Cf. *Group Psychology and the Analysis of the Ego,* chap. viii.

Along with the dissolution of the Oedipus complex the object-cathexis of the mother must be given up. Its place may be filled by one of two things: either an identification with the mother or an intensified identification with the father. We are accustomed to regard the latter outcome as the more normal; it permits the affectionate relation to the mother to be in a measure retained. In this way the passing of the Oedipus complex would consolidate the masculinity in the boy's character. . . .

These identifications are not what our previous statements would have led us to expect, since they do not involve the absorption of the abandoned object into the ego: but this alternative outcome may also occur; it is more readily observed in girls than in boys. Analysis very often shows that a little girl, after she has had to relinquish her father as a love-object, will bring her masculinity into prominence and identify herself with her father, that is, with the object which has been lost, instead of with her mother. This will clearly depend on whether the masculinity in her disposition—whatever that may consist of— is strong enough.

It would appear, therefore, that in both sexes the relative strength of the masculine and feminine sexual dispositions is what determines whether the outcome of the Oedipus situation shall be an identification with the father or with the mother. This is one of the ways in which bisexuality takes a hand in the subsequent vicissitudes of the Oedipus complex. The other way is even more important. For one gets the impression that the simple Oedipus complex is by no means its commonest form, but rather represents a simplification or schematization which, to be sure, is often enough adequate for practical purposes. Closer study usually discloses the more complete Oedipus complex, which is twofold, positive and negative, and is due to the bisexuality originally present in children: that is to say, a boy has not merely an ambivalent attitude towards his father and an affectionate object-relation towards his mother, but at the same time he also behaves like a girl and displays an affectionate feminine attitude to his father and a corresponding hostility and jealousy towards his mother. It is this complicating element introduced by bisexuality that makes it so difficult to obtain a clear view of the facts in connection with the earliest object-choices and identifications, and still more difficult to describe them intelligibly. It may even be that the ambivalence displayed in the relations to the parents should be attributed entirely to bisexuality and that it is not, as I stated just now, developed out of an identification in consequence of rivalry. . . .

The broad general outcome of the sexual phase governed by the Oedipus complex may . . . be taken to be the forming of a precipitate in the ego, consisting of these two identifications in some way combined together. This modification of the ego retains its special position; it stands in contrast to the other constituents of the ego in the form of an ego-ideal or super-ego.

The super-ego is, however, not merely a deposit left by the earliest object-choices of the id; it also represents an energetic reaction-formation against those choices. Its relation to the ego is not exhausted by the precept: "You *ought to be* such and such (like your father)"; it also comprises the prohibition: "You *must not be* such and such (like your father); that is, you may not do all that he does; many things are his prerogative." . . .

If we consider once more the origin of the super-ego as we have described it, we shall perceive it to be the outcome of two highly important factors, one of them biological and the other historical: namely, the lengthy duration in man of the helplessness and dependence belonging to childhood, and the fact of his Oedipus complex, the repression of what we have shown to be connected with the interruption of libidinal development by the latency period and so with the twofold onset of activity characteristic of man's sexual life. . . .

Psychoanalysis has been reproached time after time with ignoring the higher, moral, spiritual side of human nature. The reproach is doubly unjust, both historically and methodologically. For, in the first place, we have

from the very beginning attributed the function of in-
stigating repression to the moral and aesthetic tendencies
in the ego, and secondly, there has been a general refusal
to recognize that psychoanalytic research could not produce a complete and finished body of doctrine, like a
philosophical system, ready-made, but had to find its way
step by step along the path towards understanding the
intricacies of the mind by making an analytic dissection
of both normal and abnormal phenomena. So long as the
study of the repressed part of the mind was our task,
there was no need for us to feel any agitated apprehen-
sions about the existence of the higher side of mental life.
But now that we have embarked upon the analysis of the
ego we can give an answer to all those whose moral sense
has been shocked and who have complained that there
must surely be a higher nature in man: "Very true," we
can say, "and here we have that higher nature, in this ego-
ideal or super-ego, the representative of our relation to
our parents. When we were little children we knew these
higher natures, we admired them and feared them; and
later we took them into ourselves." ...

Whereas the ego is essentially the representative of the
external world, of reality, the super-ego stands in contrast
to it as the representative of the internal world, of the id.
Conflicts between the ego and the ideal will, as we are
now prepared to find, ultimately reflect the contrast between what is real and what is mental, between the external world and the internal world.

Through the forming of the ideal, all the traces left
behind in the id by biological developments and by the
vicissitudes gone through by the human race are taken
over by the ego and lived through again by it in each individual. Owing to the way in which it is formed, the
ego-ideal has a great many points of contact with the
phylogenetic endowment of each individual—his archaic
heritage. And thus it is that what belongs to the lowest
depths in the minds of each one of us is changed, through
this formation of the ideal, into what we value as the
highest in the human soul. ...

It is easy to show that the ego-ideal answers in every way to what is expected of the higher nature of man. In so far as it is a substitute for the longing for a father, it contains the germ from which all religions have evolved. The self-judgment which declares that the ego falls short of its ideal produces the sense of worthlessness with which the religious believer attests his longing. As a child grows up, the office of father is carried on by masters and by others in authority; the power of their injunctions and prohibitions remains vested in the ego-ideal and continues, in the form of conscience, to exercise the censorship of morals. The tension between the demands of conscience and the actual attainments of the ego is experienced as a sense of guilt. Social feelings rest on the foundation of identifications with others, on the basis of an ego-ideal in common with them. Religion, morality, and a social sense—the chief elements of what is highest in man (I am at the moment putting science and art on one side)— were originally one and the same thing. . . .

IV. *The Two Classes of Instincts*

We have already said that, if the differentiation we have made of the mind into an id, an ego, and a super-ego represents any advance in our knowledge, it ought to enable us to understand more thoroughly the dynamic relations within the mind and to describe them more clearly. We have also already reached the conclusion that the ego is especially affected by perception, and that, speaking broadly, perceptions may be said to have the same significance for the ego as instincts have for the id. At the same time the ego is subject to the influence of the instincts, too, like the id, of which it is in fact only a specially modified part.

I have lately developed a view of the instincts [10] which I shall here hold to and take as the basis of further discussions. According to this view we have to distinguish

[10] *Beyond the Pleasure Principle.*

two classes of instincts, one of which, Eros or the sexual instincts, is by far the more conspicuous and accessible to study. It comprises not merely the uninhibited sexual instinct proper and the impulses of a sublimated or aim-inhibited nature derived from it, but also the self-preservative instinct, which must be assigned to the ego and which at the beginning of our analytic work we had good reason for setting in opposition to the sexual object-instincts. The second class of instincts was not so easy to define; in the end we came to recognize sadism as its representative. As a result of theoretical considerations, supported by biology, we assumed the existence of a death-instinct, the task of which is to lead organic matter back into the inorganic state.... This hypothesis throws no light whatever upon the manner in which the two classes of instincts are fused, blended, and mingled with each other; but that this takes place regularly and very extensively is an assumption indispensable to our conception. ...

Once we have admitted the conception of a fusion of the two classes of instincts with each other, the possibility of a—more or less complete—"defusion" of them forces itself upon us. The sadistic component of the sexual instinct would be a classical example of instinctual fusion serving a useful purpose; and the perversion in which sadism has made itself independent would be typical of defusion, though not of absolutely complete defusion. From this point we obtain a new view of a great array of facts which have not before been considered in this light. We perceive that for purposes of discharge the instinct of destruction is habitually enlisted in the service of Eros (we suspect that the epileptic fit is a product and sign of instinctual defusion), and we come to understand that defusion and the marked emergence of the death-instinct are among the most noteworthy effects of many severe neuroses, e.g. the obsessional neuroses. Making a swift generalization, we might conjecture that the essence of a regression of libido, e.g. from the genital to the sadistic-anal level, would lie in a defusion of instincts, just as, conversely, the advance from an earlier to the definitive genital phase would be conditioned by an accession of erotic components. . . .

Instead of the opposition between the two classes of instincts let us consider the polarity of love and hate. . . . Now, clinical observation shows not only that love is with unexpected regularity accompanied by hate (ambivalence), and not only that in human relationships hate is frequently a forerunner of love, but also that in many circumstances hate changes into love and love into hate. If this change is anything more than a mere succession in time, then clearly the ground is cut away from under a distinction so fundamental as that between erotic instincts and death-instincts, one which presupposes the existence of physiological processes running counter to each other.

Now the case in which someone first loves and then hates the same person (or the reverse), because that person has given him cause for doing so, has obviously nothing to do with our problem. Nor has the other case in which feelings of love that have not yet become manifest express themselves to begin with by enmity and aggressive tendencies; for it may be that here the destructive components in the object-cathexis have outstripped the erotic and are only later on joined by the latter. But we know of several instances in the psychology of the neuroses in which there are better grounds for assuming that a transformation does take place. In persecutory paranoia the sufferer takes a particular way of defending himself against an unduly strong homosexual attachment to a given person, with the result that the person he once loved most is changed into a persecutor and then becomes the object of aggressive and often dangerous impulses on the part of the patient. Here we have grounds for interposing an intermediate phase in which the love is transformed into hate. Analytic investigation has only lately revealed that the sources of homosexuality and of desexualized social feelings include very intense feelings of rivalry giving rise to aggressive desires, which, after they have been surmounted, are succeeded by love for the object that was formerly hated or by an identification with it. The question arises whether in these instances we are to assume a direct transformation of hate into love. It is clear that here the changes are purely internal and an alteration in the behavior of the object plays no part in them.

There is another possible mechanism, however, which we have come to know of by analytic investigation of the processes concerned in the change in paranoia. An ambivalent attitude is present from the outset and the transformation is effected by means of a reactive shifting of cathexis, by which energy is withdrawn from the erotic impulses and used to supplement the hostile energy. Not quite the same thing but something like it happens when a hostile attitude of rivalry is overcome and leads to homosexuality. . . .

So we see that we are not obliged in either of these cases to assume a direct transformation of hate into love which would be incompatible with a qualitative distinction between the two classes of instincts. It appears, however, that by including in our calculations this other mechanism by means of which love can be changed into hate, we have tacitly made another assumption which deserves to be formulated explicitly. We have reckoned as though there existed in the mind—whether in the ego or in the id—a displaceable energy, which is in itself neutral, but is able to join forces either with an erotic or with a destructive impulse, differing qualitatively as they do, and augment its total cathexis. Without assuming the existence of a displaceable energy of this kind we can make no headway. The only question is where it comes from, what it belongs to, and what it signifies. The problem of the quality of instinctual impulses and of its persistence throughout their vicissitudes is still very obscure and has hardly been attacked up to the present. . . .

In the present discussion I am putting forward nothing but a supposition; I have no proof to offer. It seems a plausible view that this neutral displaceable energy, which is probably active alike in the ego and in the id, proceeds from the narcissistic reservoir of libido, i.e. that it desexualized Eros. (The erotic instincts appear to be altogether more plastic, more readily diverted and displaced than the destructive instincts.) From this we can easily go on to assume that this displaceable libido is employed in the service of the pleasure-principle to obviate accumulations and to facilitate discharge. . . . If this displaceable energy is desexualized libido, it might also be described as sublimated energy; for it would still retain the main purpose of Eros—that of uniting and binding— in so far as it helped towards establishing that unity, or tendency to unity, which is particularly characteristic of the ego. If the intellectual processes in the wider sense are to be classed among these displacements, then the energy for the work of thought itself must be supplied from sublimated erotic sources. . . .

V. *The Subordinate Relationships of the Ego*

The complexity of our subject matter must be an excuse for the fact that none of the chapter headings of this book correspond entirely to their contents, and that in turning to new aspects of the problem we constantly hark back to matters that have already been dealt with.

As has been said repeatedly, the ego is formed to a great extent out of identifications taking the place of cathexes on the part of the id which have been abandoned; the earliest of these identifications always fulfill a special office in the ego and stand apart from the rest of the ego in the form of a super-ego, while later on, as it grows stronger, the ego may become more able to withstand the effects of identifications. . . .

The super-ego's relation to the subsequent modifications effected in the ego is roughly that of the primary sexual period in childhood to full-grown sexual activity after puberty. Although it is amenable to every later influence, it preserves throughout life the character given to it by its derivation from the father-complex, namely, the capacity to stand apart from the ego and to rule it. It is a memorial of the former weakness and dependence of the ego and the mature ego remains subject to its domination. As the child was once compelled to obey its parents, so the ego submits to the categorical imperative pronounced by its super-ego. . . .

We can best appreciate these relations by turning our attention to certain clinical facts, which have long since lost their novelty but which still await theoretical discussion. There are certain people who behave in a quite peculiar fashion during the work of analysis. When one speaks hopefully to them or expresses satisfaction with the progress of the treatment, they show signs of discontent and their condition invariably becomes worse. One begins by regarding this as defiance and as an attempt to prove their superiority to the physician, but later one comes to take a deeper and truer view. One becomes convinced, not only that such people cannot endure any praise or appreciation, but that they react inversely to the progress of the treatment. . . . There is no doubt that there is something in these people that sets itself against their recovery and dreads its approach as though it were a danger. . . . If we analyze this resistance in the usual way —then, even after we have subtracted from it the defiant attitude towards the physician and the fixation on the various kinds of advantage which the patient derives from the illness, the greater part of it is still left over; and this reveals itself as the most powerful of all obstacles to recovery. . . . In the end we come to see that we are dealing with what may be called a "moral" factor, a sense of guilt, which is finding atonement in the illness and is refusing to give up the penalty of suffering. We are justified in regarding this rather disheartening explanation as conclusive. But as far as the patient is concerned this sense of guilt is dumb; it does not tell him he is guilty; he does not feel guilty, he simply feels ill. This sense of guilt expresses itself only as a resistance to recovery which it is extremely difficult to overcome. It is also particularly difficult to convince the patient that this motive lies behind his continuing to be ill; he holds fast to the more obvious explanation that treatment by analysis is not the right remedy for his case.

The description we have given applies to the most extreme instances of this state of affairs, but in a lesser measure this factor has to be reckoned with in very many cases, perhaps in all severe cases of neurosis. In fact it may be precisely this element in the situation, the attitude of the ego-ideal, that determines the severity of a neurotic illness. We shall not hesitate, therefore, to discuss rather more fully the way in which the sense of guilt expresses itself under different conditions.

An explanation of the normal conscious sense of guilt (conscience) presents no difficulties; it is due to tension between the ego and the ego-ideal and is the expression of a condemnation of the ego pronounced by its criticizing function. The feelings of inferiority so well known in neurotics are presumably closely related to it. In two very familiar maladies the sense of guilt is over-strongly conscious; in them the ego-ideal displays particular severity and often rages against the ego with the utmost cruelty. The attitude of the ego-ideal in these two diseases, the obsessional neurosis and melancholia, presents, alongside of this similarity, differences that are no less significant.

In certain forms of the obsessional neurosis the sense of guilt expresses itself loudly but cannot justify itself to the ego. Consequently the patient's ego rebels against this imputation of guilt and seeks the physician's support in repudiating it. It would be folly to acquiesce in this, for to do so would have no effect. Analysis shows that the super-ego is being influenced by processes that have remained hidden from the ego. It is possible to discover the repressed impulses which really occasion the sense of guilt. The super-ego is thus proved to have known more than the ego about the unconscious id.

In melancholia the impression that the super-ego has obtained a hold upon consciousness is even stronger. But in this case the ego ventures no objection; it admits the guilt and submits to the punishment. The explanation of this difference is plain. In the obsessional neurosis the reprehensible impulses which are being criticized by the super-ego have never formed part of the ego, while in melancholia the object of the super-ego's wrath has become part of the ego through identification. . . .

The hysterical type of ego defends itself from the painful perception which the criticisms of its super-ego threaten to produce in it by the same means that it uses to defend itself from an unendurable object-cathexis—by an act of repression. It is the ego, therefore, that is responsible for the sense of guilt remaining unconscious. We know that as a rule the ego carries out repressions in the service and at the behest of its super-ego; but this is a case in which it has turned the same weapon against its harsh taskmaster. In the obsessional neurosis, as we know, the phenomena of reaction-formation predominate; but here the ego contents itself with keeping at a distance the material to which the sense of guilt refers.

One may go further and venture the hypothesis that a great part of the sense of guilt must normally remain unconscious, because the origin of conscience is closely connected with the Oedipus complex which belongs to the unconscious. If anyone were inclined to put forward the paradoxical proposition that the normal man is not only far more immoral than he believes but also far more moral than he has any idea of, psychoanalysis, which is responsible for the first half of the assertion, would have no objection to raise against the second half.[11]

It was a surprise to find that exacerbation of this Ucs sense of guilt could turn people into criminals. But it is undoubtedly a fact. In many criminals, especially youthful ones, it is possible to detect a very powerful sense of guilt which existed before the crime, and is not therefore the result of it but its motive. It is as if it had been a relief

---

[11] This proposition is only apparently a paradox; it simply states that human nature has a far greater capacity, both for good and for evil, that it thinks it has, i.e. than it is aware of through the conscious perceptions of the ego.

conscience = guilt

to be able to fasten this unconscious sense of guilt on to something real and immediate. . . .

[Now] how is it that the super-ego manifests itself essentially as a sense of guilt (or rather, as criticism—for the sense of guilt is the perception in the ego which corresponds to the criticism) and at the same time develops such extraordinary harshness and severity towards the ego? If we turn to melancholia first, we find that the excessively strong super-ego which has obtained a hold upon consciousness rages against the ego with merciless fury, as if it had taken possession of the whole of the sadism available in the person concerned. Following our view of sadism, we should say that the destructive component had entrenched itself in the super-ego and turned against the ego. . . .

The reproaches of conscience in certain forms of obsessional neurosis are just as painful and tormenting, but here the situation is less perspicuous. It is remarkable that the obsessional neurotic, in contrast to the melancholiac, never takes the step of self-destruction; he is as if immune against the danger of suicide, and is far better protected from it than the hysteric. We can see that what guarantees the safety of the ego is the fact that the object has been retained. In the obsessional neurosis it has become possible, through a regression to the pregenital organization, for the love-impulses to transform themselves into impulses of aggression against the object. . . .

From the point of view of mortality, the control and restriction of instinct, it may be said of the id that it is totally non-moral, of the ego that it strives to be moral, and of the super-ego that it can be hyper-moral and then becomes as ruthless as only the id can be. It is remarkable that the more a man checks his aggressive tendencies towards others the more tyrannical, that is aggressive, he becomes in his ego-ideal. The ordinary view sees the situation the other way round: the standard set up by the ego-ideal seems to be the motive for the suppression of aggressiveness. The fact remains, however, as we have stated it: the more a man controls his aggressiveness, the more intense become the aggressive tendencies of his ego-ideal against his ego. It is like a displacement, a turning round upon the self. But even ordinary normal morality has a harshly restraining, cruelly prohibiting quality. It is from this, indeed, that the conception arises of an inexorable higher being who metes out punishment. . . .

Our ideas about the ego are beginning to clear, and its various relationships are gaining distinctness. We now see the ego in its strength and in its weaknesses. It is entrusted with important functions. By virtue of its relation to the perceptual system it arranges the processes of the mind in a temporal order and tests their correspondence with reality. By interposing the process of thinking it secures a postponement of motor discharges and controls the avenues to motility. . . . All the experiences of life that originate from without enrich the ego; the id, however, is another outer world to it, which it strives to bring into subjection to itself. It withdraws libido from the id and transforms the object-cathexes of the id into ego-constructions. . . . From [another] point of view, however, we see this same ego as a poor creature owing service to three masters and consequently menaced by three several dangers: from the external world, from the libido of the id, and from the severity of the super-ego. Three kinds of anxiety correspond to these three dangers, since anxiety is the expression of a recoil from danger. . . .

The ego is the true abode of anxiety.[12] Threatened by dangers from three directions, it develops the flight-reflex by withdrawing its own cathexis from the menacing perception or from the equally dreaded process in the id, and discharging it as anxiety. This primitive reaction is later replaced by the introduction of protective cathexes (the mechanism of the phobias). What it is that the ego fears either from an external or from a libidinal danger

[12] [The author's views upon anxiety as given in the following paragraphs have been largely revised in his later work, *Inhibitions, Symptoms and Anxiety* (1926).—TRANS.]

cannot be specified; we know that it is in the nature of an overthrow or of extinction, but it is not determined by analysis. The ego is simply obeying the warning of the pleasure-principle. On the other hand, we can tell what lies hidden behind the ego's dread of the super-ego, its fear of conscience. The higher being which later became the ego-ideal once threatened the ego with castration, and this dread of castration is probably the kernel round which the subsequent fear of conscience has gathered; it is this dread that persists as the fear of conscience.

The high-sounding phrase, "Every fear is ultimately the fear of death," has hardly any meaning; at any rate it cannot be justified. It seems to me, on the contrary, perfectly correct to distinguish the fear of death from dread of an external object (objective anxiety) and from neurotic libidinal anxiety. It presents a difficult problem to psychoanalysis, for death is an abstract concept with a negative content for which no unconscious correlative can be found. It would seem that the mechanism of the fear of death can only be that the ego relinquishes its narcissistic libidinal cathexis in a very large measure, that is, that it gives up itself, just as it gives up some *external* object in other cases in which it feels anxiety. I believe that the fear of death concerns an interplay between the ego and the super-ego.

We know that the fear of death makes its appearance under two conditions (which, moreover, are entirely analogous to the other situations in which anxiety develops), namely, as a reaction to an external danger and as an internal process, as for instance in melancholia. Once again a neurotic manifestation may help us to understand a normal one.

The fear of death in melancholia only admits of one explanation: that the ego gives itself up because it feels itself hated and persecuted by the super-ego, instead of loved. To the ego, therefore, living means the same as being loved—being loved by the super-ego, which here again appears as the representative of the id. The super-ego fulfills the same function of protecting and saving that was fulfilled in earlier days by the father and later by Providence or destiny. But, when the ego finds itself in overwhelming danger of a real order which it believes itself unable to overcome by its own strength, it is bound to draw the same conclusion. It sees itself deserted by all the forces of protection and lets itself die. Here, moreover, is once again the same situation as that which underlay the first great anxiety-state of birth and the infantile anxiety of longing for an absent person—the anxiety of separation from the protecting mother.

These considerations enable us to conceive of the fear of death, like the fear of conscience, as a development of the fear of castration. The great significance which the sense of guilt has in the neuroses makes it conceivable that ordinary neurotic anxiety is reinforced in severe cases by a development of anxiety between the ego and the super-ego (fear of castration, of conscience, of death).

The id, to which we finally come back, has no means of showing the ego either love or hate. It cannot say what it wants; it has achieved no unity of will. Eros and the death-instinct struggle within it; we have seen with what weapons the one group of instincts defends itself against the other. It would be possible to picture the id as under the domination of the mute but powerful death-instincts, which desire to be at peace and (as the pleasure-principle demands) to put Eros, the intruder, to rest; but that would be to run the risk of valuing too cheaply the part played by Eros.

LADIES AND GENTLEMEN—Let me in conclusion sum up what I [have] to say about the relation of psychoanalysis to the question of a *Weltanschauung*. Psychoanalysis is not, in my opinion, in a position to create a *Weltanschauung* of its own. It has no need to do so, for it is a branch of science, and can subscribe to the scientific *Weltanschauung*. The latter, however, hardly merits such a high-sounding name, for it does not take everything into its scope, it is incomplete, and it makes no claim to being comprehensive or to constituting a system. Scientific thought is still in its infancy; there are very many of the great problems with which it has as yet been unable to cope. A *Weltanschauung* based upon science has, apart from the emphasis it lays upon the real world, essentially negative characteristics, such as that it limits itself to truth and rejects illusions. Those of our fellow men who are dissatisfied with this state of things and who desire something more for their momentary peace of mind may look for it where they can find it. We shall not blame them for doing so; but we cannot help them and cannot change our own way of thinking on their account.

The end of the last Lecture in
"New Introductory Lectures on Psychoanalysis."

1932.

APPENDIX: THE REFORMULATION OF THE THEORY OF ANXIETY

THE publication of the two monographs entitled "Beyond the Pleasure Principle" (pp. 141–168) and "The Ego and the Id" (pp. 210–235) marked the beginning of a new epoch in psychoanalytic theory. The fundamental importance of the theoretical changes introduced in these two works was not fully apparent for some years even to those working in the field. In retrospect, however, we can say that modern psychoanalytic theory began with these works. The dual theory of the instinctual drives contained in the first work and the hypotheses concerning the origin, nature, and function of the psychic apparatus contained in the second form the bases of our current, psychoanalytic concepts concerning the development and operation of the mind.

A detailed exposition of the innovations referred to above and a thorough comparison between Freud's theories before and after 1920-23 would exceed the scope of the present volume. As Dr. Rickman explained in the Preface, the selections in this volume are intended to illustrate the way in which Freud thought and to indicate the course of the development of his theories with the hope that the reader will then turn or return to the body of psychoanalytic literature with that broader perspective which should be conducive to a better understanding. There is in fact no fully systematic discussion of the relation between Freud's earlier theories and his later ones, but those who are interested in this topic are referred to the *New Introductory Lectures* of Freud (1933) and to *An Elementary Textbook of Psychoanalysis* by Brenner (1955). All that will be attempted in the following few pages will be to describe the major theoretical innovations which appeared in Freud's works after 1923 and which resulted from the basic changes in theory which were introduced in 1920 and 1923.

These innovations had to do principally with anxiety and with psychic conflict. They are contained in a monograph which Freud wrote in 1926, the English translation of which is alternatively called *Inhibitions, Symptoms, and Anxiety*, or *The Problem of Anxiety*, the former title being the one which corresponds more precisely to that of the German work.

Before attempting to summarize the new theories contained in this work it may be profitable to review the psychoanalytic hypotheses concerning anxiety and psychic conflict which were current prior to 1926. They were essentially as follows. In the first place, a sharp distinction was to be made between neurotic and realistic anxiety. This distinction did not rest on descriptive or subjective grounds, but rather on etiological or causative ones. That is to say, realistic anxiety or fear was defined as anxiety which was caused by the perception and appraisal of a real danger which threatened harm to the individual. Neurotic anxiety on the other hand, though descriptively and subjectively indistinguishable from realistic anxiety, was considered to be the consequence of an inadequate discharge of the libidinal energies of the mind. The undischarged or dammed-up libido was believed to have been directly converted into anxiety by some unknown process. Thus, by definition, neurotic anxiety in psychoanalytic terminology prior to 1926 was transformed, undischarged libido as opposed to realistic anxiety, which was the reaction to the perception of danger (cf. p. 144).

In line with these ideas the relation between anxiety and psychic conflict was considered to be an indirect and subsequential one. If a conflict over certain instinctual wishes should result in the repression of those wishes, the wishes would continue to exist unconsciously but with all opportunity denied to them of satisfactory discharge of their libidinal cathexis (cf. the selection entitled "Repression," p. 87). Thus repression would cause damming-up of libido, which might then either remain in this dammed-up state without causing any difficulty or which might be transformed into anxiety under certain circumstances. The first of these two possibilities would be an instance of successful repression. The second would be an instance of a failure of repression of the sort seen in neuroses, and the circumstances responsible for such a failure of repression would be the precipitating or contributory factors of whatever neurosis resulted (cf. p. 67). In this etiologic formula the *major* emphasis was on a quantitative factor: the greater the amount of the libido which was dammed up, the greater the likelihood that the repression responsible for the dammed-up state would fail in its purpose and that anxiety and neurotic symptoms might result.

In addition Freud believed that in some cases a damming-up of libido occurred as a result of factors other than psychic conflict and repression and that in those cases, too, the undischarged libido might be transformed into anxiety. Examples of this would be cases of enforced sexual abstinence or of incomplete sexual gratification, as in coitus interruptus. Such cases were labeled by Freud "actual neuroses" as opposed to the psychoneuroses in which the damming-up of the libido was the consequence of repression.

The three important points to remember from this discussion are the following: (1) prior to 1926 neurotic anxiety was believed to be transformed libido, as opposed to real anxiety, which was defined as a reaction to the perception of danger; (2) neurotic anxiety was believed to be a *consequence* of *un*successful repression (in the psychoneuroses) or of sexual excitement without adequate gratification (in the actual neuroses); (3) neurotic anxiety was believed to play no part *per se* in psychic conflict or in any *successful* repression which might result therefrom; as noted under (2) it was believed to appear only when repression failed. One might express this by saying that when repression and neurotic anxiety were associated, the relationship, prior to 1926, was believed to be that the former was a necessary but not a sufficient condition for the appearance of the latter.

So much for the essentials of the earlier theory. The next question is, "What were the changes which Freud introduced in 1926?" For the sake of clarity these changes and the reasons for them will first be summarized and then discussed.

First of all the idea that libido could be transformed into anxiety was abandoned. Freud did not question the accuracy of the clinical observation that a damming-up of libidinal energies was often accompanied by the development of neurotic anxiety. It was merely that in 1926 he abandoned the previous theoretical explanation of this observation, namely, that libido was transformed into anxiety, and substituted for it another less simple but more satisfactory explanation.

Second, the relationship between anxiety and repression was reversed. In the older theory repression preceded anxiety, and anxiety was believed to appear only if repression failed. In the new theory anxiety preceded repression and was, indeed, considered to be the prime *motive* for repression. This change, unlike the first, was not a new explanation for old observations. On the contrary, it followed from a meticulous re-examination of the clinical data provided by two especially well-analyzed cases of pathological fears, or phobias, in childhood and a recognition of the fact that earlier observations on these cases, as on other, similar ones, had been in error in this particular respect: the repression of the incestuous and parricidal wishes of childhood which are known as the Oedipus complex (cf. p. 28) had not *preceded* the appearance of anxiety, but had rather followed from it. Repression in such instances was seen as a consequence of the little boy's fear of castration by his father, or of analogous fears in the case of a little girl. Thus since 1926 anxiety, according to psychoanalytic theories, has been considered to play an essential part in psychic conflict and to precede and motivate repression, whether or not repression then proved to be successful.

Finally, the causal distinction between neurotic anxiety and real fear was abandoned, and the anxiety associated with the instinctual drives was related to several typical danger situations which will be outlined below.

Having thus summarized the changes in theory which Freud proposed in *Inhibitions, Symptoms, and Anxiety* we may proceed to a more extended discussion of their nature as well as of the reasons which Freud advanced for adopting them.

His argument ran about as follows. He said that it was clear that in the psychoneuroses anxiety is not transformed libido, as previously assumed, but rather the reaction to an anticipated danger. In the two cases of childhood, animal phobias which he examined in detail, the danger, as he pointed out, was that of castration. To be sure, the two little boys in question were mistaken in their belief that they were in danger of castration, but as far as *they* were concerned, it was a real, outer danger which threatened them and caused them to be afraid. Because of their fear they repressed their Oepidal wishes, and whenever those wishes threatened to escape from repression the little boys became afraid again.

Freud went on to say that in the actual neuroses the situation was different, however. He repeated his earlier conclusion that in such cases the patients experiencing fear did so simply as a consequence of unsatisfactory or inadequate sexual gratification and not because they unconsciously feared some danger such as castration in connection with their sexual desires. On the contrary, Freud maintained that in the so-called actual neuroses anxiety was the direct consequence of an excessive damming-up of libido.

Having thus made clear the discrepancy between the situation in the actual neuroses and in the psychoneuroses with respect to the development of anxiety, Freud then addressed himself to the task of finding a hypothesis which would reconcile the two. The one which he proposed was the following.

He suggested that the affect of anxiety developed whenever the influx of stimuli into the psychic apparatus was too great for the apparatus to cope with: whenever the psychic apparatus was flooded with stimuli or overwhelmed by them. As preliminary arguments in favor of such a hypothesis he pointed out that it was consonant with the view, difficult to controvert, that anxiety served a self-preservative or adaptive function in the life of the individual, not only among humans but among other animal species as well. Since anxiety was a reaction that was essential to survival it was reasonable to assume that the conditions for its appearance or development were of a general, objectively definable nature, such as those given above.

In addition Freud pointed out that such a hypothesis was applicable to the situation which he considered to be prototypic for anxiety, that is, the experience of birth. He said that such a connection between birth and anxiety seemed justified on an observational or behavioral basis despite the impossibility of determining the borning infant's subjective experience: in both birth and anxiety there were the same motor and secretory phenomena, e. g. increased rate of pulse and respiration, crying, motor activity or restlessness, etc. He then went on to point out that birth was the end of the relatively stimulus-free, intra-uterine existence of the fetus and that during birth a host of novel, powerful, and persistent stimuli impinged on the infant's nervous system both from its own viscera and from the external environment. From a psychological point of view, therefore, one could describe birth as a time when the psychic apparatus was flooded with stimuli. Since Freud assumed that anxiety appeared at birth together with this overwhelming flood of stimuli, the hypothesis given above that the general condition for the development of anxiety is a flooding of the psychic apparatus by stimuli appeared even more probable.

However, the applicability of the new hypothesis to the situation of birth was not its crucial test. The more important question was how well it could reconcile the clinical data already outlined concerning the appearance of anxiety in the psychoneuroses and in the actual neuroses. It had to pass *this* test in order to prove its worth as a valid hypothesis, regardless of any success it might have in explaining the phenomena of birth.

The line of argument by which Freud demonstrated the value of the new hypothesis for psychoanalysis was this. He asserted that in infancy, as at birth, the development of anxiety was due to flooding of the psychic apparatus with stimuli, since at such an early age the capacity of the ego to master or discharge stimuli was much less than it was to become later in life. This relative incapacity of the ego was particularly apparent with respect to stimuli of instinctual origin. Thus, for example, there was the typical situation of early life, he said, in which the infant was seized with an imperative instinctual demand in the absence of its mother, whose help was essential for the gratification of that demand. The infant in such a situation, said Freud, would react with anxiety as a consequence of being overwhelmed by the instinctual stimuli in question.

Freud proposed that such typical and universal episodes in the life of the infant, that is, episodes when stimuli overwhelmed it, be termed *traumatic* ones and went on to say that in the course of time, as the infant grew both in experience and in ego capacity, it would recognize the mother's absence as a precondition for a traumatic situation. Freud therefore suggested that the mother's absence, or any similar event which became associated in the infant's mind with the development of a traumatic situation, be called a *danger* situation. He further suggested that the ego, as it developed, acquired the capacity to react with anxiety to a danger situation, even *before* a traumatic situation had evolved. That is to say, the ego became able to *signal* the possible advent of a traumatic situation in advance. In other words, the ego either learned or at any rate gradually became able to react with anxiety to danger, or even to the anticipation of danger.

In this way Freud was able to explain the apparently twofold origin of anxiety in later life: anxiety might develop either directly from a traumatic situation or in response to danger. Anxiety would develop directly from a traumatic situation regularly in earliest infancy, often in childhood, and in adult life in such situations as the actual neuroses, in which the psychic apparatus was flooded by the excessive amounts of libido which had been dammed up. The appearance of anxiety as a signal of danger would begin later in infancy, and would predominate in later childhood and adult life and (pathologically) in the psychoneuroses. Thus Freud was able to reconcile the apparent disparity between the clinical data relating to anxiety which were derived from the actual neuroses and from the psychoneuroses, and this theory of anxiety is the one which is generally accepted today as a part of psychoanalytic theory.

In the course of elaborating the theory just outlined Freud made two other points which have proved to be of great importance since their publication in *Inhibitions, Symptoms and Anxiety* in 1926. The first of these concerned the nature and sequence of typical danger situations in childhood; the second was the introduction, or, more accurately, the re-introduction of the term "defense" into psychoanalytic language, a term which he had first introduced in 1894 but had essentially given up some ten years later in favor of the term "repression."

As Freud reconstructed the origins of the fears of early childhood on the basis of his psychoanalytic observations on adult patients, he felt that they formed a sequence that was constant enough to be considered typical. The first typical danger situation of infancy, and hence the first typical fear, was that which was mentioned above in outlining the theory of anxiety: the absence of the individual (usually the mother) whose presence and help were necessary for the satisfaction of the infant's wishes or, correspondingly, the fear that such a person would disappear or be lost. The second typical danger situation to which Freud called attention was the loss of love or the disapproval of such an important childhood figure (usually a parent); the fear corresponding to this danger was the fear of loss of love or the fear of disapproval by the parent or similar figure. Third in sequence came the typical danger of the Oedipal period, the danger of castration, to which corresponded castration fear or castration anxiety in the case of the little boy, and analogous fears of genital injury as well as intense shame and unhappiness over what she considered to be the castrated state of her genital organs in the case of the little girl. The final danger and fear which Freud mentioned were those resulting from the establishment of the superego (cf. p. 221) with the passing of the Oedipal phase; they correspond essentially to what we ordinarily call guilt feelings. Thus the sequence of typical fears is (1) fear of loss of an instinctually important object (cf. p. 83); (2) fear of loss of the object's love; (3) castration fear in the male, and the analogous fears associated with penis envy in the female; and (4) fear of the superego, or guilt.

As for the reintroduction of the term "defense," Freud considered it to be desirable on the following grounds. The reader will recall from the selection entitled "Repression" (p. 87) that in 1915 this was the term that Freud applied to the efforts of the individual to render inoperative an objectionable instinctual impulse. When he reconsidered this problem in 1926 he observed that the means which were used for this purpose were in some instances rather different from the process of repression as previously defined. Thus, for example, in cases of obsessional neurosis the pathogenic experiences of childhood had not been forgotten, but had instead been deprived somehow of their originally frightening or guilty emotional effect. Since in 1915 the essence of repression had been declared to be the barring of something from consciousness (cf. p. 89), it seemed to be somewhat inappropriate to say that something was repressed when in fact the memory of the event itself was readily accessible to consciousness, even though the emotions originally associated with it were no longer so. This and other similar instances seemed to Freud to argue in favor of using the general term "defense" to designate all efforts of the ego to render an instinctual wish or impulse inoperative and to consider repression to be one among several, or perhaps among many methods of defense.

These two ideas: the concept of ego defenses and of a typical sequence of infantile fears, together with the ideas that anxiety was a signal of danger and the initiator of the ego's defensive operations are largely responsible for the very great changes in psychoanalytic practice that have gradually taken place during the past thirty years. Before that time analysts were mainly concerned with the discovery and communication to the patient of his repressed infantile wishes, fantasies and memories, that is, with what would today be called the repressed (or otherwise repudiated) content of the id. As little attention as possible was paid to the patient's resistances to uncovering this id material, resistances caused principally by what are now called the defenses of the ego. When such resistances interfered with the progress of analysis to such an extent that it became necessary to deal with them, the patient was urged and encouraged to relinquish his defenses, but the defenses themselves were not systematically analyzed then as they are now. On the contrary, the analyst depended largely on his personal influence with the patient, that is on suggestion, to overcome the patient's defensive resistances (cf. Lecture 28 in Freud's *General Introduction to Psychoanalysis,* 1917).

Today, on the contrary, the analyst tries to help the patient to discover and thus to become conscious of the childhood and infantile origins of his defenses and of the nature of the fears that motivate them, in addition to helping him to become conscious of the repudiated content of his id, as before. Though sometimes slower than the older, suggestive method of dealing with defenses, the newer method of making conscious their history and unconscious content has proved to be far more dependable and successful than the older one and has even made possible the achievement of good therapeutic results in many cases that would formerly have been considered unanalyzable, e.g. so-called character neuroses.

It is apparent, therefore, that the new theories outlined in this appendix have proved to be immensely fruitful and stimulating in the development of psychoanalytic practice as well as of psychoanalytic psychology. Indeed it would be hard to overestimate their value in both of these respects at the present time, and their influence seems to have not yet reached its peak. Like the last of Beethoven's string quartets, these last of Freud's theories were decades ahead of their time.

If the history of psychoanalysis is like the history of other natural sciences, and we have no reason to doubt that it will be, the time will come when the theories Freud elaborated in the 1920s will be incorporated into and superseded by other more complete and more precise hypotheses which will be based on more extensive data and perhaps on different ways of viewing psychic phenomena. At present, however, and probably for many years to come Freud's theories will continue to be the most satisfactory conceptual framework for understanding the operations of the mind that is available to the practicing psychoanalyst, the psychiatrist, the social scientist, and the psychologist.

Charles Brenner, M.D.

New York, 1957

The following is an up-to-date listing of all works by Sigmund Freud in book form that have been translated into English. The date in parentheses refers to the original publication of the work, while the other date refers to the most recent publication in English.

(1891)   *On Aphasia*, London and New York, 1953.

(1895)   With Breuer, Josef, *Studies on Hysteria*, Baltimore, 1950.

(1900)   *The Interpretation of Dreams*, London and New York, 1955.

(1901)   *On Dreams*, London, 1951; New York, 1952.

(1901)   *The Psychopathology of Everyday Life*, London, 1954; New York 1951.

(1905)   *Wit and Its Relation to the Unconscious*, included in *Basic Writings*, New York, 1938.

(1905)   *Three Essays on the Theory of Sexuality*, London, 1949.

(1907)   *Delusion and Dreams in Jensen's "Gradiva"* included in *Delusion and Dream*, New York, 1956.

(1910)   *Leonardo da Vinci: A Study in Psychosexuality*, New York, 1956.

(1912–13) *Totem and Taboo*, London, 1950; New York, 1952.

(1916–17) *Introductory Lectures on Psycho-Analysis*, London, 1929 (*A General Introduction to Psychoanalysis*, New York, 1935).

(1920)   *Beyond the Pleasure Principle*, London and New York, 1950.

(1921)   *Group Psychology and the Analysis of the Ego*, New York, 1940.

(1923)   *The Ego and the Id*, London, 1927.

(1925)   *An Autobiographical Study*, New York, 1952.

(1926)   *Inhibitions, Symptoms and Anxiety*, London, 1936 (*The Problem of Anxiety*, New York, 1936.*)

(1926)   *The Question of Lay Analysis*, London, 1947;
New York, 1950.

(1927)   *The Future of an Illusion*, New York, 1956.

(1930)   *Civilization and Its Discontents*, London, 1952.

(1933)   *New Introductory Lectures on Psychoanalysis*, London and New York, 1933.

(1939)   *Moses and Monotheism*, London 1930; New
York, 1955.

(1940)   *An Outline of Psychoanalysis*, London and
New York, 1949.

(1950)   *The Origins of Psychoanalysis*, London and
New York, 1954.

The *Collected Papers* (5 vols.) London, 1924-50, includes almost all of Freud's works that are not available
in book form, as well as some of his writings that have
recently been assembled and published as books. Additional letters and extracts from letters can be found in
the first two volumes of Ernest Jones, *Sigmund Freud:
Life and Work*, London and New York, 1953, 1955.

New translations of Freud's complete works are cur-
rently being prepared for the *Standard Edition* (24 vols.),
London, 1955 ff. To date the following of the above-
mentioned works are available: *Studies on Hysteria, The
Interpretation of Dreams, On Dreams, Three Essays on
the Theory of Sexuality, Totem and Tabu, Beyond the
Pleasure Principle, Group Psychology and the Analysis of
Ego*. Volume 24 of the *Standard Edition* will contain a
complete bibliography of Freud's writings.

INDEX AND GLOSSARY

An *Index* is a collection of pointers, and each item in the text should have a pointer which leads to it, and to it alone. A *Glossary* is a list of explanations of technical terms.

In a developing science the meaning of some of the terms also develops, so the pointer should furnish the reader with the context in which the term is used. In scientific literature it is often more important to know the date of a publication than its author. Even with the works of the most illuminating of writers it can never be left out of account, perhaps least of all with such writers, because it is by a new turn of their thought that we differentiate one period of science from another.

To meet this need for an immediate placing of concepts a simple device of printing has been employed which I hope will not confuse the eye. The last two numerals of the date of publication are set up in what printers call 'superiors', the sort of numeral that usually indicates footnotes, e.g. [1]. These immediately precede the page reference, and the date runs till the next date is mentioned. (The dates set up in these superiors give the year of publication of the paper referred to, they do not as a rule date the first use of the concept or term in psychoanalytical literature.)

The first thing about the pointers themselves is that they must really point, i.e. they must have in them something of the particular item to which they direct the reader; a word (preceded by that overworked conjunction *and*) is not as a rule enough. Given adequate pointers, there follows the difficulty of arranging them so that they can be easily found. An alphabetical order, necessary for the catch-words, (though at first the great Roget did not think so) does not allow the pointers to help each other, so to speak. The items are here arranged under each catch-word in a way that fits the special topic considered.*

In the case of a DISEASE the order usually runs:

Definition; Description; History; Etiology; Fixation; Regression; Special Form of Repression; Characteristic Mechanisms; Clinical Features; Clinical Varieties; Associated Disorders; Differential Diagnosis; Treatment; Relation to Social Life; Miscellaneous and Summary.

In the case of a MENTAL PROCESS:

Definition; Description; History; Classification; Development; considered in relation to the Topography, Dynamics and Economics of the Mind; Relation to other Mechanisms, to Clinical Types, to General Biology, to Social Life, to Art; Miscellaneous and Summary.

To make the index effective as a glossary, I have tried to use the pointers so that they will tell the student something of the meaning of the catch-word and the way it is employed in the text, i.e. the catch-word is given a conceptual as well as chronological setting. The entry under 'Instincts' shows the method.

It was the glossary element that finally decided me to venture on an index so long that the first thought of the reader will no doubt be 'Better more Freud and less Index.' This book is not even a new translation, it is a collection of bits cut out of already published translations, so that it neither gives nor withholds anything new to psychoanalytical literature.

J. R.

* I have used this plan once before in the index to Ferenczi: 'Further contributions to Psycho-Analysis.' 1926.

Abraham, Karl [1877-1925]: on melancholia [17]125; on oral incorporation [17]131.

ABREACTION: in child's play [20]147; and trauma [26]242.

ACTIVE—PASSIVE: not to be confounded with ego-subject—external-object [15]81; coalescence with masculine—feminine [15]81; instinct reversal [15]77, in mastering pain and trauma [20]147-48.

ACTUAL NEUROSIS: hypochondria, neurasthenia and anxiety neurosis [14]109-10; libido [26]238.

AESTHETICS: with economic (*q.v.*) point of view treats of turning pain to pleasure [20]148.

AFFECT: quantitative factor in instinct presentation detached from idea [15]93.

AFFIRMATION: a substitute for union (contrast denial) [25]58.

AFTER-EXPULSION: synonym for repression of derivatives of or associations to object of primary repression [15]89; force of a-e. not only from conscious 90.

ALCOHOLIC INTOXICATION: cf. mania [17]136.

AMBIVALENCE: co-existence of primary impulse and its opposite form [15]80; co-existence of both 'contents' of instinct reversal 80; origin of love and hate show reason for a. in object relationship [15]85, [23]219; in oedipus situation 220; allows repression to come into being by means of reaction-formation [15]96; in oral object relationship 85, [23]219, in obsessional neurosis [15]96, [17]140; in melancholia 138, 140, related to the repressed 32, 138; ? constitutional 138; complicates piecemeal withdrawal of cathexis in spontaneous cure 138; in group ties [21]183.

ANACLITIC TYPE [Literally, 'leaning-up-against type'; from the Greek ἀνακλίνω 'I lean up against'. In the first phase of their development the sexual instincts have no independent means of finding satisfaction; they do so by

propping themselves upon or 'leaning up against' the self-preservative instincts. The individual's first choice of a sexual object is said to be of the 'anaclitic type' when it follows this path; that is, when he chooses as his first sexual object the same person who has satisfied his early non-sexual needs—James Starchey, 1921]: [14]114.
anaclitic tendency of sexual instincts: definition [14]112; in earliest object choice [10]25, [15]78, [23]219; in love relation [14]122.

ANTI-CATHEXIS: and resistance 26238.

ANXIETY: neurotic and objective a. distinguished [26]237; a. and danger 245, loss of object 243-44; in relation to ego 238; a. a way of relieving ego [10]21; in relation to transformation of quantitative factor in instinct presentation [15]93; a. at presentations returning from repression due to their exaggerated growth in fantasy owing to detachment from conscious control and their illusory strength 93; a-dream and traumatism [20]157; birth-shock [26]241; general summary 238-39; reformulation of theory, 236-46.

ANXIETY HYSTERIA: the second movement of defence [15]95; in relation to repression and return of repressed 94.

APPETITE: disturbance of a. in melancholia [17]131.

APPREHENSION: defined (see Anxiety, Fright, Fear) [20]144; expectation of danger 144; protects against fright-neurosis 144, 156.

ARMY: regarded as artificial group (cf. Church) [21]178; relation to leader 179, 202 (who must be consistent 196), to ideals, patriotism, etc. 179; libidinal ties 179-80; contrast church in respect to identification with leader 202; replacement of ego-ideal by object (the leader) 202; democratic character 179; position of women 207.

ART: does not spare pain yet is enjoyable [20]148; a connecting link between fantasies and reality [10]31; reconciliation of pleasure- and reality-principle [11]44; reality calls for renunciations, art gives new satisfactions [11]44, [21]204; has origin in component sexual impulse [10]25.

ARTIST: moulds fantasies to new kind of reality [10]31, [11]44, [21]204; becomes the hero [11]44, [21]204.

ATTENTION: meets sense-impressions half-way [11]40; relation to consciousness and reality-principle [11]40.

ATTRACTION: towards external object viewed in relation to incorporation-tendency [15]83; a. exercised by object of primary repression on associative linkages 90; where narcissism of another is an a. [14]113; a., if based on narcissism, may lead to dissatisfaction 113.

AUTO-EROTISM [Havelock Ellis, 1898]: in infancy [10]25; relation to narcissim [15]81 to pleasure-ego [11]44 and erotogenic zones [10]25; ego's independence from outer-world makes inner stimuli seem painful therefore vis-a-tergo to allo-erotism [15]82.

Bernheim: on 'emotional contagion' [21]177.

BIOLOGICAL FACTOR: in polarity active-passive [15]86; in super-ego formation [23]221, 222; in concept of disease [10]30; in group psychology [21]176.

BIRTH: effect of [21]199; trauma of [26]242.

BISEXUALITY: in oedipus situation [23]220-21.

BOASTING: why thought dangerous [25]55.

BODY-EGO: see Ego [23]216.

Brenner, Charles: 236-46; *An Elementary Textbook of Psychoanalysis*, 237.

Breuer, Joseph: collaboration in early studies of hysteria [10]4; on (dynamic) post-hypnotic suggestion [12]48; on memory traces [20]151; on 'bound' and 'free' energy 152, 158.

cause of instinct tension 81, [23]213-15, 242; transformation from Pleasure-Ego into Reality-Ego along with change from auto-erotism to object-love [11]44; has task of welding together instincts at different stages of development [20]143; coherent-e. and the unconscious [21]199, [23]211; tolerance of dammed-up libido by e. a factor in health and ill-health [12]67; moulded by identification [21]186, [23]218, 227; control over id by introjection of objects 218, aided by education [11]43-44; change in e. leads to change in distribution of libido [14]109; development in relation to primary narcissism 121; childish e. and narcissistic self-sufficiency [21]188; ego—non-ego (subject-object) antithesis [15]81; body-ego [23]215-16; development in relation to ego-ideal [14]121; e. is representative of the outer-world in the mind, super-ego of the id [23]222; analysis of ego reveals ethical side of man's nature 222; strives to be moral 231; appears as object to ego-ideal [21]198; may tolerate fantasy so long as it is not put into action [15]102; its instability increases with each differentiation [21]199, [23]218; phases of e. development and predisposition to neurotic illness [11]44; alteration of e. in obsessional neurosis [15]97; oral impulse (see Introjection) [25]56; in mourning [17]125; in melancholia lost object set up within itself and there reviled by ego-ideal [21]201; interplay between e. and object may occur between ego-ideal and e. [21]198, [23]217; e. free after grief-work complete [17]127; e. and neurosis [15]101-2, [21]209; and anxiety [23]232, [26]243.

EGO, Differentiating Grades in: distinguish from splitting of consciousness [10]9; seen in melancholia [17]129 and group-psychology [21]188, 198.

EGO-ENRICHMENT, sense of: by identification [21]191; by gratification of object love and fulfilling ego-ideal [14]121.

EGO-IDEAL (see Ego, Super-Ego): an ideal by which a person measures his actual ego [14]116, [23]222; receives self-love which real-ego enjoyed in childhood [14]116, 121; deems itself the possessor of all perfections 116, and of past concept of self 116; formed at expense of ego-cathexis 121, [23]219; earliest identifications perform special office for ego—super-ego (q.v.) 227, that with parents the most important 219; rôle of e-i. in ego development [14]121, [21]188; regards ego as object 198; comprises the sum of all limitations on ego 200, and parental criticism [14]118, the power of whose injunctions (and that of all superiors) is vested in it [23]223; in relation to repression [14]116; imposes restrictions on libidinal gratification 121; in relation to dream-censor 119; e-i. and sublimation distinguished 116-17, 123; requires sublimation but cannot enforce it 117; e-i. and sexual ideal 122; e-i. vested in parent image is displaced on to community 123; e-i. may take place of object [21]191; non-fulfilment of e-i. demands and dread of community [14]123; group-psychology related to social aspect of e-i. 123; its relation to heroic myth [21]203; in conflict with ego 188, 209; guilt when tension between ego and e-i. 200, [23]223; severity of e-i. and need for punishment 228; paranoia [14]123; biological factors [23]222.

EGO-IMPOVERISHMENT: in respect to libido in favour of love-object [14]112, 120, [21]191; in relation to loss of object [17]131; and inferiority [14]121; countered by narcissism 113; in melancholia [17]127; in neurosis [14]122; from rupture of protective barrier [20]155.

EGO-INSTINCTS: differentiated from sexual [15]84; ego- and sexual instincts readily develop antithesis hate-love 85.

EGO-SYNTONIC (opp. Ego-Dystonic) [where erotic cathexes are in accordance with the ego-tendencies—James Strachey, 1921]: love accepted by the ego [14]121.

Ellis, Havelock: gave name to narcissism [1898] [14]104-5 and to auto-erotism [1898] [10]25.

EMOTION: viewed quantitatively [10]8.

EMPATHY: the mechanism by means of which we are enabled to take up any attitude at all towards another mental life [21]188 n.; and identification [21]186, 188.

ENVIRONMENTAL FACTOR: in mental development [20]159; in melancholia [17]125.

ENVY: and genesis of group feelings via identification [21]195.

EPILEPTIC FIT: and defusion [23]224.

[EPINOSIC GAIN (see note on Pleasure)].

EROTOGENIC ZONES [The term 'hysterogenic' had been given by Charcot to areas of the body which were connected—on pressure—with the causation or arrest of spasmodic attacks. Féré adapted the term to 'erogenic', later and more correctly it was changed to 'erotogenic']: parts of the body significant in giving sexual pleasure [10]25.

EROTOGENICITY: of organs in hypochrondia (? in all organs) [14]110.

ETIOLOGICAL FORMULA: Predisposition, Specific-, Contributory- and Releasing causes distinguished [95]59; rôle of sexual life in e. [10]23; e. not confined to immediately preceding noxae [10]24.

EUCHARIST: and object-loss [23]218 n.

EXCEPTION: people who claim to be the e. [15]99; why some women make this claim 100.

EXHIBITIONISM [Lasègue, 1877]: formulated in terms of instinct-reversal [15]77-79; active exhibition-pleasure as component sexual impulse and its relation to art and theatre [10]25.

FEAR (see Anxiety, Apprehension, Fright): definition [20]144, [26]281; in anxiety, 243-44.

Fechner: on tendency towards stability [20]142.

Federn, Paul: on religious intolerance [21]181.

192; group formation of two members 192, 198, 208; the ego-ideal 192; being-in-love 189, 192, 208; retention of moral conscience 193; h. of terror 193; relation of individual to group 171; who is hypnotist of group? 172; summary of relations between h., group-psychology, neurosis and being-in-love 208-9.

HYPOCHONDRIA: alteration of distribution of interest and libido [14]109; theory of erotogenicity in internal organs 110; actual neurosis 110, and admixture of h. in other neuroses 110; and traumatic neurosis [20]144.

HYSTERIA: former medical attitude to h. [10]4; Janet on h. states 10, his theory of h. as fission due to congenital lack of power of synthesis 13; Breuer's case 4; 'the h. suffers from reminiscences' 7; the 'absences' are related to fantasies 5; the 'h-conversion' is pent-up affect turned to the physical instead of to psychical 8; patient withdrawn from outer-world only where influenced by illness (contrast paraphrenia) [14]105; gives type of re-attachment of libido in dementia praecox 111; relation to anxiety-neurosis and hypochondria [14]109-10; Hysterical Symptoms: proceed from unconscious ideas [12]48; surrogates of suppressed ideas [10]12, 15; remnants and memory symbols of traumatic experiences (cf. mourning) 7, related to suppressed strong excitement 8, which must be released before cure can occur 8.

ID [Groddeck, following Nietzsche, employed the German word *Es* for whatever in our nature is impersonal. *Es* means 'it,' the corresponding Latin word *id* was introduced by Joan Riviere in the translation of Freud's 'Neurosis and Psychosis'. 1924]: description [23]215, 223; narcissistic reservoir 226-27; non-moral 231; no unity of will 234; object-cathexes proceed from id 218; how modified by ego 218; relations to ego and super-ego 222; ? conditions for relinquishing object 218; anxiety 245; relation to eros and death 234.

place of ego-ideal 198, as replacement of ego-ideal by object 202; individual's relation to l. 192, 193-95; psychology of leader and group psychology 197, 202.

Le Bon: his description of group mind discussed [21]171.

LIBIDO (adj. form 'libidinal' [Lytton Strachey]): definition [21]177, sexual pleasure or libido [10]25; l. cathexis of ego may vary with erotogenicity of organs [14]110; distribution in organic disease 108; l. homosexual in type in formation of narcissistic ego-ideal 118; narcissistic ego-l. in being-in-love [21]208; ego-l. and object l. indistinguishable in happy love [14]121; quantity of l. in nosogenesis [12]66-67; re-enrichment of ego through withdrawal of l. from objects [14]120; l. and anxiety and actual neurosis [26]240; detachment in mourning [17]126; hindrance to withdrawal of object l. and increased tendency to break down of reality-testing 126; in depression (sadistic, inturned but now withdrawn) 132; fate of withdrawn l. in paraphrenia [14]105; l. liberated by frustration in paraphrenias does not remain attached to objects in fantasy 110, reattached in recovery 111, the recathexis different to original one 111; l. theory and emotional contagion [21]177; group-ties 180, 183, 198, 202, in army and church 180, 202.

Linder: observations on thumb-sucking (1879) [10]25.

LONELINESS: loss of object [26]244; in relation to unfulfilled desire [21]195; dread of being alone and 'herd instinct' 194-95.

LOVE AND LOVE-OBJECT: *general*: wide application of term justified [21]177-78; the 'range' of the phenomena of love 189; l. begins with synthesis of component impulses under primacy of genital [15]84, regarded as component impulse 80; brief description of its development 84. *polarities*: l. not the direct antithesis of hate 85, [23]225, related to hate in 'content' reversal of instinct [15]80, [23]226; antitheses of love: loving—hating, loving —being-loved, love-and-hate—neutrality [15]81, [23]225; love

—indifference related to polarity ego—external-world [15]83. *Love and the object*: viewed in relation to incorporation-tendency towards pleasure-object [15]83; an instinct 'loves' its object, but not 'hates' it, l. and h. relate to attitude of ego as a whole 83; contrast l. and 'need' 84, concept shifts into sphere of pure pleasure-relation to object, finally to sexual object (in restricted sense) and to sublimation 84; sensual l. extinguished when satisfied [21]192. *relation to narcissism*: love—being loved and n. [15]80, being-in-love throws light on n. [21]208, forfeiture of n. libido and humility of l. [14]120; sexual love, self-love and love for children [21]177. *psychology of being-in-love*: overflow of ego-libido to object [14]121; sexual object exalted to position of ego-ideal [14]122; l. may remove repressions and restore perversions [14]122; relation to hypnosis ([21]189, 192), neurosis and group-psychology [21]208. *love-choice*: may be conditioned by need to be loved [14]113; narcissistic type finds path to love-object in relation to child 114, model of l-c.—the self 112; original l-c. the self and the woman who tends 112; l-c. of homosexuals 112. *Love and self-regarding feelings*: general [14]119; humble through l. because of forfeiture of narcissistic libido 120; effect of impotence to l. on self-regard 120; deprivation of l. lowers self-regard 121; when need to be loved more than to l., and felt only in proportion to l. received 112; unhappiness in l. and self-regard [21]191; the non-fulfilment of demands of ego-ideal felt as dread of loss of love [14]123. *Love in melancholia*: l-object lost in mourning [17]125, in melancholia 127 (loss of capacity for love is here secondary 128) love escapes annihilation by taking refuge in ego 138-39; intense l. compared with suicide (overwhelming of ego by object and vice versa) 133, the l-object being reproached 122. *Love and group psychology*: love is the only civilizing factor [21]184; l. developed late (historically) in sexual relationship hence its opposition to group-ties also late 206; increasing importance of sexual love to ego (being-in-love) precludes

MEGALOMANIA: a mastery of libido returning to ego after detachment from objects [14]110, and thus is related to fate of cathexes withdrawn from objects 105; when occurring in narcissism due to reflux of libido m. is a reanimation of earlier condition 106.

MELANCHOLIA: clinical description [17]125, [21]201; Karl Abraham on m. [17]125; compare with mourning 124. *etiology*: ? organic 134; originates in repeated ambivalent unconscious conflicts between love for and hate to object 138, has three main conditioning factors (a) loss of object, (b) ambivalence, (c) regression of libido into ego 139. *topography*: relation to CS-UCS 138; patient conscious of conflict between parts of ego, not hate of object 139. *Mania*: turns into mania 134, [21]201, with same content, but here ego succumbs [17]135. *object-relationship*: loss of object 132, [21]201, [23]218, but loss not realized [17]127; lost object set up in ego and there reviled by ego-ideal [21]201, [23]217; identification [21]187, [23]217. *clinical relationships*: obsessional neurosis [17]139, [23]229, hysteria [10]7. *course and cure*: wears off under influence of reality-testing [17]134; by becoming free from accumulation of 'bound' cathexes 140; spontaneous cure by piecemeal withdrawal of cathexis (this is complicated by the ambivalence) 137; contrast cure of m. with resolution of grief 136-37. *relation to ego-ideal*: tension between ego and ego-ideal [23]229; severe super-ego [23]229, and severe self-reproaches [17]127, and self-punishment [23]229. *suicide*: the preconditions [17]133. *miscellaneous*: regression [17]133, 139, [23]218; the relation of the inner labour in melancholia to inhibition [17]127; fall in self-esteem 127, [21]201; melancholia throws light on ego-structure [17]129, [21]200.

MEMORY: relation to the periodical activity of consciousness and to notation [11]40; consciousness [20]151; traces in psychical apparatus but not in the system of perceptual consciousness 151; unconscious fantasies not easy to distinguish from memories that have become uncon-

liefs of primitive peoples and the magical virtue of words 106; relation to self-regarding attitude 120. *omnipotence-feelings*: corroborated by experience of fulfilling ego-ideal [14]121.

ORAL IMPULSE [that impulse which orients the ego to an object in the outer world so that its immediate outlet in activity will be that of sucking the object into the self, or biting it. The *pleasure* derived from this activity is called oral erotism, the *character* derived from the changes in the ego caused by the (relative) rigidity of this orientation is called the oral character]: identification [23]217; introjection [17]131, [28]56; in judgment 55; influence on development of object-relationship [15]84; in melancholia [17]131.

ORGAN PLEASURE: the aim of components of sexual impulse [15]76; contribution to genesis of love 85.

ORGANIC DISEASE: distribution of libido [14]108.

ORGANIC SUBSTRUCTURE: will some day be found on which to base our provisional psychological theories [14]107, [20]165; may explain why neuroses often better towards evening [17]134; melancholia 124.

ORGY, Sexual: preconditions for [21]206.

OUTER—INNER: (see Inner—Outer).

OVER-ESTIMATION: an indication of narcissism in object-choice [14]115.

PAIN, 'Pain,' Unpleasure: increase of tension in the mind [20]141; not merely due to replacement of pleasure- by reality-principle 143; mostly perceptual 143; relation to conflict 143, to danger 143, to repression [11]42-43; may occur with gratification of instinct instead of pleasure [20]143; reason for its power over psychical apparatus 155; physical p. and breaking through protective barrier 155; in mourning [17]125-26, in melancholia 125.

cept of time 153-54; relation to UCS ideas and to CS feelings [23]214.

PERSECUTION (feelings of): and withdrawal of homosexual libido [14]119; [23]225.

PERVERSIONS: the negative of the neurosis [10]27; instinct defusion [23]224; absence of ego-ideal [14]122; and the state of being in love 122.

PHANTASY: reason for close connection of p. with sexuality [11]42; after reality-principle begins to influence the mind p. subordinated to pleasure-principle alone 42; develops exaggeratedly when presentation not under conscious control owing to repression [15]90.

PHILOSOPHY: uses introspection as source of material (relation of this to paranoiac speculative systems) [14]119; metapsychology [20]141.

PHOBIA: related to instinct-impulses, their derivatives [15]94, [23]232; 'working-over' anxiety [14]111; analogy with culture [20]163; reaction-formation [26]240; danger-situations 240.

PITY: reaction-formation not an instinct-reversal [15]79.

PLAY: children's [20]145, does not call for hypotheses of imitation-impulse 148; transformation of passive experience to active-abreaction 147.

PLEASURE: striving for p. more intense at beginning of life [20]166; pleasure-principle 193; relation to 'bound' and 'un-bound' excitation processes 167; occurs with resolution of tension caused by life-instincts 167; pleasure-gain in illness (epinosic gain) [10]30; p. of rediscovery [20]158; pleasure-gain in illness [10]30 [Freud distinguishes two 'pleasure-gains,' those due to the primary tendency (paranosic gain) the 'flight into illness' if reality becomes painful or frightening (therefore a consolation), and those due to the secondary tendencies (epinosic gain) with which the state of illness becomes connected as soon as the patient can gain a useful purpose by it. In the last case the attack is aimed at particular people. Primary and secondary relate to the levels of mental organization of the tendencies. See 'General Remarks on Hysterical Attacks' *C.P.*, II, 102, 1909. The two words epinosic and paranosic were introduced by Ernest Jones].

PLEASURE-EGO: relation to reality-ego (q.v.) [15]82, to inner-outer [25]56.

PLEASURE-PAIN: (1) *P.-P. Principle*: definition [11]39, to keep excitations as low and constant as possible [20]142; regarded as automatic regulator of mental processes 141; influence of sex instinct 143 and relation to death instinct 166, 167; repetition of painful situation 146; put out of action by trauma 155; dreams 156; hallucinatory wish-thinking abandoned through lack of satisfaction [11]39; relation to art 44, to introjection and projection [15]82, to the ego and anxiety [23]233. (2) *Polarity*: p-p. belongs to feeling series [15]81; relation to love and hate 83, to change from narcissism to object-love 83. (3) *metapsychological aspects*: inner stimuli influencing system CS [20]154, [23]213; change in the amount of cathexis in unit time [20]167.

POET, THE EPIC: his relation to the primal horde [21]203; invented heroic-myth (ego-ideal) 203; sets himself free from group 204; raises his hearer's imagination to heroic levels 204.

POLARITIES: subject—object [15]81; pleasure—pain 81, 86; active—passive 77, 81, 86; masculine—feminine 81; love —indifference 83; love—hate not simple polarity 83; but becomes one under influence of pleasure principle 84-85; loving—being-loved linked with p. active—passive (cf. scopophilia, sadism) 86; interrelation of auto-erotism, narcissism and object-love 81-82; ego—external 81-82, 86.

POSTHYPNOTIC SUGGESTION: inferences from Bernheim's experiment (particularly the *dynamic* concept) [12]47.

POVERTY: sense of p. in melancholia [17]129 and the dread in relation to anal regression 133.

PRECONSCIOUS [not Foreconscious]: symbol for System = PCS: easily becomes CS (contrast UCS) [12]50, [23]210; distinguish from UCS [12]49, 51, [23]210, 213; distinction between PCS and UCS not primary [12]51; intellectual activity in PCS 216.

PREDISPOSITION TO NEUROTIC ILLNESS (see Etiological Formula [95]59-60): relation to phases of sexual development [11]44, and to development of sex and ego impulses getting out of phase 44.

PREGENITAL ORGANIZATION: oral [15]85; anal-sadistic 85.

PRIMARY PSYCHIC PROCESS: in dreams [20]158; sources of pleasure 166-67.

PRIMITIVE PEOPLES: beliefs regarding oral incorporation [23]218 n.; megalomania [14]106.

PRIVATION: the frustration of a real satisfaction [15]100.

PROJECTION (contrast Introjection) [ascribing mental processes that are not recognized to be of personal origin to persons or situations in the outer world]: origin in (a) immediate relation of inner excitations to receptive organs [20]154, (b) thrusting painful objects by ego on outer world [15]82.

PROTECTIVE INTEGUMENT: cathexis of [20]152, 156; protection against and reception of stimuli 153.

PSYCHOANALYSIS [1896]: historical origins [10]3 [began when hypnosis was dispensed with], name of therapeutic method [24]37, 246 and a science 37; its 'Weltanschauung' is that of science [22]234-35; employs metapsychology (defined) [20]141; aim of technique [20]148-49, continues education for overcoming childhood remnants [10]30 and affords better substitute for unconscious cravings than illness, and more culturally valuable 34; people fear harm from analysis 33; outcome is release of energies 35;

oral phase [23]218, and anal level [17]133, and from object-love to narcissism in melancholia [17]140; regression from narcissistic object-choice spells object-loss 133; in melancholia libido escapes destruction by regression into ego 138-39; in group-formation [21]194, 197.

REJECTION: and judgment contrasted with repression [15]87, the essence of which is r. of presentations from consciousness 94.

RELIGION: reason for regarding every r. to be based on love [21]182, or longing for love [23]223, and explanation of r-intolerance [21]182; r. temper growing milder 182; renunciation here and reward hereafter viewed in relation to pleasure- and reality-principle [11]43; reason why formerly r. spared many from neurosis [10]31, [21]208; r. descended from totemism of Darwin's primal horder 196-97; morality, social sense and r. were once the same thing [23]223.

REMORSE: in melancholia [17]129.

RENUNCIATION: of narcissim and the ego-ideal [14]116; of pleasure in the 'exception'-type of character [15]99; may be temporarily undone [21]199.

REPETITION-COMPULSION: and the pleasure-principle [20]147, 150, 158; in treatment 149, in dreams and transference-reminiscence 157, in normal people 149; 'destiny' 149; its daemonic character 158; relation to instincts and biology 158.

REPRESSED, THE: prototype of the unconscious [23]210; produces powerful effects but not itself conscious 211.

REPRESSION: keeping something from consciousness [15]89, [26]244; proceeds from self-respect of ego [14]116, 117, [21]188, [23]211; keeps instincts at lower stage of development [20]143; not a once-and-for-all action [15]92; occurs when instinctual impulse meets with resistance the aim of which is to make it inoperative [15]87, [21]189, [23]211; r. of fantasies should cathexis of them occasion 'pain'

[11]42-43 but 'pain' alone cannot be a factor in causing r. [15]88; withdrawal of energic cathexis (libido in case of sexual instinct) 94. *stages of repression*: (a) primal-r. [15]89 (denial of entry to consciousness of ideational content of instinct) accompanied by fixation; (b) r-proper, derivatives of or associations to repressed instinct-presentations, i.e. an after-expulsion [15]89. contrast reaction by flight and rejection by judgment [11]40-41 (r. is something in between [15]87). *relation to systems* CS, UCS: r. not present before distinction between conscious and and unconscious 89; all that is r. is unconscious [23]212 but idea though r. may come to consciousness on condition that it is denied [25]55; but r. does not withhold from consciousness all derivatives of primary-r (distortion) [15]91, [21]189; r. acts specifically to each associative presentation [15]91; instinct-presentation under r. develops excessively because not under conscious control 90; force of r. not only from side of consciousness 90, only interferes with relation of instinct-presentation to system-CS 90, [21]189; relation to coherent ego [21]199, [23]218; mobility of repression [15]92; satisfaction of instinct under r. is both possible and pleasurable, but 'pain' caused in another part of the mind 88; relation of r. to lack of satisfaction 94; before r. occurs there may be other vicissitudes of instinct, reversal, turning on self, etc., 89, [15]78; the repressed constantly strives to become conscious [15]92, 94; 'undoing' (q.v.) r. by denial [23]55; joking viewed as transitory lifting of r. [15]91. *clinical*: r. in anxiety hysteria 94, in conversion 95, in neuroses (summary) [21]209; defence [26]245; r. during latency period [21]206; ineffectiveness of cure by love [14]122-23; relation of r. to culture [20]163.

RESISTANCE: the force preventing buried memories from coming to consciousness, prevents hypnosis and causes forgetting [10]11-12; connected with irreconcilable wishes 12; prevents unconscious ideas from coming to consciousness [12]51, [20]148, [21]199, [23]211, and distorts them before emergence [10]15; proceeds from ego [23]211, and is